Unshielded Twisted Pair (UTP Wire)

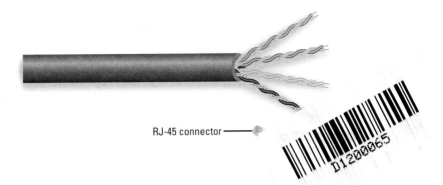

RJ-45 connector

Coaxial Cable

BNC connector

Shielded Twisted Pair (STP) Wire

IBM Data connector

Fiber-Optic Cable

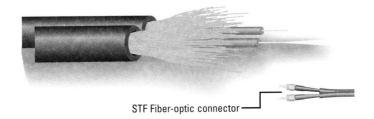

STF Fiber-optic connector

RJ-45 Wiring Schemes

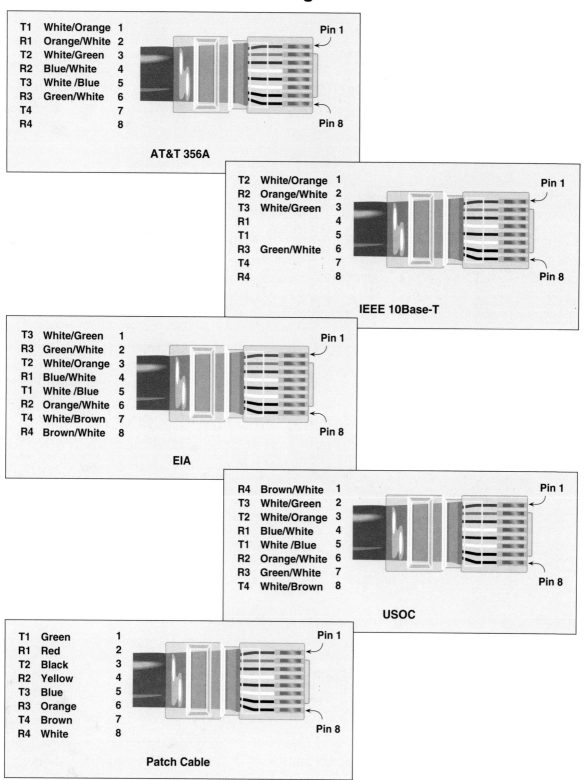

T1	White/Orange	1
R1	Orange/White	2
T2	White/Green	3
R2	Blue/White	4
T3	White /Blue	5
R3	Green/White	6
T4		7
R4		8

Pin 1

Pin 8

AT&T 356A

T2	White/Orange	1
R2	Orange/White	2
T3	White/Green	3
R1		4
T1		5
R3	Green/White	6
T4		7
R4		8

Pin 1

Pin 8

IEEE 10Base-T

T3	White/Green	1
R3	Green/White	2
T2	White/Orange	3
R1	Blue/White	4
T1	White /Blue	5
R2	Orange/White	6
T4	White/Brown	7
R4	Brown/White	8

Pin 1

Pin 8

EIA

R4	Brown/White	1
T3	White/Green	2
T2	White/Orange	3
R1	Blue/White	4
T1	White /Blue	5
R2	Orange/White	6
R3	Green/White	7
T4	White/Brown	8

Pin 1

Pin 8

USOC

T1	Green	1
R1	Red	2
T2	Black	3
R2	Yellow	4
T3	Blue	5
R3	Orange	6
T4	Brown	7
R4	White	8

Pin 1

Pin 8

Patch Cable

PRACTICAL

Network Cabling

Frank J. Derfler, Jr.

Les Freed

Contents at a Glance

Introduction   1

1   The Role of Cabling: Planning Considerations   5

2   Cable Basics   29

3   Standards: There Are So Many!   47

4   LAN Combinations   77

5   Managing Through The Hub   99

6   The Structured Cable System:
Wiring Closets and Cross-Connections   117

7   Power Wiring and Grounding   145

8   From the Wall to the Desktop   165

9   Practical Home and Small Office
Network Cabling   187

10   Fiber-Optic Cable   199

11   Cable Testing and Certification   213

12   Wireless Communications   227

Glossary   239

Index   253

A Division of Macmillan USA
201 West 103rd Street
Indianapolis, Indiana 46290

Practical Network Cabling

International Standard Book Number: 0-7897-2247-x

Library of Congress Catalog Card Number: 99-65927

Printed in the United States of America

First Printing: November 1999

01   00   99   4   3   2   1

Trademarks

Warning and Disclaimer

Associate Publisher
Jim Minatel

Acquisitions Editor
Tracy Williams

Senior Development Editor
Rick Kughen

Managing Editor
Lisa Wilson

Project Editor
Linda Seifert

Copy Editor
Cynthia Fields

Indexer
Joy Dean Lee

Proofreader
Rachel Lopez Bell

Technical Editors
Steve Rigney
Bruce Ford

Team Coordinator
Vicki Harding

Interior Design
Anne Jones

Cover Design
Rader Design

Production
Dan Harris
Mark Walchle

Table of Contents

Introduction   1

A Fundamental Investment   *1*

A Quick Look at the Contents   *2*

Conventions Used in this Book   *3*

1 The Role of Cabling: Planning Considerations   5

Pay Me Now or Pay Me Later   *6*

Introduction   *7*

Networks Big and Small   *8*

Cable and Wire   *9*
So, How Important Is It?   *9*

Above the Cable   *10*

LAN Adapters   *11*
The Physical Connection   *12*
Baseband and Broadband Signaling   *12*
Sharing the Cable   *14*

Protocols and Procedures   *15*
Ethernet   *15*
Size Considerations   *18*
ARCnet   *20*
Token-Ring   *22*

The Costs of Cabling   *26*

Looking Upstream   *27*

2 Cable Basics   29

Cables Aren't Just Wire Anymore   *30*

Many Types of Cables   *30*

Keeping Things In, Keeping Things Out   *31*

Coaxial Cable   *34*

Unshielded Twisted-Pair (UTP) Cable   *37*
UTP's Pluses and Minuses   *38*
Telephone Wire Is Not LAN Cable   *38*

Shielded Twisted-Pair (STP) Cable   *40*

Fiber-Optic Cable   *42*

Selecting the Best Cable   *44*

3 Standards: There Are So Many!   47

Grading Your Cables   *48*

Working Together   *49*

Who Said So?   *51*

Company Plans   *53*
IBM Cabling System   *54*
AT&T/Lucent Systimax   *58*
Amp and Mod-Tap/Molex   *63*
Anixter's Cable Model   *67*

National Electrical Code (NEC)   *69*
Type Codes   *70*

The EIA/TIA-568 (SP-2840) Standard   *71*

Underwriters Laboratories (UL)   *73*

Evolution   *75*

4 LAN Combinations   77

Different Terms   *78*

Network Architectures   *79*

Ethernet   *80*
Thick Ethernet   *83*
Thin Ethernet   *85*
10BaseT   *86*

Token-Ring   *92*
MTD = ECL + (Lobe Length * Nodes) +
Loopback   *93*

ARCnet *96*

Newer Standards *98*

5 Managing Through the Hub 99

Management Plays *100*

Network Management *102*
  Management for All 102
  The Network/PDS, Management
  Puzzle 103

Network Management Architectures *106*
  CMIP 108
  CMOT 108
  SNMP 108
  Agents and Consoles 109
  Device Setup 111
  RMON—Listening on Distant
  Segments 112

Network Management and
Troubleshooting *115*

**6 The Structured Cable System: Wiring Closets
and Cross-Connections 117**

Wiring at the Core *118*

More Than Just Skeletons in That
Closet *119*

Conduits and Cable Trays *123*

Up the Backbone *126*
  Locating the Closets 127
  The Backbone Cable 131

In the Closet *132*
  Cross-Connect Devices 132
  An Octopus with a Harmonica 135
  Cabinets and Racks 137
  Neat Cables 141
  Uninterruptible Power Supplies 142
  Connections Up and Down the Line 143

7 Power Wiring and Grounding 145

Killing Power *146*

What You Don't Know Could Kill You *148*

Where Problems Can Begin *148*

What Is a Ground? *148*

Grounding Problems *153*

Normal Mode and Common Mode Power
Problems *156*
  Spikes, Surges, and Sags 156

Surge Suppressors *157*

Uninterruptible Power Supplies *158*

8 From the Wall to the Desktop 165

Cable Crimps *166*

The Weak Link *167*

Information Outlets *168*

The Station Cable *169*

Cable Connectors *170*
  The RJ-45 Connector 171
  Which Wire Is Which? 171
  Attaching RJ-45 Connectors 176
  The BNC Coaxial Connector 182
  The Token-Ring Data Connector 183

**9 Practical Home and Small Office Network
Cabling 187**

Home Sweet LAN *188*

Networking Your Home *189*

Ethernet: Still the Speed Champ *190*

Alternatives to Ethernet *193*
  Wireless LANs 193
  Phone Line Networks 196
  Power Line Networking 198

10 Fiber-Optic Cable   199

Looking Through Glass   *200*

The Skinny on Fiber   *201*

Light Through the Tunnel   *202*

Single-Mode and Multimode   *203*

Ordering Options   *203*
  Connectors   204
  Low-Cost Connectors   207

Signaling and Connection Standards   *208*
  FDDI   208
  FOIRL and 10Base-F   209

Practical Installations   *211*

11 Cable Testing and Certification   213

The Best Test   *214*

Nobody Knows the Troubles…   *215*

What Cable Testers Measure   *219*
  Cable Distance   219
  Wire Map   220
  Attenuation   221
  Near-End Crosstalk   222
  *Network Monitoring and Protocol Decoding
  223*
  Noise-Level Test   223
  Programmed Standards   224
  Special Features   225

Testing Fiber   *225*

Baseline and Certification   *226*

12 Wireless Communications   227

Air Willy   *228*

Going Wireless   *229*
  Wireless Bridges   231
  Wireless LANs   234

Wireless LAN Topology   *235*

Solving Other Wired Problems   *236*

Glossary   239

Index   253

Acknowledgments

Willy and the folks at OK Cable follow in the steps of "Gus" at the Model Garage and Herb S. Brier's "Carl and Jerry" stories from decades ago. In more modern times, we want to thank Steve Rigney for inspiration and perspiration.

Tell Us What You Think!

As the reader of this book, *you* are our most important critic and commentator. We value your opinion and want to know what we're doing right, what we could do better, what areas you'd like to see us publish in, and any other words of wisdom you're willing to pass our way.

As a Publisher for Que, I welcome your comments. You can fax, email, or write me directly to let me know what you did or didn't like about this book—as well as what we can do to make our books stronger.

Please note that I cannot help you with technical problems related to the topic of this book, and that due to the high volume of mail I receive, I might not be able to reply to every message.

When you write, please be sure to include this book's title and author as well as your name and phone or fax number. I will carefully review your comments and share them with the author and editors who worked on the book.

Fax: 317-581-4666

Email: networking@mcp.com

Mail: Publisher
            Que
            201 West 103rd Street
            Indianapolis, IN 46290 USA

introduction

Compared to other investments you will make in computer products, your LAN cabling lasts practically forever! Software seems to go through an evolution every two to three years. Studies show that most of us swap PC hardware every three, but you will live for 15 years or more with your network cabling. The investment you make in a cabling scheme today will pay back dividends for years, but the rate of return you earn on your investment will depend on how wisely you choose the pieces and parts and supervise the installation of your cabling.

Our goal in writing this book is to prepare you to make your own informed choices about cabling and to help you evaluate plans proposed by others. This is a practical book for people faced with tough, long-term decisions. It is as technical as it needs to be, but stresses practical tips and objective product information. We want this book to have as long and useful a life as your cabling system!

A Fundamental Investment

Cabling is "plugged in" at the most fundamental level of networking. The powerful computer hardware, the complex networking software, and the modules that implement sophisticated error-control and network-management protocols will sit idle because one whisker-thin piece of wire touches another in a space behind a wall or because a little-used ventilation motor starts up and generates an electrical field that creates noise in the LAN cable. Your network can never be more reliable or perform better than its cabling allows.

Investing in LAN cabling is very similar to investing in your retirement fund. Putting your money in a mutual fund is the equivalent of adopting a wiring scheme built on standard principles developed by a major corporation like IBM or AT&T. You can use the services of a consultant to guide your investment choices for both your retirement account and your cabling service, or if you are well-informed, you can pick and choose from among complex options to make your own customized plan.

A Quick Look at the Contents

- In Chapter 1, we give you an overview of networking technology and describe some of the economic and technical forces that shape your cabling options.

- Chapter 2 describes and categorizes the various types of cabling you can buy. Because cabling is part of a building structure, as well as part of the network, it is subject to an extraordinary number of descriptions, specifications, regulations, and standards.

- In Chapter 3, we describe those standards and buzz words introduced in Chapter 2.

- Chapter 4 links cabling into the specifications of real networking systems like ethernet and token-ring.

- In Chapter 5, we describe the important and quickly evolving wiring hubs that bring network management, statistical reporting, and improved reliability to your LAN cabling system.

- Chapters 6 through 9 deal with products, tips, and techniques and get into detailed "hands-on" and "how to" descriptions of bringing wire into a central facility and applying the wide range of connectors. Chapter 7 specifically covers the important topic of power and grounding.

- Chapter 10 tackles the important area of how to wire your home and small office for networking. We realize that people don't want networks in their homes; they want the Internet, production capabilities, and games. However, you often have to do more than throw a couple of cables in back of a desk to make these things happen.

- After you install the cabling, you must make sure that it will work properly and reliably. Chapter 11 deals with cable testing and installation certification.

- Chapter 12 doesn't deal with cabling at all! Instead, this chapter describes your options for wireless communications systems that might or might not include segments of copper or fiber-optic cabling. New developments have made wireless critically important.

In these chapters, we give you the tools to build the best possible infrastructure for networks of every size. You yourself might not pull the cable, but we can help you to configure, size, and control this long-term critical investment in your networking infrastructure.

Conventions Used in this Book

Commands, directions, and explanations in this book are presented in the clearest format possible. The following items are some of the features that will make this book easier for you to use:

- *Commands that you must enter*—Router commands that you will have to type are easily identified by a bold monospace font. For example, if I direct you to get the encapsulation (the WAN protocol set) for a serial interface, I display the command like this: `show interface serial 0`. This is exactly what you should type.

- *Cross references*—If a related topic is a prerequisite to the section or steps you are reading, or a topic that builds further on what you are reading, you will find the cross reference to it at the end of the section or after the steps, like this:

SEE ALSO

➤ *UTP is much thinner and takes up less room in a conduit than does STP; see page 37 and page 40.*

- *Glossary terms*—For all the terms that appear in the glossary, you will find the first appearance of that term in the text in *italic*, along with its definition.

- *Sidenotes*—Valuable information related to the task at hand or "inside" information from the authors is offset in sidebars. This way, it does not interfere with the task and is easy to find. Each of these sidebars has a short title to help you quickly identify its content. You will find the same kind of information in these that you might find in notes, tips, or cautions in other books, but the sidenote titles are more informative.

chapter

1

The Role of Cabling: Planning Considerations

Pay Me Now or Pay Me Later ●

Introduction ●

Networks Big and Small ●

Cable and Wire ●

Above the Cable ●

LAN Adapters ●

Protocols and Procedures ●

The Costs of Cabling ●

Looking Upstream ●

Pay Me Now or Pay Me Later

The first thing Willy Barnett noticed was the silence. He had been here only once before, but people who had then been busy answering the phones and booking reservations were now turning the pages of magazines or talking together quietly in the corners of the room. Even before he found the network administrator, Willy saw the error message on the bottom of a computer screen: Server Not Found.

The network administrator looked like a man with a migraine. "We're losing money by the minute, Willy. We've got all the phones on busy because it doesn't do any good to tell people we can't do business while the network is down. We've checked the hardware and software on the servers and they seem okay. Our network management programs rely on the network being up, so they don't work. I think the problem must be in the network cabling, but it's nothing I can find."

OK Cable, Willy's company, hadn't installed this network cabling. The original installers weren't even in the phone book anymore. Having no diagrams of the cable layout, he decided to start at the closest point and pulled a PC away from the wall. Then he took a small meter about the size of a deck of playing cards out of his pocket, applied the leads to the ethernet connector, and grunted.

"Fifty ohms. You've got a cable break. Anybody move their desks around last night or this morning?" The wordless network administrator shook his head and shifted his feet as though he were walking on hot coals.

Willy searched the offices for the last PC on the thin ethernet cable, the one with a terminating resistor. When he found it, he attached a device about the size of a paperback novel to the cable. Within a few seconds, the liquid crystal screen flashed Cable open at 90 feet.

Moving about 40 feet across the office, Willy reached in back of a PC. When he touched a connector with smooth flat sides, he rolled his eyes and said, "I'll bet on this one. A twist-on connector. A problem waiting to happen."

As he talked, he clipped off the old connector with a careful right-angle cut and used a special wire-stripping tool to take off just the right amount of cable jacket, shielding braid, and inner insulation.

Then he used a formidable-looking black crimping tool to create a permanent physical bond between the cable and a new connector. He attached the cable to its T-connector, used the little ohm meter again, and announced, "Twenty-five ohms. You're back on the air."

Following OK Cable policy, Willy presented an invoice before leaving the job. When he looked at the bill, the network administrator said, "I don't pay my lawyer this much an hour!" The old punch line "That's why I gave up law" passed through Willy's mind, but he decided to take a different approach.

"You're going to pay me now or pay me later," he said. "You've bet your business on a network cabling system that can fail from any one of three or four causes, including twist-on connectors, people who don't know how to disconnect a PC from the cable without taking the whole network down, and a cable installation that exceeds the maximum recommended length by 100 feet. This won't be the last bill you'll get for an emergency call if you don't make some changes." The network administrator sighed, closed his office door, and said to Willy, "Let's talk."

Introduction

What do you do with an unconnected computer? Certainly not as much as you do with a connected computer! Practically all computers used in business and government have an external connection, typically to a *local area network (LAN)*. A LAN is a network of local connections with long reach. The local network provides important services like file and print sharing, and it provides the portal to a wider world, including the Internet. The LAN can carry data traffic that's critical to the success of an organization or enterprise.

At the fundamental levels of connectivity, a LAN and the Internet are very different. The Internet and *wide area networks (WAN)* move data over complex circuits installed and maintained by sophisticated telecommunications carriers. The LAN moves traffic locally—within a building or across a campus—over relatively simple copper wire connections installed and maintained within the company or organization. As e-commerce and computers burrow into the core business of many companies, the quality and reliability of those LAN cable

It can't be any better!

Here is a fundamental truth: A network is never any better than its cabling! You can add the finest servers and the most sophisticated application software, but if the cabling is poor, the network is poor. Cabling is fundamental!

connections become more important. If you measure your network's downtime in dollars-per-second, your network cabling is a critical resource, calling for significant planning and care.

This book is not designed to make you into a cable installer. However, it does have four goals that we think we've hit:

- First, it is designed as an introduction for people who would become installers. It's a good general introduction to the craft.

- Second, it's a book for those who have to hire installers. We try to give you the necessary vocabulary and insight to effectively evaluate, prepare for, and work with installers.

- Third, we try to meet the information needs of the person who is pulling together a small network for either the home or office.

- Finally, it's designed for enterprise network managers, professional IS managers, those whose jobs hang on the end of a cable and who need both a vocabulary and reference material.

Networks Big and Small

A small network—meaning fewer than a dozen nodes with no major barriers between them—typically has simple cabling requirements. Some prepackaged cables thrown along the baseboard and connected to a hub mounted behind the desks often do the job. However, as networks grow in size and importance, the cabling system takes a larger part of the budget, planning activities, and administrator's time. As soon as the cable system starts to pierce permanent walls or go between floors of a building, the cable system requires careful planning and installation. After a dozen nodes or so, we recommend a structured cabling system.

Often, the first and most definitive decision to make about a network is the type of wiring to use and the physical configuration of the wiring plant. Starting out on the wrong course can incur future penalties in time, money, or performance as the network grows. Follow along and we'll describe the ways cabling systems fit into the architecture of a network and the relative costs and long-term importance of cabling systems.

Cable and Wire

Throughout this book, when we use the term *network cabling*, usually we mean copper wire twisted or shielded inside an outer jacket made of plastic. In many cases, however, the jacket will surround strands of plastic or glass that conduct light in much the same way that copper conducts electricity. When we refer to *cable*, we use the term's most generic meaning: the stuff that conducts signals between network nodes. We'll be specific when referring to the various types of cable, such as shielded or unshielded twisted-pair wire, coaxial cable, or fiber-optic cable. The word *wire* typically refers to individual copper wires with a cable jacket.

So, How Important Is It?

So, what is your network worth? Will you lose your job or significant revenue if a major portion of the network is down for more than a few minutes? Here are some questions to ponder as you review the material in this book. In later chapters, we'll tell you what to do with specific answers.

- Which network nodes generate the most traffic? After you identify your traffic patterns, we'll help you to configure your cabling and contention schemes for the best efficiency and reliability.

- What is the physical environment? Cable systems have finite physical limits. You must develop a diagram of the physical layout of the network nodes so that you can plot the best locations for wiring hubs and make plans for any special links. Also, consider the types of walls and construction between rooms containing elements of the network.

- Do you have physical threats to your network? Do you have information someone would like to steal? Do you have internal physical threats such as forklifts, welders, or frequent construction in your building?

- What is in place? What cabling and conduit are in your walls now, and what are their condition? Can you gain access? Are they being used? Can they be surveyed?

Above the Cable

The network cabling is part of a system. Some elements of the system, such as the applications, can drive the selection and configuration of the cabling. You need the big picture before you can plan the cabling for the LAN.

It's easier to understand networks if you think of each element above the cabling as a process. Each element takes data in at one end, processes it, and then passes it out at the other end. The purpose of the processing is to package or unwrap the data going to and from the network connections.

In any model of network operations, such as the one shown in Figure 1.1, every other block in the diagram depends on, and is supported by, the network cabling. The cabling—sometimes referred to in academic circles as *transmission medium* or *network media*—is separate from, but tightly linked to, the rest of the operational components of the network.

Learning more about the elements above the cable

If you want to understand the details and alternatives of the network elements above the cable, we recommend picking up a copy of *Practical Networks*, also published by Que.

FIGURE 1.1
This block diagram shows the functional elements of a client PC and file server. Note that the powerful processors and software, designed according to elegant protocols, are all linked by a thin piece of cable.

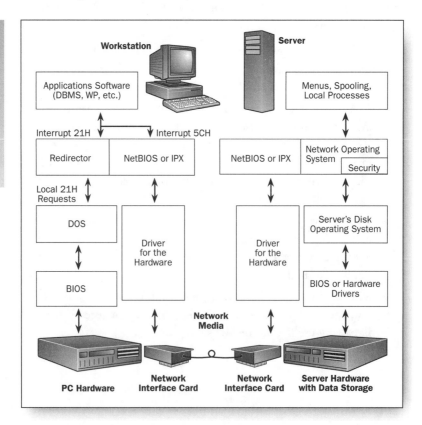

LAN Adapters

The cabling connects to LAN adapters in the various network nodes. Some LAN adapters, also called *network interface cards (NICs)*, are separate printed-circuit boards designed for computers that range in size from desktop PCs, to IBM AS/400 midframe machines, to the communications controllers for IBM mainframe computers. Nearly a dozen companies market LAN adapters for PCs, and their products have street prices that range from $20 to $100. An example of a LAN adapter appears in Figure 1.2.

USB networking is a good alternative!

The Universal Serial Bus (USB) ports on modern computers can carry high-speed data over short distances and act as a small network using special software. Several companies also offer USB to ethernet converters.

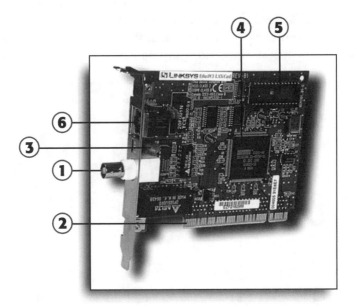

FIGURE 1.2
This typical ethernet LAN adapter (or NIC) inserts into a computer's expansion bus. It connects to the ethernet cabling through its RJ-45 socket. This adapter from Linksys is designed for a computer's PCI expansion bus and includes a BNC connector for thin ethernet coaxial cabling.

1. BNC connector
2. Edge connector
3. Protective spark gap
4. Special-purpose ethernet processor
5. Empty socket for boot ROM
6. RJ-45 socket for UTP connection

Some companies make LAN adapters a part of their computers. For example, Hewlett-Packard, Dell, and Gateway build LAN adapters into computers in certain product lines. Apple includes ethernet connections in its Power Mac and iMac computers. If the computer doesn't have a built-in adapter or an expansion slot to add a circuit board, you can use an external LAN adapter or make a network connection through the computer's Universal Serial Bus (USB) port.

Because the LAN adapter must have some specific circuitry to connect to the type of cable used in the network, the selection of the cabling can drive the selection of the LAN adapter.

Each LAN adapter has three important jobs to do in its interconnection to the network cable:

- Make a physical connection.
- Provide electrical signaling.
- Implement orderly access to the shared network cable system.

The Physical Connection

The physical connection depends on one of several types of cable connectors. Figure 1.3 shows the most common types of connectors. Generally, these connectors use a male plug on the cable and a female jack on the chassis of the computer or LAN adapter. They physically lock with a snap or a twist for a solid connection.

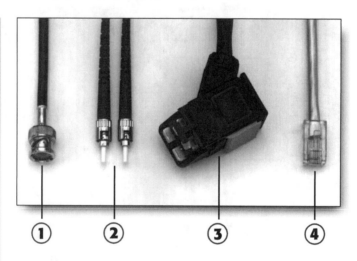

FIGURE 1.3
The most widely used types of network cable connectors:

(1) BNC connector on coaxial cable

(2) ST fiber-optic connector on fiber-optic cables

(3) IBM type 1 connector on shielded twisted-pair wiring

(4) RJ-45 connector on unshielded twisted-pair wire

(1)   (2)   (3)   (4)

Baseband and Broadband Signaling

Copper network cables carry electrical signals, whereas fiber-optic cables carry pulses of light. In the 1980s, two technologies competed for popularity in the copper cable market: baseband and broadband signaling.

In broadband signaling—the more technically elegant signaling technique—each LAN adapter treats the network cable like a radio antenna. Each broadband LAN adapter is a small radio-transmitting and radio-receiving station that pumps a broad spectrum of radio-frequency energy into the cable. This scheme uses complex radio repeaters and requires careful installation and frequent maintenance. These disadvantages far outweigh the advertised advantage of broadband signaling: the capability to combine voice, video, and data on the same network cable. New installations of broadband systems are very rare, and we won't discuss them further in this book.

Baseband signaling uses a direct-current voltage, very similar to the voltage of a car battery, to signal the presence of a digital 0 or a 1 on the cable. The adapter applies a positive or negative voltage in the range of +15 to –15 volts to the cable, and the transition between the voltage levels indicates a change from one binary state to the other.

The peak of each positive and negative cycle is flat, generating the picture of square waves. However, as these square waves travel over the cable, the electrical capacitance and inductance in the cable drag at the voltage and the current of the signal and round off its square edges. The factors create *attenuation*, reduction in the amplitude of the positive and negative voltages. Other factors—*crosstalk* (interference from other network signals) and *electromagnetic interference (EMI)*—can mask the desired signals.

Ethernet baseband signaling uses the Manchester encoding technique to signal the presence of digital zeroes and ones on the wire (see Figure 1.4). This type of encoding depends on the capability of the network interface cards to detect a change (called a *transition*) from one voltage level to another. The change might be from low to high or from high to low. Both the change event and its direction are important. If the transition is masked because of low voltage levels (attenuation) or high noise levels (crosstalk, EMI), the adapters can't decode the changes and detect the data. This simple idea, moving bits down the wire with voltage swings, is at the heart of network cable systems. In essence, the rest of this book is about the techniques used to provide good clear signals free of attenuation, crosstalk, and EMI everywhere on the network.

Faster signaling speeds put even more stringent demands on cabling systems. The higher speeds decrease the time duration between the square waves and make it more difficult for the LAN adapters to discriminate between them.

Choose LAN adapters carefully

You must choose LAN adapters that are compatible with the type of cable, the type of computer expansion bus, and the type of networking software you use. Make a careful inventory of your computers and settle on your cabling scheme before you buy your LAN adapters. Chapter 2, "Cable Basics," discusses the various types of cabling, but it's worth pointing out upfront that anyone putting in a new installation should strongly consider unshielded twisted-pair cable.

Proper installation of connectors is crucial

Here's a rule: Improper installation of the connector on the cable is the most common source of poor cable connections. Poorly installed connectors can create electrical noise, make intermittent electrical contact, and disrupt the network. It pays to invest in the best connectors and installation tools.

We'll describe the types of cable connectors and give instructions on how to install the most commonly used connectors in Chapter 7, "Power Wiring and Grounding."

FIGURE 1.4
Manchester encoding signals the presence of digital zeros and ones on the wire.

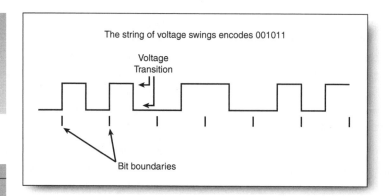

Baseband LAN, broadband WAN

Although there was a big fight between baseband and broadband in the 1980s, there are peace and harmony in the 2000s. Baseband is the signaling used in local area networks and broadband is essentially the signaling used in cable modems. Both technologies have evolved and found their own niche.

Higher-quality copper cables and connectors have more favorable capacitance, inductance, and resistance ratings and do less to round off and attenuate square waves. In later chapters, we describe the qualitative differences between copper cables and connectors with different ratings.

Sharing the Cable

"Networks are for sharing" is a phrase that you will find in all our books. Local area networks allow people to share data and program files, devices such as printers and CD-ROM drives, and communications links to wide area networks and to the Internet, but sharing starts with the network cabling scheme. On a shared cable, only one node can transmit a packet of data at a time, so each LAN adapter gives its network node orderly access to the network cable by following a specific *media-access control (MAC)* scheme. Cable sharing takes place within milliseconds, so it appears that many communications are taking place simultaneously, but actually it's just one at a time. MAC is an operational scheme recognized by modern standards committees.

The old survive

We guarantee that you will never see a new installation of ARCnet. Token-ring appears only in older but high quality installations. However, it is possible or even likely that anyone in the computer industry will run across active installations of ARCnet or token-ring. If you know the basics of these networking schemes, you could become a corporate hero.

The three most common MAC schemes are described in the ARCnet, ethernet, and token-ring standards. We'll describe the specific cabling schemes associated with each standard in Chapter 4, "LAN Combinations." You don't have to consider the operation of the MAC layer to select a cabling scheme, but understanding the MAC layer will help you to understand why some wiring systems are laid out in specific ways.

Protocols and Procedures

Protocols are agreements among different parts of the network community on how data are to be transferred. Protocols describe how things work. Committees established by organizations such as the Institute of Electrical and Electronics Engineers (IEEE), the Electronic Industries Association (EIA), the International Consultive Committee on Telephone and Telegraph (CCITT in French), and the International Standards Organization (ISO) typically labor for years to develop these agreements on how electronic devices signal, exchange data, and handle problems.

Committees develop protocols, but companies develop products conforming to those protocols. Some companies, particularly IBM and Digital, used to establish their own proprietary protocols and products (at least partially in an attempt to lock customers into their technology), but today so-called *open* systems of protocols, established by national and international committees, prevail.

In theory, if a company develops a product that operates according to a standard protocol, the product will work with products from all other vendors meeting that same standard. In practice, companies often implement the protocols in ways so different that the products don't work together without a lot of adjustment on both sides. However, the concept of compatibility among LAN products is sound, and constant improvement efforts are working.

Three standard protocols for network cabling and media access control should interest you: ethernet, token-ring, and ARCnet. In the last half of the 1990s, ethernet won what had been a pitched technological battle against token-ring, but ethernet itself was changed in the process. We'll describe ARCnet and token-ring because networks conforming to those technologies still carry a lot of data in important settings. Our main focus, though, will be on the cabling to support the evolved versions of ethernet.

> **The ISO superseded CCITT**
>
> The ISO has absorbed and superseded the CCITT, so the only references you will see to CCITT standards are in older material. However, in the cable infrastructure, things survive for decades, so it wouldn't be unusual to find references to the CCITT.

Ethernet

As ethernet contended with token-ring for network primacy, it evolved and even took on many aspects of token-ring, such as a central wiring point. Now, several cable schemes qualify as "ethernet":

- *10Base5*—This is the *thick* ethernet. It's called that because it uses a thick coaxial cable. It is never used in new installations today, and because it is difficult to work with, most managers want to get it out of their walls. However, where it still exists, it works fine for 10Mbps applications.

- *10Base2*—This is the *thin* ethernet, or "cheaper net." The specification calls for relatively thin (about 1/4 inch) coaxial cable connecting the networked nodes without a central hub. This is called a *peer-to-peer* network.

- *10BaseT*—This is the primary specification for ethernet running at 10Mbps over unshielded twisted-pair cable. The specification also introduces a central wiring point, a hub or switch, for improved reliability and management control. This is the contemporary meaning of *ethernet* in common use.

- *10BaseF*—This specification describes ethernet running over fiber-optic cable at 10Mbps. The primary advantages are increased distance and reliability in areas of high electromagnetic interference.

- *100BaseT*—The *fast* ethernet specification is now the most popular for new installations. Devices conforming to this specification can signal at 100Mbps over unshielded twisted-pair cable.

- *1000BaseT*—This new specification describes signaling at 1,000Mbps over unshielded twisted-pair cable. However, the distances are limited, and the signaling takes place over multiple wire pairs within the cable.

The primary characteristics of the basic thin ethernet link include

- A data rate of 10Mbps

- A maximum station separation of 2.8 kilometers

- A shielded coaxial cable connecting the stations

- A specific kind of electrical signaling on the cable called a *Manchester encoded digital baseband*

- A media access control protocol called *CSMA/CD*

Of these characteristics, the Manchester encoding (described earlier) and CSMA/CD signaling still carry through to the other specifications. The other specifications have their own specific signaling rates

Basic ethernet and its enhancements

The basic component of the ethernet family of protocols is 10Mbps ethernet. Newer and very popular members of the family include fast ethernet, operating at 100Mbps, and gigabit ethernet. If you understand how the 10Mbps product works, you have the basis for understanding the whole family.

and distance limitations, but they are different for every ethernet specification.

Overall, ethernet uses a *broadcast architecture;* every node on the same contention segment receives every broadcast from every other node at the same time. In the earlier forms of ethernet, practically every node in the LAN was contending with every other node for access. In the more modern network, nodes on a hub contend with only a small number of other nodes for access, and nodes on an ethernet switch contend only with the switch for access to the dedicated link.

The CSMA-CD Media Access Control Protocol

The major part of the data link layer specification for ethernet describes how stations share access to coaxial cable through a process called *Carrier-Sense Multiple Access with Collision Detection (CSMA/CD)*. CSMA/CD is a media access control (MAC) protocol that determines how nodes on the network share access to the cable. The medium is the coaxial or unshielded twisted-pair cable connecting the network nodes, and the access control protocol is the sharing scheme. Before packets of information can traverse the cable of the basic ethernet network, they must deal with CSMA/CD.

As we pointed out earlier, ethernet switching reduces the contention for the network media. However, the switch and the end device attached to the switch still interact and contend for access to a single wire pair. They use CSMA/CD to decide the issue of access. Although the CSMA/CD system might not work as hard on a switch port as it does on a hub, it is still important.

CSMA/CD works in a listen-before-transmit mode: If the network adapter receives data to send from higher-level software, it checks whether any other station is broadcasting on the cable. Only when the cable is clear does the network adapter broadcast its message.

CSMA/CD also mediates when the inevitable happens: Two or more nodes simultaneously start to transmit on an idle cable, and the transmissions collide. The adapters can detect such collisions because of the higher electrical-signal level that simultaneous transmissions produce. When they detect a collision, the network adapter cards begin transmitting what is called a *jam signal* to ensure that all the conflicting nodes notice the collision. Then, each adapter stops

Switching changes the model

The description of the ethernet broadcast model describes how the typical ethernet system works. However, many modern networks use switching techniques that reduce the need for sharing and contention. Introducing switching into the ethernet system affects the cabling scheme because it avoids the need to continually redesign the network into small contention groups as traffic builds.

10/100 ethernet is the technology we recommend!

As the street price of high-quality ethernet adapters continues to spiral downward, we don't see any advantage to saving a few bucks and installing only 10Mbps adapters on network equipment. All your LAN adapters, equipment, and cables should conform to the 100BaseT specification. Buying adapters, hubs, and switches with 10/100 autoswitching capability is a sound investment in future expansion.

transmitting and goes to its internal programming to determine a randomly selected time for retransmission. This "back-off" period ensures that the stations don't continue to send out colliding signals every time the cable grows quiet.

The 802.3 10BaseT Standard

In late 1990, after three years of meetings, proposals, and compromises, a committee of the IEEE finalized a specification for running ethernet-type signaling over twisted-pair wiring.

The IEEE calls the standard *802.3i 10BaseT*. The IEEE 802.3 standards family generally describes CSMA signaling, like ethernet, used over various wiring systems. The *10BaseT* name indicates a signaling speed of 10Mbps, a baseband signaling scheme, and twisted-pair wiring in the configuration of a star—with end nodes attached to a central point, which is an ethernet hub or switch.

The biggest potential advantage of a 10BaseT wiring installation to a network manager comes from the star-cabling scheme. The star-wiring scheme (the general configuration appears in Figure 1.5) provides both reliability and centralized management. Like spokes from the hub of a wheel, the wires go from a central wiring hub (or ethernet switch) out to each node. If one wire run is broken or shorted, that node is out of commission, but the network remains operational. In station-to-station wiring schemes like thin ethernet, one bad connection at any point takes down the entire network.

Size Considerations

Because of the carrier-sense media-access control system, every ethernet adapter in a traditional installation must "hear" at least part of every packet transmitted by any other adapter in the same collision domain at the same time. This is true even if the collision domain is simply the connection between a PC and a port on an ethernet switch.

An ethernet cable that is too long doesn't allow all networked nodes to hear the packet at the same time (see Figure 1.6). A node can detect silence and then generate a conflicting packet. This same limitation is even involved when an end node communicates with a hub.

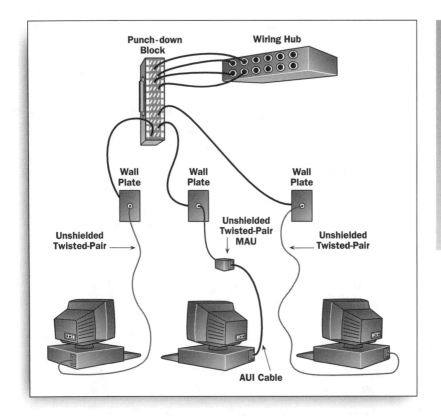

FIGURE 1.5
The IEEE 10BaseT archi-
tecture uses a central
wiring hub and a sepa-
rate run of cable to each
node. In this diagram,
the wiring is terminated
on a punch-down block
to improve its accessibil-
ity. One PC uses a media
access unit (MAU) or
external transceiver to
make the connection to
unshielded twisted-pair
wire.

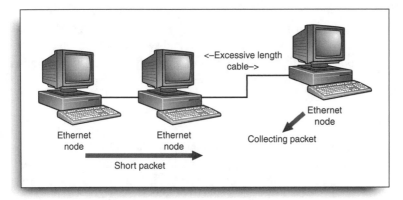

FIGURE 1.6
Each ethernet client
must hear a portion of
the same packet at a
single instant to avoid
collisions. This require-
ment limits the maximum
separation between any
two nodes.

Imagine three nodes, one each at either end and one at the center of
a very, very long cable. Suppose the adapter at the left end sends a
short packet of data that goes completely by the center node before
its front part reaches the distant node. When the packet clears the

center node, the adapter at the center sees a quiet cable and immediately sends out its own packet. Together, the near and center nodes can foreclose any opportunity for the end node to transmit. If an adapter is so far away from the point of origin that, even at nearly the speed of light, the front part of the packet doesn't reach it before the back of the packet clears all other nodes, the chance exists for conflict. So, in ethernet, the maximum cable distance is a factor of the minimum packet size and the usable strength of the signal.

Overall, the rules for a thin ethernet cable segment say that the system can have 185 meters (606 feet) of cable before it must have a repeater. Only 30 nodes can populate a single thin-cable segment, and there must be a minimum of .5 meters (2 feet) of cable between each node.

The star wiring configuration of the 10BaseT wiring scheme changes the rules. Each cable segment linking the 10BaseT wiring hub, and a network node can have a maximum length of 100 meters (328 feet), although some hub manufacturers advertise that their equipment can work over greater distances. The 10BaseT system offers approximately the same end-to-end distance as thin ethernet, but because of the hub-and-spoke design, its coverage in a radius around the wiring hub is much greater.

When you consider that cables go a long distance when routed around walls and over ceilings, this limitation can create the need for several separate hubs in big buildings or work areas. We explain more about linking those hubs and switches in Chapter 4, but the point to understand right now is that these rules and limitations drive the requirements for a structured wiring plan.

ARCnet

The ARCnet system—originated by Datapoint Corporation and fostered in the microcomputer world by Standard Microsystems Corporation—uses messages addressed to specific stations to regulate traffic. The ARC acronym stands for Datapoint's Attached Resource Computing architecture. Like ethernet, ARCnet uses a broadcast architecture in which all stations receive all messages broadcast into the cable at approximately the same time, without action by any other node.

The technical literature describes ARCnet as a token-passing system, but it operates very differently from IEEE 802.5 token-ring. Rather than pass a token from station to station like token-ring, one ARCnet station broadcasts the transmission permission message to the others on the network.

Each ethernet and token-ring adapter has a unique adapter identifier assigned by the manufacturer and drawn from a common pool established by industry associations. ARCnet adapters, however, don't come with an identification number assigned. You set the identification number, from 1 to 255, using switches located on each adapter. The identification numbers have no relationship to the position of the nodes on the cable or to any other physical positioning factor.

When activated, the adapters broadcast their numbers, and the lowest-numbered active station becomes the controller for the network. This controller sends a token to each active station, granting permission to transmit. When each station receives the permission token, it either sends its waiting message or remains silent. After a pause of a few milliseconds, the controlling station sends a permission token to the next station in numeric sequence.

When a new station enters the network, all the stations rebroadcast their station numbers in what is called a *reconfiguration*, or *recon*. Like the collisions in ethernet, the concept of a recon bothers people who worry about esoteric matters of network efficiency. In reality, a recon takes no longer than, in the worst case, 65 milliseconds and scarcely disturbs the flow of traffic on a network.

The Topology

The ARCnet scheme traditionally uses RG/62 coaxial cable in a configuration that connects each networked node to a hub. The configuration is different from 10BaseT because it doesn't use CSMA/CD and can use longer distance cables.

The RG/62 coaxial cable specified for ARCnet is the same cable used by IBM in its 3270 wiring plan that links IBM computer terminals to mainframe computers. Because this ARCnet plan also uses a star wiring configuration with a central hub, it is wired like a mainframe. Therefore, many companies found it easy to install ARCnet when they downsized their computer systems from IBM mainframes to

Keep a list of active adapter numbers

There are two things an ARCnet installer can't afford to lose: the instruction manual telling how to set the adapter numbers and the list of adapter numbers active on the network. If you know which station numbers are assigned, it's easy to add more stations. If you don't know which station numbers are active, you face a frustrating session of research or trial-and-error installation.

networks of PCs. They kept the same coaxial-cable wiring in place and replaced the IBM mainframe communications controller with a simple wiring hub. Modern versions of ARCnet can also use unshielded twisted-pair wire in a station-to-station physical topology.

Size Considerations

A complex set of rules regulates how big an ARCnet network can be.

- Generally, the maximum length of cable from one end of the network to the other is 20,000 feet.

- The maximum cable length to regenerate signals between *powered*, or so-called *active* hubs, is 2,000 feet.

- The length between a powered hub and a network node is also 2,000 feet.

- Unpowered passive hubs can connect to nodes over 100 feet of cable.

As you can see, ARCnet systems can cover a large geographical area.

Token-Ring

The token-ring concept and its underlying cabling plan evolved at IBM in the period from 1982 to 1985. In the early 1990s, Token-Ring was the central supporting pillar of IBM connectivity. IBM shuffled into full support of ethernet in the late 1990s. The company still offers Token-Ring adapters and software for every level of computer product. The token-ring system is described in an open IEEE standard 802.5, but the standardization process was guided and led by people from IBM. At this point, it's doubtful that anyone would elect to install Token-Ring in a new installation, but IBM and other companies still sell the adapters and are improving the technology.

If you're going to "bet the business" on your network, you want it to be reliable and robust. Token-ring uses a precise mechanism called *token-passing* for regulating the access of each node to the cable. The nodes on the network pass a small message packet called a *token* from station to station on a ring of cable. When a node has data to transmit, it changes the free token to a busy token and sends the data from its application program inside a formatted package called a *frame*. Each node on the ring repeats each bit of the frame as it is

---

Swapping speed for distance

Note: A general rule of communications is that you trade speed for distance. Architectures like ARCnet that use slower signaling can span greater cable lengths without the need for a repeater. Faster 10, 100, and 1,000Mbps ethernet architectures carry increasingly stringent cable-length limitations.

received, but only the addressee copies the frame to a buffer on the LAN adapter and then into the host device. When the originating node receives its busy token from upstream in the ring, it turns it back into a free token and sends it into the ring downstream.

The real system is, of course, much more complex. Here's what is involved:

- The adapter cards learn the addresses of their upstream neighbors to speed recovery from interruptions.
- The station with the highest internal address (assigned during manufacture of the adapter) acts as a monitor to keep the token going, and a secondary station monitors the activity of the primary monitor.
- Built-in problem determination procedures (PDPs) identify a malfunctioning adapter and remove it from the ring.

The token-passing technique stands in stark contrast to the comparative free-for-all of the somewhat older ethernet CSMA/CD standard, in which a node listens for a break in the traffic and tries to insert data onto the network cable before any other node.

Token-ring is designed to survive. Although this system is electrically a ring, it is physically a star with cabling reaching out to each node from a central wiring hub. This configuration appears in Figure 1.7. The wiring hub uses a relay to sense voltage coming from an adapter after the adapter has passed a rigorous self-test and is ready to enter the ring. The hub actually breaks the electrical continuity of the ring for a fraction of a second while it switches in the new entrant. In token-ring terminology, a wiring center is a *multistation access unit (MAU)*, or, in an improved version, a *controlled access unit (CAU)*. Dozens of companies market MAUs and CAUs with different capabilities, including elaborate management and reporting schemes and the capability to extend communications over longer-than-recommended cable spans.

The Wiring Hub

Because of the wiring hub, damage to a cable run going to an inactive station never affects the nodes in the active ring. If an adapter fails or something happens to the cable going to an adapter, that piece of the ring is immediately discarded.

FIGURE 1.7
The token-ring architecture uses a star wiring configuration, although the data passes from node to node around an electrical ring. This diagram shows various wiring centers, including two-port hubs that allow you to share a single cable run to the wiring center between two nodes in the same office.

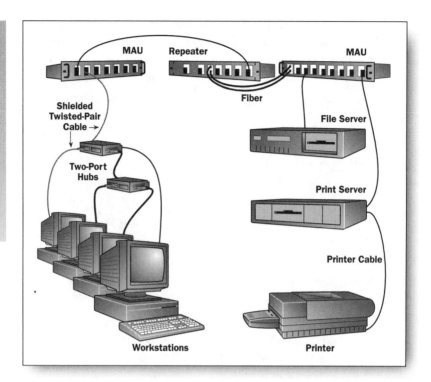

FIGURE 1.7
The token-ring architecture uses a star wiring configuration, although the data passes from node to node around an electrical ring. This diagram shows various wiring centers, including two-port hubs that allow you to share a single cable run to the wiring center between two nodes in the same office.

The system becomes more complex as you link wiring hubs together. The hubs maintain the ring architecture for the flow of data in one extended network, even though the wiring hubs are in different work areas or wiring closets several hundred feet apart. In practice, one ring can have many wiring centers, and the wiring centers are often spread around the building. When two separate wiring centers are linked, a physical diagram of them would look like two stars reaching out toward each other.

The token-ring standard allows for either 4Mbps or 16Mbps signaling speeds, and new LAN adapters that you buy will typically operate at either speed. However, you can't intermix the 4Mbps and 16Mbps signals on the same network segment. In practice, many companies use 16Mbps signaling between wiring hubs and 4Mbps signaling from the wiring hub to the network nodes.

Chapter 5, "Managing Through the Hub," is dedicated to the topic of hubs and repeaters.

Cabling Alternatives

As we describe in Chapter 4, the IEEE 802.5 token-ring standards give you a lot of leeway to choose cabling alternatives. The original specification called for a cable made from shielded twisted-pair wire (STP). STP provides a high-quality electrical environment that can easily handle the 4Mbps or 16Mbps signaling of token-ring. It's also suitable for emerging 100Mbps systems. However, this cable is bulky and quickly fills wiring conduits.

Although IBM tried to stick to shielded twisted-pair, users in general clamored for the unshielded twisted-pair (UTP) used in high-end telephone systems and in the IEEE 802.3 10BaseT. The primary appeal of UTP is its small size; it doesn't clog wiring ducts. IBM initially specified an unshielded twisted-pair cable as IBM Type 3 cable. Type 3 cable works reliably in 4Mbps service, but it must be carefully installed to work reliably in 16Mbps systems. In Chapter 3, "Standards: There Are So Many!" we describe newer UTP standards for high-speed token-ring installations.

UTP was certainly never in IBM's original plans for reliable connectivity wiring, but the company joined with Synoptics Communications to get IEEE approval for a plan using passive inductive and capacitive circuits to properly form the signal for transmission over UTP at 16Mbps. They have also released a family of Lobe Attachment Modules that can link shielded and unshielded twisted-pair cable. (Each run of cable from a hub to a node is called a *lobe.*)

Size Considerations

Complicated formulas guide the number of wiring centers, the cable distance between them, the number of nodes, and the maximum length of cable between a wiring center and a node. In the simplest form, any single ring is limited to a maximum of 72 nodes on UTP and a maximum of 260 nodes on STP. Therefore, if you have more nodes—or if you simply want to limit the traffic on any one ring— you link the rings with a token-ring bridge. The bridge passes traffic between rings, reinserting only certain frames into the downstream ring to reduce the amount of traffic and to avoid ring-size and cable-length limitations.

The Costs of Cabling

So far, we've tried to make the point that network systems have complex rules and that the best way to follow the rules is to use a structured wiring system. This kind of system meets the rules for deployment, minimizes the attenuation and interference, and provides room for growth. Now you should ask, "At what price?"

Let's examine the costs of installing a 20-node local area network to illustrate how the cost of cabling can be a wildcard factor in your budget.

The cost of installing cabling is often the hidden surprise in networking. We'll start out with a wiring hub. The price for wiring hubs varies, but the popular 10BaseT hubs usually cost as little as $10 per port. We stress the importance of using switching in any corporate or enterprise LAN; switches with full 10/100Mbps capability, but no management, cost about $30 per port. You will pay more for hubs with internal management systems, but we won't include that capability in this relatively small network. For a small switch, we will start the budget for cabling with $600.

Let's assume that this installation will use a fireproof cable with runs of 100 feet each. You will pay about $.20 per foot for this cable, so we will add $400 to the budget. Wall plates cost $4.75 each; a patch panel is $210; and there will probably be $50 worth of plastic wire wraps and connectors in the installation. We will add another $350.

Labor is the biggest variable in the cost of cabling, and if you run into installation problems, it can be the biggest unpleasant surprise. Experience shows that it takes about 7 minutes to prepare each end of the cable, 20 minutes to run each cable, 1 hour to unpack and clean up, and 10 minutes per cable for certification. Add an hour for things that go wrong. If we assume $45 an hour for each of two people, you will pay at least $1,800 for labor.

Thus, if everything goes smoothly, your bottom line will be close to $3,200—nearly $160 per node. If running the wires through the walls of your building is difficult or your hourly labor rates are higher, the installation costs can skyrocket.

On the bottom line, a good cable system has a high upfront investment cost, but it offers long-term service. Overall, your network is
no better than its cabling system. The cabling is critical to reliability
and *throughput* (more carrying capacity in the cabling system), and a
surprisingly large number of network problems are cabling problems.
A good cabling installation costs more in the beginning, but pays
dividends for years.

Looking Upstream

In the last half of the 1990s, the load on local networks has increased
and the patterns of traffic have changed. The years after 2000 will
see more streams of data. New applications drive the need for more
throughput and flexibility. The effect of the Internet and intranets
changes the patterns of data traffic and puts more emphasis on gateways and portals to the wide world.

Ethernet and UTP have won their technology wars and depend on
fiber-optic cable to extend their reach. At the same time, wireless
connection alternatives have become more important in many installations.

chapter

2

Cable Basics

Cables Aren't Just Wire Anymore   •

Many Types of Cables   •

Keeping Things In, Keeping Things Out   •

Coaxial Cable   •

Unshielded Twisted-Pair (UTP) Cable   •

Shielded Twisted-Pair (STP) Cable   •

Fiber-Optic Cable   •

Selecting the Best Cable   •

Cables Aren't Just Wire Anymore

"Wire is wire. Isn't that so?" the New Guy asked. "No," Willy replied patiently, "you can't run and you can't hide from the laws of physics. The laws of physics say that there's a lot of difference between cables like these because of the size of the conductors, the kind of insulation between them, their arrangement inside the outer tubing, and their capability to keep out electrical noise."

Willy slid open another drawer and pulled out a rat's nest of cables the size of a wastebasket. (The New Guy was new at OK Cable partially because the guy before him hadn't kept his materials and installations neat.) Sloppy installations are bad installations in Willy's book. As he and the New Guy untangled the cables and marked them, Willy welcomed the opportunity to do some on-the-job training.

"The networks we put in are real finicky about their cabling. The faster the signaling speed on the LAN, the more finicky they get. Those are the laws of physics at work. As the signaling speed goes up, the square waves that represent the zeros and ones on the wire are closer together, and it's more difficult for the LAN cards to tell them apart. If there is high electrical noise on the cable, or if a bad installation or bad design reduces the strength of the signals, the equipment can't detect the difference between a zero and a one, and the network is down."

"So everything depends on the cabling, huh?" the New Guy observed.

"Yup, time was when we really could run 1Mbps adapters like the old 10Net boards for a quarter mile over two strands of barbed wire. But today's 10, 16, and 100Mbps systems need high quality cable and careful installation."

Willy opened another drawer and pointed to more tangled cables. "Every connection counts, kid. Every connection counts."

Many Types of Cables

Wire, wire, everywhere and not an inch to link! All wire isn't cable and all cable isn't equal. Any single wire can be an individual conductor, but in electrical systems it takes two wires to form a complete circuit. When two or more wires are combined in a manner that conforms to specific standards, we call the collective product a *cable*. The world of cabling includes many types of individual cables and cable systems in which connectors and other devices are combined with the cables.

When you plan a network, you're faced with cabling decisions fraught with high initial costs and long-term importance. In Chapter 3, "Standards: There Are So Many!," we advise you on how to use national and international standards to select the right cables for your installation. In this chapter, we'll define some cable buzzwords for you and discuss the categories of cables. We'll start with copper cables, which carry electrical signals, and then move to glass cables, which carry pulses of light.

Keeping Things In, Keeping Things Out

In networks, the primary job of the connecting cable is to carry the signal from node to node with as little degradation as possible. However, the electrical signal is under constant attack from inside and out. Inside the cable, signals degrade because of various electrical characteristics, including opposition to the flow of electrons, called *resistance*, and opposition to changes in voltage and current, called *reactance*. Electrical impulses from many sources such as lighting, electrical motors, and radio systems can attack the cable from outside.

Network designers can do only a few practical things to limit signal degradation. The techniques typically involve increasing the size of the conductors and improving the type of insulation. These changes increase the size and cost of the cable faster than they improve its quality, so designers typically specify a cable of good practical quality and then specify limitations on the overall length of the cable between nodes.

Each wire in the cable can act like an antenna, absorbing electrical signals from other wires in the cable and from sources of electrical noise outside the cable. The imposed electrical noise can reach such a high level that it becomes difficult for the network interface cards to discriminate between the electrical noise and the desired signal. Electrical noise arising from signals on other wires in the cable is known as *crosstalk*. The potential level of crosstalk is a major limiting factor in the use of some types of cables.

Outside sources of potential interference include radio transmitters, electrical relays and switches, thermostats, and fluorescent lights. This type of interference is commonly referred to as *EMI/RFI noise* (electromagnetic interference/radio frequency interference).

There are many types of EMI/RFI, and their study is a serious academic field of great commercial importance. You see EMI happen every time you turn on a motor and the lights blink. Flipping a switch on a high-current device creates a pulse of energy called a *transient*. A nearby data cable can pick up that transient, and the induced pulse can drown out the desired signals on the cable. If this happens once a day, it's no big deal. Networking software can repeat data packets that didn't make it to the other end. If it happens several times a minute, as with the motor on an elevator, network performance will suffer.

Similarly, the radio frequency energy from a radio transmitter can couple to a network cable and make it harder for the receiver portion of a network interface card to pick out the desirable signals. We saw this happen with the radar-equipped burglar alarm of a bank. When the vault closed for the night and the alarm went on, the network in the property management office next door slowed down. The radio waves nearly drowned out the desired signals at a server, and the networking software had to make repeated efforts to get the packets through.

Cable designers use two techniques to protect each wire from undesirable signals: *shielding* and *cancellation*. Shielding is a brute force, but highly effective technique. In a shielded cable, each wire pair or group of wire pairs is surrounded by a metal braid or foil, which acts as a barrier to the interfering signals. Of course, the braid or foil covering increases the diameter of each cable and its cost.

Cancellation is a more elegant approach than shielding. As Figure 2.1 shows, current flowing through a wire creates a small, circular electromagnetic field around the wire. The direction of the

Sneaky problems

Many cabling problems aren't serious enough to stop the data, but they're bad enough to really slow it down. That often makes cabling problems difficult to recognize. A network with low utilization can get by with marginal cables, but when you add more applications and depend on it more for connectivity, it won't have the top end performance to do the job.

The enemies of success

Poorly installed connectors can deliver weak signals that are overcome by crosstalk or EMI/RIF. Poorly installed connectors can interrupt ground connections so that crosstalk and EMI/RFI increase. Poorly routed UTP cable can be exposed to overwhelming levels of EMI/RFI.

current flow in the wire determines the direction of the electromagnetic lines of force encircling the wire. If two wires are in the same electrical circuit, the electrons flow from the negative voltage source to the destination (called a *load*) in one wire and from the load to the positive source in the other wire. If the two wires are in close proximity, their electromagnetic fields are the exact opposite of each other and cancel out each other and any outside fields as well. This canceling effect erases unwanted electromagnetic impulses from outside the cable and prevents them from hiding the desired signals under noise inside the cable. Engineers enhance this cancellation effect by twisting the wires. Cancellation is a very effective method of providing self-shielding for wire pairs within a cable.

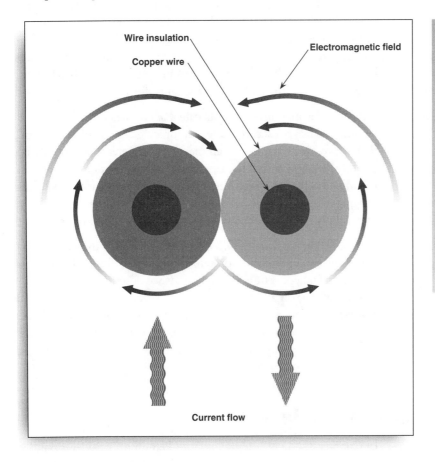

Wire insulation

Copper wire

Electromagnetic field

Current flow

FIGURE 2.1
Current flowing through a wire creates an electromagnetic field around the wire. Because the current flows in opposite directions within each wire in an active electrical circuit, the two fields rotate in opposite directions, cancel each other out, and also cancel outside sources of electrical noise. In addition, twisting the two wires together strengthens the fields' capability to resist outside noise.

All network cables use one or both of these shielding and cancellation techniques to protect their data. On the bottom line, cables vary in their size, cost, and difficulty of installation primarily because of differences in the shielding and cancellation techniques they use.

We have briefly described resistance and reactance, but you will hear the word *impedance* more frequently. Cables are often specified by impedance. You will hear about 52-ohm coaxial cables, 100-ohm unshielded twisted-pair cables, and even 150-ohm shielded cables. In each case, the designation indicates the impedance of the cable.

Impedance is a complex electrical characteristic involving resistance and reactance, which can be measured only with sophisticated equipment. Cables must have a specific impedance value in order to match the electrical components in the interface cards. A high or low impedance in itself is not good or bad, but a cable must have the correct impedance to avoid signal loss and interference. The distance between two conductors, the type of insulation, and other factors determine a specific electrical impedance for each type of cable.

Impedance is measured in units called *ohms*, which confuses some people because resistance—a less complex electrical characteristic that is easy to measure with an inexpensive meter—is also measured in ohms. Don't confuse the resistance of a connection or circuit with the impedance of a cable. Resistance is only one factor in determining impedance. The two factors are slightly interrelated, but they aren't the same, even though we express them both in ohms.

Another term we'll use is *cable jacket*. The jacket is the outside covering of the cable, typically some form of plastic, Teflon, or composite material. The concept is simple, but as we describe in Chapter 3, the jacket material on all cable is subject to several complex codes and regulations. Cables differ in ways that are even subtler than their size, weight, and cost. The chemical composition of the materials in the cable, the spacing of the wires in the cable, and other factors all have an effect on cable performance.

Coaxial Cable

In Chapter 1, "The Role of Cabling: Planning Considerations," we associated the early ethernet networking architecture with coaxial cable. The only new coaxial cable installations are in areas with very big RFI/EMI problems. Even then, modern installers are more likely to use fiber-optic cable than copper coaxial cable. However, coaxial cable installations done in the mid-1990s have a decade more of useful lives, so it pays to understand coax if you're going to understand cabling.

Coaxial cable consists of a center copper conductor (either solid wire or stranded, but solid is recommended for networks), a layer of flexible insulation, a shield of woven copper braid or metallic foil, and an outer cable jacket. The term *coaxial* arose from the fact that the shielding braid and the center conductor both have the same axis.

The outer braid of coaxial cable makes up one half of the electrical circuit, in addition to acting as shielding for the inner conductor, so the braid must make a solid electrical connection at both ends of the cable. Poor shield connection is the biggest source of connection problems in a coaxial cable installation. (Later, we'll describe other types of shielded wire in which the shielding is not a part of the circuit.) The cable jacket adds a final layer of insulation and protective coating and completes the package.

Figure 2.2 details the components of a coaxial cable. The coaxial cable used in thin ethernet and ARCnet networks has an outside diameter of about 0.18 inch or 4.7mm. A larger diameter of coaxial cable is specified for ethernet backbone cables. This cable, stiff with shielding and carrying an easily identified yellow jacket, is often referred to as a "frozen yellow garden hose." The ethernet backbone cable has an outside diameter of approximately 0.4 inch or 9.8mm.

Some LAN signaling schemes, such as thin ethernet and ARCnet, depend on coaxial cables with specific impedances that are not interchangeable. Thin ethernet uses a cable originally described as RG-58, which has an impedance of 52 ohms. Some manufacturers now market for ethernet use a cable that they describe as 802.3 cable, because it conforms to the standards established by the IEEE 802.3 Committee.

ARCnet was originally designed for RG-62 coaxial cable, which has an impedance of 93 ohms. This cable is also used in IBM mainframe computer installations to link IBM 3270 terminals to their controllers. RG-58 and RG-62 cables often look very similar, and sometimes the only way to tell the difference is by reading the labels on the outside of the cable. You will find RG-59 coaxial cable, with an impedance of 75 ohms, used for cable television wiring in many buildings, but it isn't suitable for any modern networking connections.

Always suspect the coaxial connector

Unshielded twisted-pair wire can stretch, become compressed, or otherwise be damaged over the life of a building. Coaxial cable is much tougher stuff. If you have a cable problem in a coaxial cable system, always suspect the connectors. It's common for the braid to look as though it's connected when it doesn't have a good connection.

Coaxial cable plays an important role in both the ARCnet and ethernet network architectures, but there is no provision for coaxial cable in token-ring. Originally, ARCnet plans specified that coaxial cable should be installed in a star-shaped configuration; each node has a separate run of coaxial cable going to a central wiring hub. This configuration reduces the chance that one bad cable segment might bring down the entire network. Some companies later introduced ARCnet network adapters that allow different cable configurations, but star wiring with coaxial cable and hubs remains the most popular arrangement.

Originally, the ethernet scheme allowed for a plan called *thin ethernet* using the RG-58–type cable arranged in a node-to-node or daisy-chain wiring scheme. In this configuration, one break in the cable or one bad connector could disrupt the entire network. Manufacturers of wiring hubs now market connectors for coaxial cable that enable you to configure thin ethernet in a star-wired arrangement with separate lengths of coax running between each node and the wiring hub. This arrangement is particularly useful wherever high electrical noise is a problem. A star-wired thin ethernet arrangement combines the excellent shielding capabilities of coax with the highly reliable star-wiring scheme.

Despite its resistance to crosstalk and to RFI/EMI, the networking industry has moved away from coaxial cable. Coax costs much more per foot than UTP and fills up conduit and wiring trays. Developments and standards have all moved to unshielded twisted-pair wire augmented by fiber-optic cable in special conditions.

Unshielded Twisted-Pair (UTP) Cable

As the name implies, twisted-pair cable is composed of pairs of wires; the pairs are insulated from each other and twisted together within an outer jacket. There is no physical electrical shielding, either foil or braid, on UTP cable; it derives all its protection from the cancellation effect of the twisted-wire pairs. The mutual cancellation effect reduces crosstalk between pairs and EMI/RFI noise. Network designers vary the number of twists in the different wire pairs within each cable to reduce the electrical coupling and crosstalk between the pairs. UTP cable relies solely on this cancellation effect to minimize the absorption and radiation of electrical energy.

Unshielded twisted-pair cable designed for networks, shown in Figure 2.3, contains four pairs of 22-gauge or 24-gauge solid copper wires. The cable has an impedance of 100 ohms—an important factor that differentiates it from other types of twisted-pair and telephone wiring. Network UTP cable has an external diameter of about 0.17 inch or 4.3mm. This small size is advantageous during installation.

FIGURE 2.3
Unshielded twisted-pair cable (UTP) for networks uses four pairs of wire in the same jacket. Each wire pair has a different degree of twisting to reduce the coupling and crosstalk between them.

Beware when purchasing cable

In American Wire Gauge (AWG) standards, larger numbers indicate smaller wires. Other standards, described in Chapter 3, "Standards: There Are So Many!" will guide your cable purchase, but beware of any cabling in your installation that uses wires that look too thin or are stranded instead of solid.

UTP now dominates the cabling market. You can use UTP with each of the three major networking architectures (ARCnet, ethernet, and token-ring), although in some cases the wire pairs appear on different pin connections in the wall jacks. In most cases, you must order network interface cards for the specific type of cabling, but some ethernet interface cards are still configured for both coaxial cable and UTP.

UTP's Pluses and Minuses

Although UTP is popular, some of its potential and often highly lauded advantages, such as ease of installation and low cost, don't survive close scrutiny. Certainly, it requires less training and equipment to install UTP than to install fiber-optic cable, but it still takes a great deal of care and skill to install a UTP system capable of reliably carrying data moving at 100Mbps. Newer standards call for using UTP over short distances with signaling rates up to one gigabit per second, but these cable plants have to be carefully planned and installed. UTP isn't the best choice for installations with high levels of EMI. Fiber offers better EMI resistance and better distance, but for the large majority of network installations, UTP fills the bill with efficiency and economy.

It's true that UTP costs less per foot than any other type of LAN cabling, but materials are the least significant cost of any installation, with labor typically costing the most. The high demand for installations has kept personnel costs high.

On the bottom line, UTP's real advantage is its size. UTP doesn't fill wiring ducts as quickly as other cable types (it's about the same size as fiber-optic cable). In an existing building, its small size makes pulling UTP through the walls easier. In a new building, wiring with UTP makes it possible to plan for more connections without seriously diminishing vital utility space.

Telephone Wire Is Not LAN Cable

Many people confuse UTP wire designed for network data with the telephone wire already installed in their walls. They are seldom the same. The telephone wiring in use in most residences is called *quad*. Quad has four nontwisted parallel wires in one cable. Silver satin is another type of telephone wire found in some modern buildings. Silver satin cable is flat and typically has a silver-colored vinyl jacket. In older buildings, you will often find thick multiconductor cables designed for a type of telephone system called a *key system*. None of these wiring systems—quad, silver satin, or key system—is adequate for modern LAN data services. Figure 2.4 shows you what types of cable to avoid.

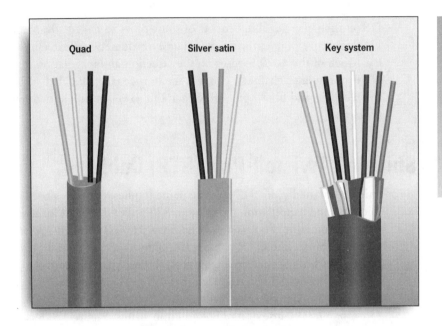

Quad   Silver satin   Key system

FIGURE 2.4
Although you might already find them in the walls of your building, these cables are not network cables. They don't conform to the electrical specifications for LAN adapters and won't reliably carry LAN signals over practical distances.

Even though some digital telephone private branch exchange (PBX) systems do use high quality, twisted-pair wire (sometimes even shielded twisted-pair), it typically isn't installed in the same pair configuration called for in local area networks. Even a sophisticated digital PBX wiring plant can require a great deal of modification before it can be used for ARCnet, ethernet, or token-ring networking. Even if they do have the correct type of wire, existing wiring plants often exhibit problems when you try to use them to carry high-speed data. If you are going to bet your business on your network, you should probably plan on installing a new LAN wiring system.

Older cable plants often suffer from out-of-date documentation, so you don't know which cables go where or, most importantly, their length. Standard PBX wiring installations provide four pairs of wires to the wall jack; two pairs are used by the PBX telephone system and two pairs might be free. However, if you have an intercom or other special telephone feature, all your pairs will be used. Also, a rule of thumb is that two to three percent of wire pairs in an installation are bad. When the number of available pairs is already marginal, attrition takes a big toll. The cost of testing an existing cable plant, troubleshooting, and making modifications to meet current standards often offsets the cost of pulling new cable.

Despite the questionable benefits of some of its so-called advantages, UTP is secure in its growing dominance of the network cable industry. Much of this book focuses on the selection and installation of UTP, but in later chapters, you will see how coaxial, shielded twisted-pair, and fiber-optic cable each can solve specific networking problems.

Shielded Twisted-Pair (STP) Cable

Shielded twisted-pair (STP), as the name implies, combines both shielding and cancellation techniques. STP cable designed for networking comes in two varieties. The simplest STP is called *100-ohm shielded* because, like UTP, it has a 100-ohm impedance and has an added shield of copper braid around all the wire pairs. The most common form of STP, introduced by IBM and associated with the IEEE 802.5 token-ring networking architecture, is known as *150-ohm STP* because of its 150-ohm impedance. Figure 2.5 illustrates 150-ohm shielded twisted-pair wire.

The style of STP cable introduced by IBM for Token-Ring uses a "belt and suspenders" approach to engineering. Not only is the entire 150-ohm STP cable shielded to reduce EMI/RFI, but also each pair of twisted wires is shielded from the others by a separate shield to reduce crosstalk. In addition, each pair is twisted to benefit from the effects of cancellation. Note that unlike coaxial cable, the shielding on 150-ohm STP isn't part of the signal path, but is grounded at both ends.

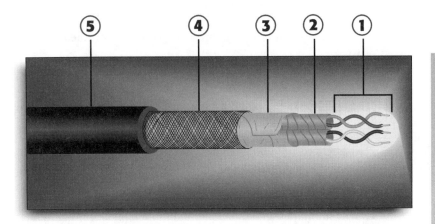

FIGURE 2.5
The shielded twisted-pair wire used in IBM's Token-Ring networking system shields each pair of wires individually to reduce crosstalk and then shields the entire cable to reduce outside interference. This conservative approach provides an excellent electrical environment, but the cable has a large outside diameter and is expensive.

① Unshielded twisted-pairs

② Insulation

③ Foil shielding

④ Shielded braid

⑤ Outer jacket

On the positive side, 150-ohm STP can carry data using very fast signaling with little chance of distortion. On the negative side, all the shielding causes signal loss that increases the need for greater spacing (that is, more insulation) between the wire pairs and the shield. The increased amount of insulation and the large amount of shielding considerably increase the size, weight, and cost of the cable. IBM-style STP, with an outside diameter of approximately 0.4 inch or 0.98mm, quickly fills wiring ducts. Wiring a building for IBM Token-Ring with STP requires the installation of large wiring closets and large wiring ducts.

The 100-ohm STP, used primarily for ethernet installations, improves the EMI/RFI resistance of twisted-pair wire without a significant gain in size or weight. The shield is not part of the data circuit, so it is grounded at only one end, typically at the wiring closet or hub. However, properly grounding the shield on the cable isn't easy, particularly if you want to make use of older wiring hubs that aren't designed for STP. If it isn't grounded at one end, the shield becomes an antenna and your problems multiply.

Mod-Tap (now Molex Premise Networks), Amp, BTR Telecom, and other companies market patch panels that can grasp the cable shield and ground it. You can terminate all the 100-ohm shielded twisted-pair cables in the patch panel and retain the wiring hub and LAN adapters you've already installed, but you will need a good ground connection for the patch panel. 100-ohm shielded twisted-pair cable

Advantages to fully shielded UTP

The advantages of using fully shielded UTP are particularly obvious in an area where you have strong electromagnetic interference. A location in a building near a commercial AM radio transmitter is a good example. However, it's also true that higher speed networks need more protection. As signaling speeds increase, the devices in any installation demand the lower levels of noise provided by shielding.

offers more protection from interference than unshielded twisted-pair. It also maintains compatibility with 10BaseT wiring hubs and avoids the conduit crowding problems of 150-ohm shielded twisted-pair wire.

Fiber-Optic Cable

Whereas copper wires carry electrons, fiber-optic cables made of glass fibers carry light. The advantages of fiber include complete immunity from crosstalk and EMI/RFI. The lack of internal and external noise means that signals go farther and can move faster, which translates to both greater speed and distance than copper cabling. Because fiber can't carry electrical power, it is the perfect medium to connect buildings that might have different electrical grounds. Also, the long cable spans between buildings can't serve as an entry point for lightning, as they can if the interbuilding links are copper cables. Finally, a two-fiber cable, in which each fiber carries a beam of light in one direction, is about the same size as UTP: approximately 0.21 inch or 5.3mm. Because it is flat like a piece of lamp cord, you can get many fiber cables in a single conduit.

If fiber-optic cable offers so many benefits, why do we still use copper? The answer lies in interface devices and the cost of connections. As an optical interface, a fiber-optic connector must make a precise right angle and polished connection to the end of the strand, which clearly makes installation more difficult. Installers typically attend a one-day training course, but the only way to learn is through practice, and each practice connection can cost 8 to 10 dollars. The course is a costly investment in training. It can take a trained installer several minutes to make a connection, so the hourly cost of labor is high in a large installation, and the installer needs an expensive toolkit to make even one connection.

Finally, the fiber-optic transceivers at each end of the cable are expensive. A fiber-optic LAN card costs five to seven times as much as an ethernet card for copper cable. Although fiber is alluring, it is difficult to justify the cost of running fiber to each desktop. In modern installations, fiber makes up the backbone between wiring hubs and between buildings. Fiber also has an important role as the media of choice for gigabit ethernet.

Fiber-optic communication has its roots in nineteenth-century inventions. A device called the *Photophen* converted voice signals into optical signals using sunlight and lenses mounted on a transducer that vibrated to the sound. Fiber optics became practical in the 1960s with the introduction of solid-state light sources—lasers and light-emitting diodes—and high quality glass free of most impurities. Telephone companies pioneered fiber-optic techniques to gain all its benefits for long distance connections.

A typical fiber-optic LAN cable, shown in Figure 2.6, has two fibers that terminate in two separate connectors. Some cables combine fibers and twisted copper inside the same jacket, and cables with multiple fibers are common. However, the link between a node and a cable hub is always made using two fibers, each of which carries light in one direction.

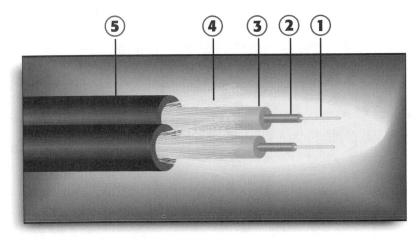

FIGURE 2.6
A fiber-optic cable for networks consists of two fibers in separate sheaths. Each glass fiber is surrounded by reflective cladding, a plastic coating, a protective layer of Kevlar, and an outer jacket.

① Fiber

② Cladding

③ Plastic coating

④ Fibers

⑤ Outer jacket

Each half of the fiber-optic cable is composed of layers of material. On the outside, a plastic jacket that must conform to the appropriate fire and building codes for the installation protects the entire cable. Under the jacket, a layer of Kevlar fibers (also used in bulletproof vests) provides cushioning and strength. Under the Kevlar, another layer of plastic, called the *coating*, typically adds cushioning and protection. Some fiber-optic cables designed for burial might include a stainless steel wire or other materials for added strength. All these materials protect the hair-thin glass strand.

WARNING: Eye damage possible

Never look directly into an unmarked optical cable to determine whether it is fiber-optic cable. Permanent eye damage may result because the light that moves through the cable is often intense but not visible to the human eye.

The center of each glass strand, called the *core*, is where the data actually travels. Light from a diode or laser enters the core at one end and is trapped by the shiny walls of the core—a phenomenon called *total internal reflection*. The size of the core is measured in microns. Two standard sizes for the core are 62.5 and 100 microns, equal to about 0.002 inch.

The core is surrounded by a glass or plastic coating, called the *cladding*, which has a different optical density than the core. The boundary between the cladding and the core reflects the light back into the core. Cladding typically is 125 or 140 microns thick, about 0.003 inch.

In later chapters, we provide more details about the selection and use of fiber-optic cable, but for now you should understand that it is economical for specific applications such as connecting wiring centers. Additionally, fiber is highly recommended for some applications, such as connecting separate buildings. Running fiber to every desktop has been an expensive alternative. 3M has led some changes in the fiber-optic cable market through a consortium called *VF-45*. VF-45, a system of cables and connectors, reduces the cost of fiber-optic cable and makes it more practical to use fiber to the desktop. See Chapter 11, "Cable Testing and Certification," for more information.

Selecting the Best Cable

Many network designers focus on decisions such as what brand of network operating system to use or what kind of server hardware to buy. In many installations, though, selecting the cable is the first major step in network design. Final decisions about software and computer hardware can wait, but the early actions of architects and construction crews hinge on the cable decision.

We suggest that you consider the following factors when making your cable decision:

- What is the present need for signaling speed? What do the applications require?

- Can you foresee future needs for signaling speed? Are high-density graphics on the horizon?

- Are you required to comply with building and fire codes? Do you have cable conduit space? Architectural considerations? Local building code restrictions?

After you understand those factors, you can address these questions:

- Do you want to rely on copper or fiber?
- How widely dispersed are the nodes? What can you afford?
- Is this a backbone or a lobe to a LAN node?

Each of these decisions leads you into a different area of standards and specifications. In the following chapters, we provide more detailed information to guide your decisions and installation techniques.

chapter

3

Standards:
There Are So Many!

Grading Your Cables •

Working Together •

Who Said So? •

Company Plans •

National Electrical Code (NEC) •

The EIA/TIA-568 (SP-2840) Standard •

Underwriters Laboratories (UL) •

Evolution •

Grading Your Cables

"Willy, I need help. I've got to put together a specification for this network and I don't know where to start."

The center of focus on Willy's desk was a bottomless tray of paperwork, so any distraction, even one from a blustery high school principal, was welcome. He cleaned off a chair so that the young woman could sit down. "Let me get this straight, Sara, you want me to help you write a wide-open specification for the high school network so that anybody, including me, can bid on it?"

"Yeah, who else in town could write it so that it's both fair and technically correct?" the principal replied.

"But will you let me bid on it?"

"Sure, we'll invite a round of comments before the final bid, and if you've sneaked in anything that locks up the job for you, we'll hold a public lynching," she quipped with a straight face.

"You do know that every electrical contractor in four counties will try to bid? Most of them don't know anything about data systems, but they'll all claim they can pull wire. Are you ready for the screams when they can't bid because of the technical specifications?"

The principal was a realist who worked for an elected superintendent of schools. She weighed the political consequences before speaking. "Have you got some technical stuff we can put in there that's rock solid and supported by the federal government or something?"

"The best. You probably have county or state rules forcing you to buy only UL-marked products anyway." Willy fished in a desk drawer and pulled out a thin pamphlet with the title *UL's LAN Cable Certification Program*. "Anybody can get this pamphlet. It doesn't tell you how to install the cable, but it does describe the technical specifications for the cable. If we ask for the UL Level IV marking in your request for bids, you will get the correct cable no matter who wins.

"But," Willy continued, "there's still a problem. Getting the right grade of cable is only a small part of the job. If the cable isn't properly installed, the network might work inefficiently because the LAN adapters have to resend data, or it might not work when you move to higher speeds in a few years. So, we're going to ask the installer to provide a report, on paper, showing the crosstalk and attenuation on every cable span. That report does two things: It ensures that the installation is done right the first time, and it gives you an excellent place to start troubleshooting problems in the future. It also cuts out the people who don't know crosstalk from a crosswalk."

Willy was still hesitant about getting too involved with creating the statement of requirements for a job he wanted to bid on. So he sent the principal back to school armed with the UL pamphlet and a sample crosstalk and attenuation report. Willy gave Sara one piece of advice as he walked her to the door: "Your network is never any better than the cabling, Sara. Don't limit your network's capability tomorrow by making short-sighted cabling decisions today."

Working Together

Both the value and the wonder of today's networks are that products from many different companies all work together. A LAN adapter from 3Com and a LAN adapter from D-Link communicate with each other across a network cable because the designers of both adapters followed the same standards for interaction across the cable.

As Figure 3.1 shows, a hierarchy of standards controls the interface to the application programs, the actions of network communications programs, the design of LAN adapters, the cable connectors, and the cables themselves. Figure 3.1 can be broken down as follows:

- The Windows Open Systems Architecture (WOSA) tells programmers how to write programs that can access the services available within the Microsoft Windows environment.

- The File Transfer Protocol (FTP) from the TCP/IP standards, Microsoft's Server Message Block (SMB), and the IBM NetBIOS protocol all provide different ways for programs to communicate across a network.

- The Internet Protocol (IP) and Internetwork Packet Exchange (IPX) protocol define how networking software carries data from node to node.

- The IEEE 802 family of specifications is used to design network interface cards.

- The cable itself, though, is governed by a confusing mix of standards ranging from fire codes to detailed electrical specifications and tests for safety and performance.

Unfortunately, the specifications and standards for cables have evolved from many sources and are often overlapping and confusing.

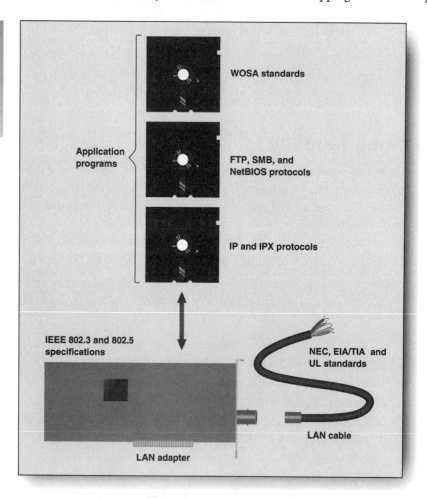

FIGURE 3.1
Modern networks function according to openly published standards supported by many companies.

In this chapter, we examine some important cable plant standards and explain the designations and specifications you will find useful when you write a request or proposal or make a purchase. But using the right materials doesn't ensure that an installation will meet the performance specification. Many factors determine the quality of the total installation, including

- How much the wire is untwisted before it reaches a termination
- The type of termination equipment
- The electrical noise in various frequency bands
- The near-end crosstalk (NEXT) caused by wires in proximity to each other

You can get a good start on a high-quality installation by using the correct cable. However, this alone does not guarantee a good installation because the actions of the installer are critical to the overall quality of your cable plant.

This chapter deals primarily with specifications that apply to shielded and unshielded twisted-pair wire. The "Company Plans" section unravels this twisted bundle of terms by looking at the plans and specifications developed by specific companies.

Who Said So?

Numerous companies, organizations, and even government bodies regulate and specify the cables you use. More than a decade ago, companies such as AT&T, Digital Equipment Corporation, Hewlett-Packard, IBM, and Northern Telecom developed volumes of detailed specifications that went beyond the cable to include the connectors, wiring and distribution centers, and installation techniques. Integrated cable plans developed by specific companies are called *premises distribution systems (PDSs)*. We'll describe some company-specific PDS architectures later in this chapter.

Generally, a corporate PDS architecture provides the following:

- Standardized media and layout descriptions for both backbone and horizontal cabling.
- Standard connection interfaces for the physical connection of equipment.
- Consistent and uniform design that follows a system plan and basic design principles.

PDS=SCS

It seems that some people in the industry now use the acronym *SCS* (structured cable system) to generally equate to a premises distribution system. Being old-fashioned and sentimental, I like PDS, but you should understand SCS, too.

51

- End-to-end tested components that minimize the risk of incompatibility. With a multivendor approach, incompatibility problems might become apparent only when changes are made to the system or high-speed networks are required. However, on the downside, sticking with one vendor means that you're stuck with that vendor's pricing, too!

- Open architecture supports equipment and applications of many vendors, including data terminals, analog and digital telephones, personal computers, and video teleconferencing and host computers, as well as common system equipment. The PDS designers have thought of everything.

- Decreased maintenance costs. Fault-finding and resolution can be particularly expensive and time-consuming in multivendor networks. Adopting a single standardized system saves finger pointing.

- PDS developers offer specific training and certification. It helps to make sure that the installers know what they're doing.

However, the systems and architectures from big companies are just part of the picture. There are many other "influencers," such as national and international organizations that develop fire and building codes. These include

- The Institute of Electrical and Electronic Engineers (IEEE)
- The Electronic Industries Alliance and the newer Telecommunications Industry Association (EIA/TIA)
- Underwriters Laboratories (UL)
- Government agencies at various levels

All these agencies and organizations issue specifications for cable material and installation. The Electronic Industries Alliance/Telecommunications Industry Association has issued EIA/TIA-568 and EIA/TIA-569 standards for technical performance. This program has gone beyond performance to include guidance such as specific wiring sequences and installation guidance. Generally, the EIA/TIA-568 and EIA/TIA–569 standards represent guidance that is independent of specific manufacturers. (See "The EIA/TIA-568 (SP-2840) Standard" section later in this chapter.) The IEEE has included minimal cable requirements in its 802.3 and 802.5 specifications for ethernet and token-ring systems.

Digital? Who?

Although it's true that Digital Equipment Corporation and even Northern Telecom no longer exist in their old corporate forms, their cabling plans survive. A building wired for Digital's plan has no growth path, whereas a building wired under Northern Telecom's plan can have robust growth.

The opposite of a PDS is...?

The opposite of a structured cable system or PDS is *ad hoc*. In other words, it grows without a plan. In the end, this kind of cable plant is very expensive to expand and maintain.

SEE ALSO
➤ *Because the IEEE 802.3 and 802.5 standards focus as much on network access as on cabling, we describe them on page 80.*

The National Electrical Code of the United States (NEC) describes various types of cables and materials used in the cables. The UL focuses on safety standards, but has expanded its certification program to evaluate twisted-pair LAN cables for performance according to IBM and EIA/TIA performance specifications, as well as NEC safety specifications. The UL also established a program to mark shielded and unshielded twisted-pair LAN cables, which should simplify the complex task of making sure that the materials used in the installation are up to specification.

As explained in Chapter 2, "Cable Basics," the designations for coaxial cable had the benefit of being set in practice before most of the standards committees began their deliberations. (The chart in Chapter 2 describes the typical coaxial cables and their different impedance ratings.) In Chapter 4, "LAN Combinations," we describe the associations between specific types of coaxial cable and local area network architectures.

Company Plans

In the 1980s and 1990s, companies like AT&T, Digital Equipment Corporation, IBM, and Northern Telecom developed and marketed complete architectures for structured cabling systems called *premises distribution systems (PDSs)*. AT&T passed its architecture on to Lucent Technologies, and Lucent markets it as the AT&T Systimax Premises Distribution System.

IBM calls its architecture the *IBM Cabling System*. IBM and AT&T fielded their systems in 1984 and 1985. Northern Telecom's Integrated Building Distribution Network (IBDN), which is quite similar to AT&T's Systimax, is a relative newcomer that emerged in 1991. Northern Telecom spun off NORCOM/CDT, formerly Northern Telecom's Cable Group, to carry on IBDN. NORCOM/CDT is one of the major suppliers of copper outside plant and central office wire and cable in North America and the leading supplier in Canada. The architectures make up a family of products offered by each vendor. Today, these product families include individual products that conform to the EIA/TIA-568 family of standards. In other words, you can follow the EIA/TIA-568 standards and still have the benefits of ordering everything from Lucent because Lucent has EIA/TIA–compliant products as part of its Systimax architecture.

Overall, the plans from IBM and AT&T had the most profound effect on the cabling industry. You will often see cables in catalogs rated in terms of IBM or AT&T/Lucent specifications. IBM's concept of cable *types* permeates the industry, and AT&T's original work influenced every cable and connector standard.

Other companies, particularly Amp, Inc., Anixter, and Mod-Tap, market and sell specific equipment for structured cabling systems. Anixter especially deserves praise for setting openly documented and fair performance and electrical standards for twisted-pair wiring. Anixter's original concept of *levels* is used by EIA/TIA and UL in their standards.

IBM Cabling System

Check out potential vendors carefully

If you have an IBM network installed, but need maintainers, ask prospective companies which IBM schools their employees have attended and what experience they have in following the IBM Cabling Plan specifications. As a rule, it doesn't pay to let a vendor learn on your installation.

Interestingly, IBM does not sell the cables or connectors it describes in its documentation. IBM's goal in creating and supporting the IBM Cabling Plan is to have a stable and known environment for the operation of its computer equipment. You can buy cables and parts certified to meet the IBM specifications from a variety of vendors, and you can find local contractors who will install the PDS according to IBM's specifications.

The heart of the IBM cabling system is a series of specifications for wire types. The IBM architecture contains the only significant support in the industry for shielded twisted-pair wire. STP, specified in IBM's Type 1, Type 2, Type 6, Type 8, and Type 9 cable (described next), replaces the older RG-62 coaxial cable IBM used to link terminals to mainframe computers under the IBM 3270 terminal plan. STP is the wiring alternative IBM recommends for both 4Mbps and 16Mbps token-ring installations. The IBM Cabling Plan also uses fiber-optic cable (see Chapter 8, "From the Wall to the Desktop," for more information) and unshielded twisted-pair wire, but the heart of the system is shielded twisted-pair wire. Here is a brief description of the IBM wire types:

- *Type 1 cable* consists of shielded cable with two twisted pairs made from 22AWG solid wire (as opposed to the stranded wire in Type 6). Used for data transmission, particularly with token-ring networks, the cable has an impedance of 150 ohms. Each pair of wires has its own shielding, and then the entire cable is shielded by an external braid. Type 1 cable is tested to a bandwidth of 100MHz and has a data transmission rating of 100Mbps. See Figure 3.2 and the discussion of the EIA/TIA-568 Category 5 and the UL Level V later in this chapter.

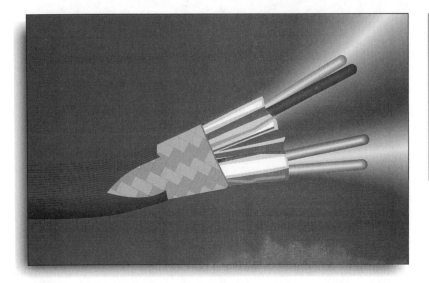

FIGURE 3.2
Many companies sell cable that follows IBM's Type 1 specification. This cable combines two separately shielded pairs of solid twisted wire. PVC and Teflon jackets provide different degrees of fire resistance.

IBM has added a new specification that uses the same cable but subjects it to more rigorous testing. This specification, Type 1A, calls for cable tested to 300MHz and has applications in areas requiring very high-speed data, such as Asynchronous Transfer Mode communications (ATM).

- *Type 2 cable* consists of four unshielded pairs of 22AWG solid wire for voice telephone and two shielded data pairs meeting the Type 1 specification in the same sheath. Type 2 was originally designed to provide voice and data transmission in the same cable. See Type 3 cable (next) for more information on the unshielded twisted pairs in the Type 2 cable. A new Type 2A, with the same configuration but tested to 600MHz, is also available. See Figure 3.3.

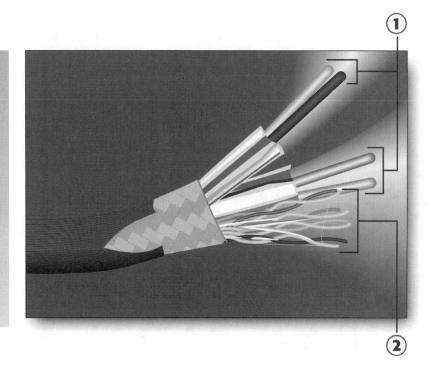

FIGURE 3.3
Cables that follow IBM's Type 2 cable specifications are used primarily to combine telephone and token-ring wiring within the same cable installation. Two pairs of shielded twisted-pair wires are joined with four unshielded twisted pairs within the same outer jacket.

① Two shielded data pairs

② Four unshielded pairs of 22AWG solid wire

- *Type 3 cable* consists of four unshielded 24AWG solid twisted pairs for voice or data with a characteristic impedance of 105 ohms. Type 3 is IBM's version of twisted-pair telephone wire. The unshielded pairs in Type 2 cable and Type 3 cable are designed only for telephone and low-speed data transmission of up to 4Mbps and do not meet the requirements for higher-speed data transmission. Do not confuse IBM Type 3 cable with EIA/TIA-568 Category 3 or UL Level III cable described later in this chapter; it looks similar, but it is not the same.

- *Type 4 cable* lacks a published specification.

- *Type 5 cable* consists of two fiber-optic strands. This cable has a 100-micron core and measures 140 microns with cladding. It has a window at 850nm and a bandwidth of 100MHz. Note that Type 5 cable differs considerably from the more popular 62.5/125 micron dual-window fiber-optic cable. Type 5 is accepted as part of the Fiber Distributed Data Interface (FDDI) specification, but the 62.5/125 micron cable, also part of the FDDI specification, is more common.

- *Type 6 cable* consists of shielded cable with two twisted pairs made from 26AWG stranded wire. More flexible than Type 1 cable and designed for data transmission, Type 6 is commonly used between a computer and a data jack in the wall. A Type 6A, tested to 600MHz, is also available.

- *Type 7 cable* lacks a published specification.

- *Type 8 cable* is a special "under-the-carpet," shielded twisted-pair cable designed to minimize the lump in the carpet that covers it. This cable contains two parallel untwisted pairs of 23AWG solid conductors and has little practical use in modern data installations.

- *Type 9 cable* is plenum cable. It consists of two individually shielded twisted pairs of 26AWG solid or stranded copper wire, covered with a special flame-retardant coating, for use between floors in a building. A Type 9A, tested to 600MHz, is also available.

The primary advantage of IBM's Cable Plan is in its conservative engineering. IBM not only relies on heavy shielding around all the pairs to keep electrical noise out, but also specifies shielding between both the pairs and the twistings to keep down the crosstalk between the pairs. This is belt-and-suspenders engineering. The specifications keep wiring runs short to avoid problems caused by the degrading of the signals with distance. If the installer follows the plan, the cable system will work in practically any electrical environment, and be viable well beyond the life of the computer equipment in the installation.

The primary drawback to the IBM Cabling Plan is the heaviness and bulk of the shielded twisted-pair cable. Type 1 cable—with an outside diameter of between .32 and .5 inch, depending on the manufacturer and the type of outside jacket—quickly fills wiring conduits and cascades into wiring closets in a huge waterfall of cable.

Another significant drawback to the IBM plan is the cost of the cabling and the connectors. On a per-foot basis, Type 1 cable costs approximately four times as much as the highest-quality unshielded twisted-pair wire designed for the same conditions. The IBM Data Connector, shown in Figure 3.4, costs about 16 times the price of an RJ-45 connector, typically used on unshielded twisted-pair wire, and

Cable confusion

When you hear or read references to Type 1 cable, you should immediately think of shielded twisted-pair wiring, but note that many speakers and writers don't clearly differentiate between the IBM cable types and often mean Type 2 or Type 6 cable.

has about that same ratio of size. Although it might be good, IBM's cable plan is bulky and expensive.

IBM Data Connector

AT&T/Lucent Systimax

The Systimax PDS, now marketed by Lucent Technologies, is deeply rooted in history. Before the breakup of the Bell System in the United States, the technical side of the telephone industry was controlled by a series of publications called the *Bell Standard Practices (BSPs)*. Because it was largely a monopoly, the telephone industry didn't need many standards beyond those in the BSPs. The BSPs described in detail how installers should cut, twist, and attach every wire, and how to secure every cable span. The Systimax specifications are, at least, the spiritual and cultural offspring of the BSPs. They are detailed and, if followed, can give you a flexible, reliable, and expandable cable plant.

Lucent inherited Systimax from AT&T, and Lucent now manufactures, sells, and installs the products in the Systimax family. The company also provides training, so you will find many installers in local companies who are certified to do work according to Systimax specifications. The IBM Cabling Plan is built on shielded twisted-pair wiring, but the AT&T Systimax is based on unshielded twisted-pair wire for horizontal wiring and fiber-optic cabling for everything else. To describe all the products in the Systimax line requires a catalog 3 inches thick, but the next four sections cover a few key elements.

Lucent offers up to 20-year assurance programs for Systimax components installed by Lucent value-added resellers. This warranty protects against defects in cable and other products manufactured by Lucent and against the system's becoming obsolete for specified applications. Systimax is a comprehensive and proven premises distribution system that serves as a standard for all installations. Whether you think it's more than you need depends on how much you value your network.

Systimax 1061A and 2061A LAN Cables

The Systimax LAN cables, shown in Figure 3.5, include four pairs of unshielded twisted-pair 24AWG copper wire in different jackets for nonplenum and plenum installations. This is the Systimax 100-ohm impedance cable for horizontal-wiring data applications. Note that the four-pair cable provides two spare pairs in most installations. With an outside diameter of about .17 inch, this cable is easy to pull through conduits and inside walls.

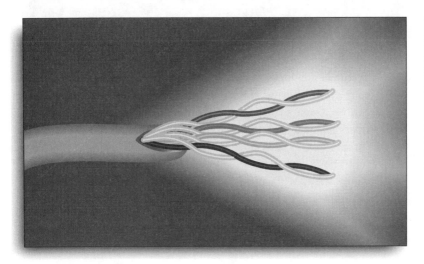

FIGURE 3.5
Systimax 1061A LAN cable is a good choice for all unshielded twisted-pair data-transmission applications. Each cable contains four unshielded twisted pairs.

Systimax 1090 and 2290 Cables

This composite cable, shown in Figure 3.6, combining copper and fiber-optic conductors, is the ultimate horizontal-wiring choice for people who want to make sure that they will never outgrow their cabling systems. It provides a total of eight unshielded twisted pairs—the equivalent of two runs of Systimax 1061A or 2061A cable—and two fibers inside one jacket. This combination provides plenty of bandwidth for data and voice telephone connections between wiring closets and the capability to add fiber connections for higher-speed data, video, or other applications. If you have a big budget and plan to own the building forever, we think that this is the right cable to install, but, like the IBM Cabling Plan, it is expensive and bulky.

FIGURE 3.6
Systimax 1090 cable combines two fibers with two separate cable runs containing four unshielded twisted pairs. This cable is bulky and expensive, but it provides a desktop with the ultimate in available bandwidth.

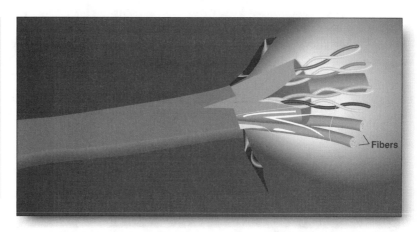

Accumax

Systimax includes a variety of fiber-optic cables to use as backbone cable to link wiring closets and as horizontal wiring for special applications. Some products in this family group together as many as 216 fibers inside a protective jacket for the long trip up an elevator or air shaft. The Systimax fiber-optic standard calls for 62.5/125 micron multimode fiber with windows at 850nm and 1300nm and a bandwidth of 160MHz and 500MHz. These fibers have gray jackets. The Systimax family also offers single-mode fiber cables with yellow jackets.

The 110 Cross-Connect and Patch Panel Systems

The Lucent 110 Connector System includes several types of rack or wall-mounted connector hardware that typically goes into a wiring closet to terminate horizontal and backbone cable. The 110 Cross-Connect System, shown in Figure 3.7, uses jumper wire and punch-down tools to make connections between circuits. The 110 Patch Panel System, shown in Figure 3.8, uses patch cords for more flexibility, but it is more expensive and requires more space than the 110 Cross-Connect System. You can include both types of interconnection systems in your wiring plan to get the best mix of flexibility and economy.

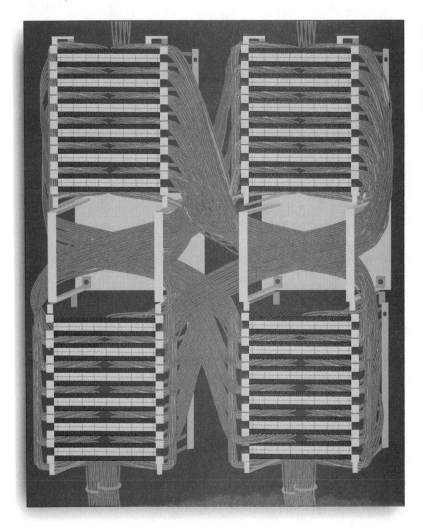

FIGURE 3.7
The Systimax 110 Cross-Connect System is the modern version of a punch-down block. Using short jumper wires, it provides high-quality interconnections between data circuits.

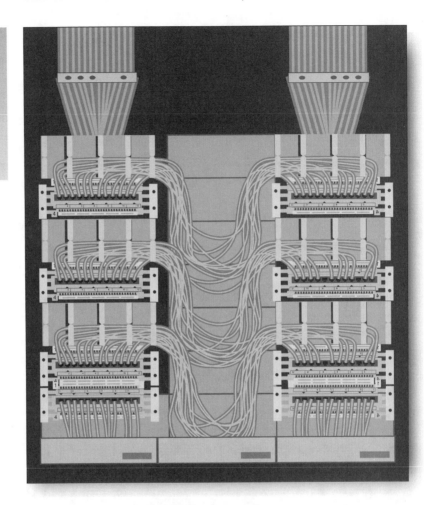

Lucent Plug and Jack Standards

Taking the wiring almost up to the desktop, Lucent offers a variety of outlets that terminate eight conductors for data and voice connections. The wiring sequence for these jacks—which wire goes to which terminal—is critical to the proper operation of the network (see Figure 3.9 later in this chapter).

Before the development of the EIA/TIA-568 standards, AT&T's old Standard 258A was the most widely specified wiring sequence for 4-pair plugs and jacks. It is also the same as the wiring sequence specified for Integrated Services Digital Network (ISDN), for 10Base-T ethernet over unshielded twisted-pair wiring, and for EIA/TIA-568B. Tens of thousands, if not hundreds of thousands, of existing jacks are wired to the AT&T Standards 258A and 356A. These standards defined the sequence used to connect two pairs of wires to plugs and jacks. The 356A standard dealt with three pairs of wires, and the 258A standard described the sequence for four pairs of wires.

The older USOC code was used in the U.S. Bell telephone system. Note that for pairs 2 through 4, the Lucent 258A sequence is different from the older Universal Service Order Code (USOC) sequence (see Figure 3.9), which is used for many voice telephone installations. Confusion over these wire sequences is a major cause of cable plant installation problems. Intermixing USOC and 258A wired plugs and jacks is a sure setting for a variety of problems ranging from no connection to mysteriously poor network performance.

The AT&T 258A and 356A specifications evolved into the EIA/TIA-568B standard commonly used in the United States. Beware of cable schemes wired according to the older USOC standard. They were probably designed for telephone systems and do not meet modern data transmission standards.

Following the existing wiring pattern is crucial

It's critical to know what wiring pattern the outlet jacks in your facility follow. The current trend is to use the EIA/TIA-568A outside the United States and EIA/TIA-568B inside the United States. However, many older buildings have been wired with systems from Digital Equipment Corporation or other companies. If you have one of these proprietary systems, you will have to take special steps during maintenance, upgrade, and repair to ensure that the installers understand your architecture.

Amp and Mod-Tap/Molex

Two companies, Amp and Mod-Tap, stand head and shoulders above their competition in consistently providing quality products, trained installers, and support for their products. Mod-Tap is now a part of Molex Corporation, an excellent connector company in its own right, and is now called *Molex Premise Networks*. These two companies don't attempt to set PDS standards; instead, they make and market cable and connection products that conform to popular standards while also innovating and providing improved convenience and quality.

Both AMP and Molex Premise Networks have training programs for installers. We strongly recommend that you ask your installer for a training history and references.

Amp Products

Amp is well known as a manufacturer of connectors. You probably have Amp connectors on your printer cables and perhaps on high-quality RS-232 serial cables. In the network cabling market, Amp has products for the ends of the cables, the wall plates, the wiring hubs, and the distribution frame. Amp's product line is known as the *NETCONNECT Open Cabling System*.

FIGURE 3.9
EIA/TIA, AT&T, and USOC wiring standards.

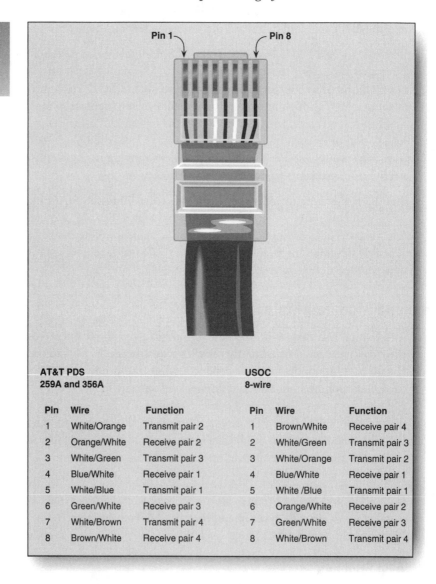

AT&T PDS 259A and 356A			USOC 8-wire		
Pin	Wire	Function	Pin	Wire	Function
1	White/Orange	Transmit pair 2	1	Brown/White	Receive pair 4
2	Orange/White	Receive pair 2	2	White/Green	Transmit pair 3
3	White/Green	Transmit pair 3	3	White/Orange	Transmit pair 2
4	Blue/White	Receive pair 1	4	Blue/White	Receive pair 1
5	White/Blue	Transmit pair 1	5	White /Blue	Transmit pair 1
6	Green/White	Receive pair 3	6	Orange/White	Receive pair 2
7	White/Brown	Transmit pair 4	7	Green/White	Receive pair 3
8	Brown/White	Receive pair 4	8	White/Brown	Transmit pair 4

LAN-Line Thinnet TapAMP demonstrated innovation in the design of the LAN-Line Thinnet Tap system, shown in Figure 3.10. This unique wall jack provides an answer to the difficult challenge of making a neat and reliable connection using thin ethernet coaxial cable. A single physical cable goes from the wall plate to the node, eliminating the possibility of someone's disabling the entire network by disconnecting the cable from a T-connector.

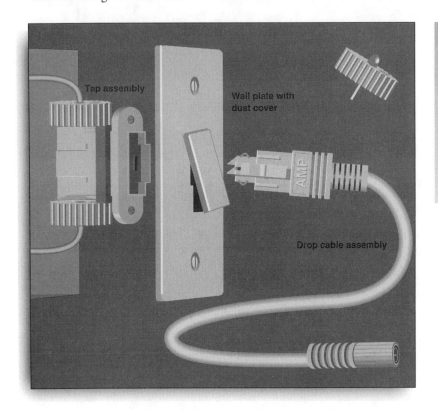

Tap assembly

Wall plate with dust cover

Drop cable assembly

FIGURE 3.10

Amp's unique LAN-Line Thinnet Tap for thin ethernet installations significantly reduces potential network cabling problems by eliminating T-connectors. It provides a high-quality single cable connection from the wall plate to the LAN adapter.

The location of telephone, power, and network connections is a prime consideration in the design of modern offices. But designers can't anticipate all the desk and divider configurations that people will use when they inhabit a building. The Amp Access Floor Workstation Module, shown in Figure 3.11, enables designers to bury a series of connectors in the floor until they're needed. Until someone places a desk by the Floor Workstation Module, it lies flat and matches the floor covering. When it's needed, the system can be configured with a variety of connectors.

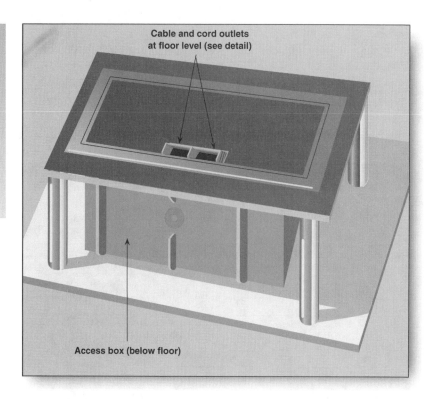

FIGURE 3.11
The Amp Access Floor Workstation Module provides a standardized method of prepositioning power, telephone, and network connections within a building. You can change the connectors within the module to meet the needs of the particular worker.

AMPIX Cross-Connect System

Among its many products, Amp markets a Cross-Connect distribution system for voice and data, with specially designed, high-quality wire terminations and printed-circuit-board connections between the wire termination and the RJ-45 jack of the patch-board system. Figure 3.12 shows an Amp modular-jack field with Amp barrel terminals for the wires. Amp also has a wide variety of fiber-optic-cable splicing, terminating, and testing equipment.

Molex Premise Networks Products

The product line from Molex Premise Networks stresses flexibility. The company markets products that meet the requirements of the EIA/TIA standards and those of many companies. Molex also has an excellent line of fiber-optic products that range from the cable itself to connectors and splicing equipment and supplies. The company is a single source of supply for a wide variety of products that range from wall plates and connectors to all the components of a distribution frame.

FIGURE 3.12
This AMPIX printed-circuit-board assembly and other similar modules are installed in a mounting track to build a distribution and cross-connect system. The use of printed-circuit-board connections gives extremely low levels of crosstalk and high reliability.

The Molex Universal System Outlet (USO), shown in Figure 3.13, provides an attractive and flexible way to terminate horizontal wiring at a node. You can snap various modules into the mounting box to customize the connections appearing at any wall plate or panel. This flexibility reduces the size and cost of installations while still making it easy to respond to moves and changes.

Anixter's Cable Model

Anixter Wire and Cable is a worldwide distributor of wiring-system products. It is also a service and technology company with a technical support staff of specialists and engineers who can help customers choose products and answer questions relating to design, industry specifications, and installation. The company's place in history as the developer of the multilevel model of performance for cables is assured. Anixter's model includes five levels that describe the performance and electrical characteristics of wiring, ranging from the most common telephone wire used in residences to sophisticated twisted-pair wire capable of moving data at 100Mbps.

FIGURE 3.13
The Molex Universal System Outlet allows you to snap various connection modules into wall plates, surface mounting modules, and equipment racks. You can select from among RJ-45, BNC, fiber, video, and many other connectors.

Hot cable colors are cool!

I've seen pink cable and I've seen purple cable. Some vendors (such as Keystone Wire and Cable) offer cables in some hot colors. We like the idea. Cable labels and tags are fine, but color speaks volumes. You can tell which cables go where when you use a bright color code. Just make sure that all those who follow the original installers keep to the color scheme!

The Anixter cable-level designations led a major evolution in the industry. The UL and EIA/TIA both use an evolved version of the Anixter cable model, and we'll describe the total model with all additions later in this chapter.

Amid the popularity of unshielded twisted-pair wiring, it is worth repeating that most of the wire installed for telephone systems does not meet the standards for LAN data transmission over 1Mbps. The telephone wiring in residences and many small businesses is typically a cable carrying four untwisted wires called *quad*. Quad is fine for simple telephone installations and for very low-speed data applications, but that's all.

Similarly, some PBX telephone systems use a twisted-pair wire. Even though it is twisted, this wire doesn't have the correct electrical properties to match the requirements of modern high-speed local-area network adapters. The Anixter Level 1 and Level 2 specifications describe these products with lower levels of performance.

National Electrical Code (NEC)

The National Electrical Code (NEC) is established by the National Fire Protection Association (NFPA). The language of the code is designed so that it can be adopted as law through legislative procedure. You will see the term *NEC* used widely in cable catalogs, and you shouldn't confuse it with specifications from a major international equipment manufacturer with the same initials.

In general terms, the NEC describes how a cable burns. During a building fire, a cable going between walls, up an elevator shaft, or through an air-handling plenum could become a torch that carries the flame from one floor or one part of the building to another. Because the coverings of cables and wires are typically plastic, they can create noxious smoke when they burn. Several organizations, including UL, have established standards for flame and smoke that apply to LAN cables. However, the NEC contains the standards most widely supported by local licensing and inspection officials. The standards, among other things, set a limit to the maximum amount of time the cable burns after a flame is applied. Other standards, developed by the NFPA and adopted by the American National Standards Institute (ANSI), also describe the type and amount of smoke a burning cable can generate.

Although the industry recognizes and generally conforms to the NEC standards, every individual municipality can decide whether to adopt the latest version of the NEC for local use. In other words, the NEC standards might or might not be a part of your local fire or building codes. In either case, we urge you to select, for your application, cable that meets the NEC standards.

Buried cable? Why?

While we are on the topic of cable jackets, let's talk about *direct buried* cable. This kind of cable is available in several forms from manufacturers. It has better strength and protection from rodents and backhoes. But be very careful. Copper connections between buildings are dangerous because of building electrical ground and lightning problems. If you have to go between buildings, do it with fiber-optic cable. Please!

Type Codes

You will see NEC type codes listed in catalogs of cables and supplies. These codes classify specific categories of products for specific uses, as shown here.

Type of Cable	Description
OFC (fiber-optic)	Contains metal conductors, inserted for strength
OFN (fiber-optic)	Contains no metal
CMP (communications plenum)	Passed tests showing a limited spread of flame and low production of smoke. Plenum cable is typically coated with a special jacket material such as Teflon. The letter *P* in this code defines a plenum as a channel or ductwork fabricated for handling air. A false ceiling or floor is not a plenum.
CMR (communications riser)	The letter *R* shows that the cable has passed similar but slightly different tests for the spread of flame and production of smoke. For example, riser cable is tested for its burning properties in a vertical position. According to the code, you must use cable rated for riser service whenever a cable penetrates a floor and a ceiling. Riser cables typically have a polyvinyl chloride (PVC) outer jacket.

Generally, you will find LAN cables listed in the category of type CM for communications or type MP for multipurpose. Some companies choose to run their cables through testing as remote-control or power-limited circuit cables CL2 or CL3 (class 2 or class 3) general tests instead of through the CM or CP tests, but the flame and smoke criteria are generally the same for all tests. The differences between these markings concern the amount of electrical power that could run through the cable in the worst case. MP cable is subjected to tests that assume the most power-handling capability, with CM, CL3, and CL2 going through tests with decreasing levels of power handling.

The EIA/TIA-568 (SP-2840) Standard

The Electronic Industries Alliance/Telecommunications Industry Association (EIA/TIA) is a U.S. standards body with a long history of issuing standards for communications systems including, for example, EIA232 for serial communications ports. The EIA/TIA tackled the problem of specifying LAN cables by starting with the Anixter Level 5 model, but the EIA/TIA calls the divisions "categories" instead of levels. Amp and other companies worked in the EIA/TIA to expand the model to account for other categories of products, including coaxial cable and fiber-optic cable. The result is the EIA/TIA-568 Standard for Commercial Building Telecommunications Wiring.

The primary advantage of EIA/TIA-568 is its publication as an open standard without the stamp of any single vendor. You can select and specify cable that meets a specific category of the EIA/TIA-568 standard and expect to get comparable bids back from a variety of vendors. Note, however, that the EIA/TIA categories are not tied to the NEC specifications, and they don't deal with shielded twisted-pair wiring. (As we describe later in this chapter, UL finally ties performance to safety.)

The EIA/TIA-568 standard describes both the performance specifications of the cable and its installation. However, the standard still leaves the network-system designer room for options and expansion. The standard calls for running two cables, one for voice and one for data, to each outlet. One of the two cables must be 4-pair unshielded twisted pair for voice. You can choose to run the data on another unshielded twisted-pair cable or on coax. If you elect to run fiber to the desktop, it can't displace the copper data cable.

Here is an overview of the cable-performance specification described in EIA/TIA-568:

- *Category 1*—Overall, EIA/TIA-568 says very little about the technical specifications in Category 1 or Category 2. The descriptions that follow are for general information. Category 1 cable is typically 22AWG or 24AWG untwisted wire, with a wide range of impedance and attenuation values. Category 1 is not recommended for data, in general, and certainly not for signaling speeds over 1Mbps.

New Name

The EIA/TIA standard is being renamed to *SP-2840*. However, the old name will probably remain in use for some time.

71

- *Category 2*—This category of cable is the same as the Anixter Level 2 cable specification, and it is derived from the IBM Type 3 cable specification. This cable uses 22AWG or 24AWG solid wire in twisted pairs. It is tested to a maximum bandwidth of 1MHz and is not tested for near-end crosstalk. You can use this cable for IBM 3270 and AS/400 computer connections and for Apple LocalTalk.

- *Category 3*—This category of cable is the same as the Anixter Level 3 and generally is the minimum level of cable quality you should allow in new installations. Category 3 uses 24AWG solid wire in twisted pairs. This wire displays a typical impedance of 100 ohms and is tested for attenuation and near-end crosstalk through 16MHz. Useful for data transmission at speeds up to 16Mbps, this wire is the lowest standard you should use for 10Base-T installations, and it is sufficient for 4Mbps token-ring.

- *Category 4*—The same as the Anixter Level 4 cable, Category 4 cable can have 22AWG or 24AWG solid wire in twisted pairs. This cable has a typical impedance of 100 ohms and is tested for performance at a bandwidth of 20MHz. Category 4 cable is formally rated for a maximum signaling speed of 20MHz, so it is good cable to install if you think that you will run 16Mbps token-ring over unshielded twisted-pair wire. Category 4 cable also works well for 10Base-T installations.

- *Category 5*—This is the performance specification we recommend for all new installations. This is 22AWG or 24AWG unshielded twisted-pair cable with a 100-ohm impedance. Originally, this cable was tested at a maximum frequency of 100MHz, but advancements in the state of the art now call for testing at 200MHz. Category 5 can handle data signaling at 100Mbps under specified conditions. The 1000BaseT specification provides a way to move data even faster, but it uses multiple wire pairs within the same cable to split the data stream. Category 5 cable is a high-quality medium with growing applications for transmitting video, images, and very high-speed data.

Trying to describe the EIA/TIA-568 standard and the category system in a book is like trying to paint a moving train. The standard

Don't mix megahertz with megabits!

The EIA/TIA specifications categorize cables according to the frequency spectrum they will pass with certain characteristics. The frequency spectrum is specified in megahertz. "But wait!" you say, "I want to know the signaling rate in megabits per second." It doesn't work that way. The signaling speed is determined by the encoding scheme, and ethernet, token-ring, ATM, and other network schemes each have unique encoding schemes with different bit-per-hertz ratios. Don't equate megabits directly with megahertz. It's a lot more complex than you think.

evolves through an interactive committee process, and change, particularly expansion, is constant. However, because committees develop these standards, things can get a little murky. One good example is the introduction of new technology beyond EIA/TIA Category 5.

The technology of sending data over twisted-pair wire moved more quickly than the standards process. In 1998, the 1992 Level 5 specification was modified to include the performance capabilities available in the then-current Category 5 cable products. That, at least, brought the standard up-to-date with the technology.

In the interim, manufacturers continued to push the technology and developed what had been called *High-End Cat 5*, *Cat 5E* (enhanced), or *Cat 5+* cables. The committees created a new Level 5 and Level 6 in the updated levels program. A new generation of recently launched products that meet the twice Cat 5 bandwidth requirement constitute Level 7. Generally, Level 5 products are tested at a highest frequency of 200MHz. Level 6 products are tested at 350MHz and Level 7 products are tested at 400MHz. Note that Level 5 is different from the standard Cat 5 in that it now must meet the more stringent requirements included in the international standard document ISO 11801. This standard allows cables meeting these requirements to be used globally. This new definition for cable performance creates a "superset" of the original Category 5 requirements.

On paper, the categorizations look confusing. When you use them to specify the quality of products and certification you want in your installation, they should be straightforward. Most installations will fit into a Category 5 certified installation for decades. In many cases, fiber-optic cable is a better choice than Level 6 or Level 7 unshielded twisted pair. This is particularly true for installation of gigabit ethernet.

Underwriters Laboratories (UL)

Local fire-code and building-code regulators try to use standards like those of the NEC, but insurance groups and other regulators often specify the standards of the Underwriters Laboratories. UL has safety standards for cables similar to those of the NEC. UL 444 is

Always install the best!

Most of the major manufacturers offer several grades of Category 5 cable. Not all cable meeting Category 5 is the same. Because the cost of labor is the major portion of a cabling scheme, it makes little sense to install cable that is a few cents a foot cheaper. The better-quality cables exceed the minimum specifications and provide margins for error and for growth.

Don't believe everything you hear!

Asynchronous Transfer Mode (ATM) is a hi-tech method of moving data in small packets. It was designed to reduce the effect of losing one or two packets. ATM typically starts at a signaling rate of 155Mbps. Some manufacturers assert that ATM demands a type of cable better than Cat 5. I think that ATM is best implemented on fiber-optic cable, but the ATM Forum (an industry group) confirms that ATM 155 will operate correctly on a Cat 5 cabling system—with some distance limitations. If someone says that you need something much better than Cat 5, ask, "Why not fiber?" The reply is probably cost, but dig deeper and the cost penalty for fiber might be affordable.

the Standard for Safety for Communications Cable. UL 13 is the Standard for Safety for Power-Limited Circuit Cable. Network cable might fall into either category. UL tests and evaluates samples of cable and then, after granting a UL listing, the organization conducts follow-up tests and inspections. This independent testing and follow-through make the UL markings valuable symbols to buyers.

In an interesting and unique action, the people at UL stirred safety and performance together in a program designed to make selecting or specifying a cable easier. UL's LAN Certification Program addresses not only safety, but also performance. IBM authorized UL to verify 150-ohm STP to IBM performance specifications, and UL established a data-transmission, performance-level marking program that covers 100-ohm twisted-pair cable. UL adopted the EIA/TIA-568 performance standard and, through that, some aspects of the Anixter cable performance model. There is a small inconsistency: The UL program deals with both shielded and unshielded twisted-pair wire, whereas the EIA/TIA-568 standard focuses on unshielded wire.

The UL markings range from Level I through Level V. You can tell a UL level from an Anixter level because the UL uses roman numerals. As we described, IBM's cable specifications range from Type 1 through Type 9, whereas the EIA/TIA has Category 1 through Category 5. But at publication time the EIA/TIA has started to talk in "levels," too. It's easy to become confused by the similarly numbered levels and types. The UL level markings deal with performance and safety, so the products that merit UL level markings also meet the appropriate NEC MP, CM, or CL specifications, as well as the EIA/TIA standard for a specific category.

Companies whose cables earn these UL markings display them on the outer jacket as, for example, *Level I*, *LVL I*, or *LEV I*. Here is a summary of the UL level markings:

- The UL Level I marking meets appropriate NEC and UL 444 safety requirements. No specific performance specifications.
- The UL Level II marking meets the performance requirements of EIA/TIA-568 Category 2 and IBM Cable Plan Type 3 cable. Meets appropriate NEC and UL 444 safety requirements.

Acceptable for 4Mb token-ring, but not for higher-speed data applications such as 10Base-T.

- The UL Level III marking meets the performance requirements of EIA/TIA-568 Category 3 and NEC and UL 444 safety requirements. Lowest acceptable marking for LAN applications.

- The UL Level IV marking meets the performance requirements of EIA/TIA-568 Category 4 and NEC and UL 444 safety requirements.

- The UL Level V marking meets the performance requirements of EIA/TIA-568 Category 5 and NEC and UL 444 safety requirements. The right choice for new LAN installations.

Evolution

The standards committees will continue meeting. They constantly make proposals and usually issue major updates every five years. New technologies, as well as the desire of companies to find a tiny marketing edge for new products, will result in evolutionary changes to the standards for network wiring and cabling. Also, other standards bodies will follow the path of Anixter, EIA/TIA, and UL. For example, Standards Committee 25 of the International Standards Organization (ISO)/International Electrotechnical Commission (IEC) Joint Technical Committee 1 has developed a framework of international standards (probably known as *ISO/IEC JTC1/SC25* with more numbers and letters). This framework applies to token-ring cabling and a generic structured cabling system. Fortunately, the emerging ISO/IEC standards closely follow the EIA/TIA standards, but there will be some differences.

Your cable plant must last a long time. Following the EIA/TIA and ISO/IEC standards will ensure payback on your investment and successful operation of networks that are critical to your business.

chapter

4

LAN Combinations

Different Terms •

Network Architectures •

Ethernet •

Token-Ring •

ARCnet •

Newer Standards •

Different Terms

Willy knew that there would be a problem, because these folks weren't speaking the same language. On his truck's two-way radio, he'd heard the New Guy ask Bill Owens, one of the more experienced installers, whether he had a "mau" in his truck. The New Guy was troubleshooting at an old and valued client, and apparently he thought that he could quickly solve the problem by replacing the MAU. Willy knew that these two guys were using the same term for different items.

As Willy pulled into the parking lot, the New Guy was wearing a puzzled expression as he tore apart a cardboard box nearly two feet wide and a few inches high.

"I asked Bill for a MAU, and this is what he gave me," the New Guy explained to Willy. "Unless there are a dozen of them in here, this isn't the right thing."

"You went to Hewlett-Packard system schools, right?" Willy asked. When the New Guy nodded, Willy explained, "HP calls an external transceiver for 10BaseT wiring a *media attachment unit*, or *MAU*, and that's what you wanted—a transceiver to attach to the AUI port on an ethernet adapter so that it can make a 10BaseT connection. Well, Bill went to IBM school. At IBM, a MAU is a multistation access unit—a wiring hub. What you have there is a wiring hub for token-ring."

"Oh," the New Guy replied, "no wonder he asked me whether I wanted a MAU for unshielded twisted-pair. I thought he was being funny."

Willy tossed the New Guy a package about the size of a deck of playing cards. "Here, use this external 10BaseT transceiver and also remember to use plain old English whenever possible. Even when folks are familiar with the standards, it's still better to describe what you want as simply as possible. After all, standards are wonderful things—that's why we have so many of them!"

Network Architectures

ARCnet, ethernet, and token-ring are specifications for network signaling and media access. The signaling and access specifications drive certain LAN adapter and cable interface specifications. These specifications are based in the cable technology of the 1970s and 1980s, so how do they fit into the premise distribution schemes (PDS) of this decade (described in Chapter 3, "Standards: There Are So Many!")?

The answer is that the ARCnet, ethernet, and token-ring network architecture specifications were each developed in a vacuum. The designers of ARCnet were unaware of the efforts of the Ethernet designers, even though the developments occurred nearly simultaneously. IBM also designed Token-Ring from a clean slate. In all cases, the designers of PDS architectures had to stretch to accommodate the network architectures. The specifications for using unshielded twisted-pair wire were overlaid onto the existing network architectures, primarily in response to customer demand.

SEE ALSO

➤ *To learn more about premise distribution systems (PDS), see page 51.*

The problem with all this evolution and modification is that you're likely to be thrown into the middle of an existing cable scheme. It's a jump from the theoretical to the real world. Because cabling can last for decades, you can inherit or walk into a building that was wired according to a networking specification, such as ARCnet, or according to a PDS specification at some stage of the evolution of either specification.

Because you never know what you're going to find, we're going to paint with a broad brush. In this chapter, we provide an easy guide to the generally accepted network specifications for cabling ARCnet, ethernet, and token-ring systems. This guide is intended as a tool for both planning and troubleshooting. It should also be useful as a reference when you want to expand or modify the network-cabling infrastructure. For example, limitations on factors such as overall cable length can make it expensive or challenging to add just one more node to the network.

Standards and specifications...how's that again?

There are network specifications, such as IEEE 802.3 for ethernet and 802.5 for token-ring. They were developed first.

There are PDS specifications such as Systimax. They try to be broad and cover all bases.

Then, there are international standards such as EIA/TIA-568. They try to be broad, but don't cover everything.

If you follow the PDS specifications, you should conform to the international standards, but you might not always conform to the network specifications. It pays to look at the network specifications separately.

The factors we provide are for planning purposes only. Although some companies offer wiring hubs and network interface cards capable of spanning greater distances than the ones we present, some electrical environments dictate much shorter limits. In Chapter 9, "Practical Home and Small Office Network Cabling (NEW)," we discuss testing and certification. After using this chapter to understand a cable installation, it is wise to test and get a profile of the cable, connectors, patch panels, and other parts of the installation. If you are using 16Mb token-ring or 100Mb ethernet, certification of the installation is especially important to your network's success.

Now let's look at the generally accepted copper cabling plans for the three major networking architectures. We'll talk about fiber-optic cabling in Chapter 8, "From the Wall to the Desktop."

Ethernet

The three types of ethernet connections are thin coaxial cable, thick coaxial cable, and unshielded twisted-pair wire. Separate rules apply to each type of cabling, so let's start with some overall vocabulary.

In ethernet, you always have to think about collision domains. The "listen-before-talk" media-sharing scheme of ethernet depends on all nodes being able to simultaneously hear some part of the same packet. If the cables are too long or there are too many repeaters and too much delay, nodes on the same cable might hear silence and simultaneously transmit data. This results in collision, adaptation, retry, and general slowdown of useful throughput on the network (see Figure 4.1).

Ethernet cabling is primarily based on the concept of a *trunk cable*. A *trunk segment* is a link that is terminated on each end so that signals can't go any further. In the 10BaseT ethernet scheme, introduced in the first chapter, a typical trunk segment runs between a node (like a PC or a networked printer) and a hub or switch. In the older but still common thin ethernet scheme, a trunk cable is typically a piece of cable with a small device called a *terminator* at each end. Inside each terminator, an electrical component called a *resistor* soaks up signals reaching the end of the cable so that they don't reflect back up the cable and create patterns of conflicting signals. In modern networks, these terminators are in each LAN adapter and on each port of the hub. On old systems, even those installed in the mid-1990s, you might find physical terminating resistors that look like a silver bullet on the end of the cables.

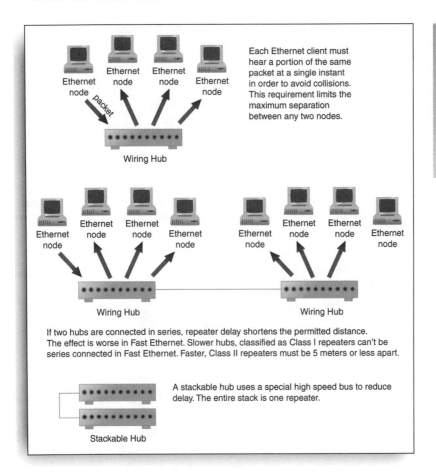

Each Ethernet client must hear a portion of the same packet at a single instant in order to avoid collisions. This requirement limits the maximum separation between any two nodes.

If two hubs are connected in series, repeater delay shortens the permitted distance. The effect is worse in Fast Ethernet. Slower hubs, classified as Class I repeaters can't be series connected in Fast Ethernet. Faster, Class II repeaters must be 5 meters or less apart.

A stackable hub uses a special high speed bus to reduce delay. The entire stack is one repeater.

FIGURE 4.1
If you overextend the cable or introduce too many hubs into an ethernet network, you will experience collisions. Stacking hubs, switches, and segmentation avoids collisions.

Devices called *repeaters* link individual trunk segments. A repeater regenerates the electrical signals to restore the strength they lost through cable attenuation, but the carrier-sense multiple-access cable-sharing scheme limits the number of repeaters allowed in a network cable system. Today, you can think of a repeater as one wiring hub.

Generally, you can have four repeaters (or hubs) in an ethernet system linking five trunk segments, but only three of those trunk segments can have nodes attached. In modern terms, those trunk segments connect hubs. Two of the trunks are, in ethernet terms, *unpopulated*, but serve to extend the network between populated segments. In popular terms, this is the "5-4-3" rule of repeater placement. That is, the network can have only five segments connected; it can use only four repeaters; and of the five segments, only three can have users attached. The other two must be inter-repeater links.

The IEEE 802.3 committee designates each style of architecture according to signaling speed, type of signaling, and the maximum cable length (in meters) of one trunk segment. Table 4.1 gives a quick summary.

Table 4.1 Ethernet Characteristics

Ethernet Designation	Common Name	Media	Maximum Number of Nodes per Segment	Maximum Distance per Segment
10Base5	Thick ethernet	Coaxial cable	100	500 meters
10Base2	Thin ethernet	Coaxial cable	30	185 meters
10BaseT	10BaseT	Unshielded twisted-pair	2 (node to hub)	100 meters
10BaseFL	Fiber ethernet	Fiber-optic cable	2 (node to hub)	2,000 meters

Bad connectors could be the culprits

Whenever you have a problem with a thin ethernet network, suspect the cable-end connectors. It takes experience to properly install a coaxial cable connector, and they can go bad without warning.

Here's an example of how the IEEE 802.3 designation system works: The thick coaxial cable uses a 10Mbps signaling speed and baseband signaling (described in Chapter 1, "The Role of Cabling: Planning Considerations"), and the standard allows a maximum of 500 meters of cable on one trunk segment. A system that conforms to these standards is designated as 10Base5. Thin coaxial cabling, also known informally as *Cheapernet* or *thin ethernet*, has poorer electrical characteristics. Therefore, the IEEE standard limits thin ethernet systems to a trunk segment length of 185 meters, which is close enough to 200 meters for this type of cabling system to be designated as 10Base2. Ethernet over UTP is a special case that is referred to as *10BaseT* (twisted). The term *10Base-FL* describes fiber-optic cable connections. Fast ethernet, signaling at 100Mbps over Category 5 UTP, is defined as 100BaseT.

The various forms of ethernet also vary in what is called the *physical topology*, shown in Figure 4.2. The 10Base2 and 10Base5 systems use a linear bus configuration, which means that the nodes connect to the cable and it proceeds in a linear fashion between the nodes. This arrangement is the most economical in the amount of cable it uses, but one break in the cable or a bad connection at any point will disable the entire network.

The 10BaseT system uses a star wiring arrangement that is more reliable but also more expensive because of the costs of additional cable and hardware. Also, 10BaseT does not rely on external terminators. Wiring hubs can contain connectors for each ethernet wiring scheme, allowing combinations of the topologies to meet special needs.

Thick Ethernet

A 10Base5 thick ethernet system uses a trunk or backbone cable with a 50-ohm terminator at each end. The "frozen yellow garden hose" thick ethernet cable (named for its appearance and handling characteristics) typically runs through a false ceiling or floor. When you want to connect to a node, you use a device called a *vampire tap* that pierces the outer shield with a metal fang and makes contact with the center conductor. This seemingly radical surgery results in surprisingly reliable connections. Another type of tap that uses connectors is available, but in our experience, the connectors make this type of tap less reliable in the long run than the vampire tap.

The thick ethernet cable tap contains electronic components that sense the electrical carrier on the cable, so generally it is referred to as a *transceiver*. A piece of multiconductor shielded cable, called the *transceiver cable*, connects the tap to the network adapter. The transceiver cable connects to the networking interface card's *attachment unit interface (AUI)* socket. The connector used on the AUI socket along with the transceiver cable is called a *DIX connector*.

The maximum length of a single thick ethernet trunk segment is 1,640 feet (500 meters), and the maximum overall cable length connected by repeaters is 8,200 feet (2,500 meters). The standard allows 100 nodes on each trunk segment, and the minimum distance between transceivers is 8 feet (2.5 meters). The maximum length of transceiver cable is 165 feet (50 meters), but transceiver cable is expensive, so you will probably want to keep the cable runs short. Plan for the backbone cable run to use unspliced lengths of thick ethernet cable between the nodes whenever possible.

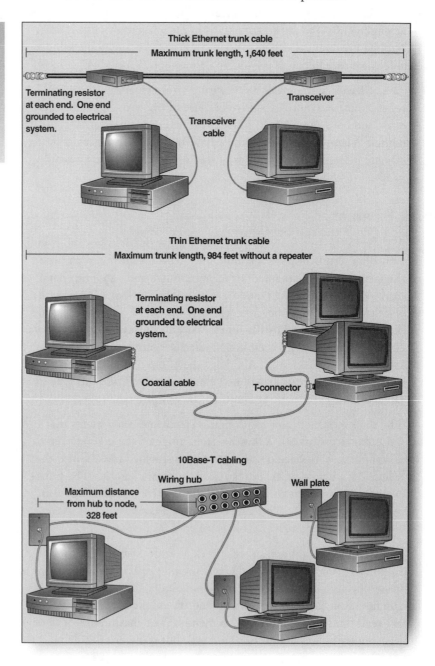

FIGURE 4.2
Here are the three standard ethernet topologies. The thick and thin ethernet systems use two slightly different types of coaxial trunk cables with terminators at each end.

Thick Ethernet trunk cable
Maximum trunk length, 1,640 feet

Terminating resistor at each end. One end grounded to electrical system.

Transceiver

Transceiver cable

Thin Ethernet trunk cable
Maximum trunk length, 984 feet without a repeater

Terminating resistor at each end. One end grounded to electrical system.

Coaxial cable

T-connector

10Base-T cabling

Wiring hub

Wall plate

Maximum distance from hub to node, 328 feet

The outside of the jacket of the thick ethernet backbone cable has distance markers on it that show the quarter wavelength points. It's important that the terminators are installed precisely on a marker at each end. If they are and you tap in to the cable at those points marked in between, the transceiver detects the correct impedance. If you miss the point by more than a few inches, theoretically the impedance mismatch could set up reflections within the cable that would lead to lost packets. According to the specification, one of the terminators must be attached to the building electrical ground. This ground wire usually connects to a mounting screw on a wall socket.

In practice, people report that thick ethernet works despite all types of mishandling. If you ever suspect you might have a problem with the thick ethernet backbone cable, look instead for a bad network interface card or a transceiver with the Signal Quality Error (SQE) switch turned on. SQE is an old feature that causes more problems than it solves. Just remember the mnemonic used by installers (namely, that SQE has three letters, like the word *off*), and you will know what to do with the switch. Thick ethernet is difficult to install because of the diameter of the cable and the complex hardware required for every connection. Because of these factors and the growing popularity of UTP, you won't see many new thick ethernet installations, but after it is in the walls, it should work until the building falls down.

Thin Ethernet

The other old, yet still useful, form of ethernet is the thin ethernet, or *Cheapernet*. Thin ethernet is a node-to-node system using coaxial cable that's about one-quarter inch thick and much more flexible than thick ethernet. As Figure 4.3 illustrates, thin coaxial cable ethernet systems cannot use any type of *drop* cable (an extension between the backbone cable and the node). The backbone cable travels from node to node without drops or transceiver cables and uses a T-connector to make the connection at each node. Each end of each trunk cable has a terminating resistor, and one of the terminating resistors on each trunk cable should be grounded to the building's electrical system.

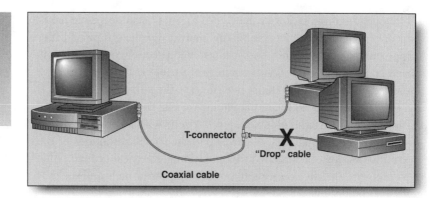

FIGURE 4.3
Never use a drop cable in a thin ethernet wiring plan. The trunk cable must go from node to node.

T-connector

X

"Drop" cable

Coaxial cable

Generally, a thin ethernet system includes a maximum of five trunk cable segments linked by repeaters. Each trunk segment can have a maximum length of 607 feet (185 meters), so the total system can have an overall length of 3,035 feet (925 meters). If you don't use repeaters, you may have one trunk segment with an overall maximum length of 984 feet (300 meters). Each trunk cable can have a maximum of 30 nodes, and the minimum distance between nodes is 1.5 feet (0.45 meters). Although 30 nodes is the standard, many models of LAN adapters are designed to allow up to 100 nodes on a trunk cable.

10BaseT

In practical terms

The repeater rules mean, in practical terms, that you can have only three ethernet hubs or switches linked together in a daisy chain. Typically, each hub or switch (*repeater*) is in or near a wiring closet. You should work over your floor plan to find the network nodes and create wiring closets so that they reach the desktop PCs and printers, with no more than 300 feet of UTP for each connection.

10BaseT—ethernet over UTP—is popular because it's cheaper and thinner than the other alternatives. Also, people feel comfortable with the technology. Although it's technically demanding and requires care in installation, the UTP is somehow less threatening than coaxial cable.

The 10BaseT plan specifies a wiring hub, cable arranged in a star configuration, and unshielded twisted-pair cable. Each node has a separate cable run, not to exceed 328 feet (100 meters) from the node to the hub. There are no external terminators, as in the coaxial cable systems. You can mix the other types of ethernet wiring schemes and 10BaseT in the same network because hubs often have AUI connectors for thin ethernet, thick ethernet, or even fiber-optic cable transceivers.

The star wiring configuration prevents a single bad connector or piece of cable from bringing down the entire network, as it can with thin ethernet. 10BaseT hubs and adapters offer a built-in link-integrity test feature that causes light-emitting diodes on the hub and LAN adapter to glow when the node's network interface card has power and the electrical connection is good. This enables you to determine at a glance whether you have a serious cabling problem. The hub can recognize certain trouble conditions and isolate or "partition" the offending segment so that it doesn't affect the rest of the network. Of course, if the bad cable segment leads to your only server, you still will lose network services, but the cause of the outage should be obvious and easy to repair.

Wiring hubs come in all shapes and sizes. Some, like the D-Link hub shown in Figure 4.4, are small cabinets about the size of a hardback book that you could stick on the side of a desk. This kind of hub is appropriate only for small networks of 2 to about 16 nodes. Expect to pay nearly $10 to $25 per port for these products. The 10BaseT standard allows up to 1,000 nodes per cable segment, which is more than you're ever likely to use. You will separate your LAN into more cable segments long before you get to 100-plus nodes.

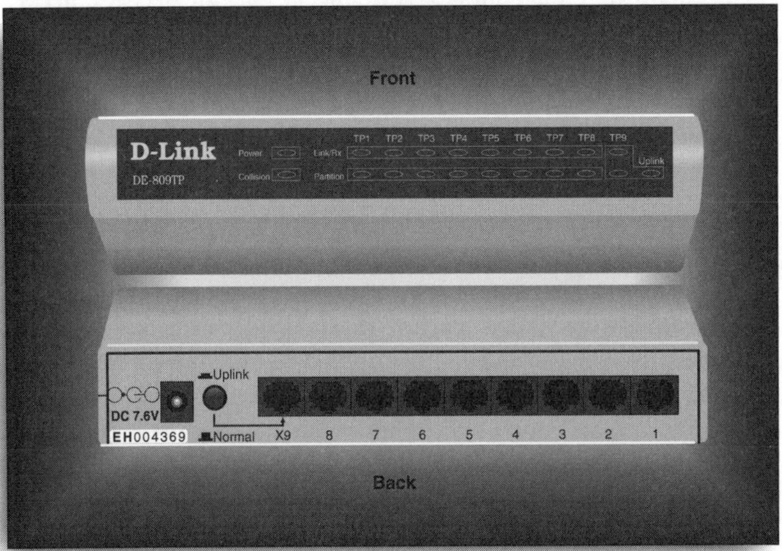

Watch those lights

The "Link" lights on LAN adapters and hubs show you only that you don't have a completely broken wire. When they glow, they indicate that a complete, direct-current connection exists. However, they don't tell you anything about split pairs, high electrical noise, or high resistance that the signaling trans-ceivers must overcome. The lights are useful to indicate that a link exists, but they don't indicate the quality of the link.

FIGURE 4.4
This small D-Link wiring hub for 10BaseT offers economy and good ser-vice, but these types of hubs have limited expan-sion capabilities.

Rule of three

The 10BaseT three-repeater rule limits the number of hubs in a daisy chain to three.

The 10BaseT wiring scheme contains a subtle trap. Many network planners start small, with a standalone hub that can accommodate 8 to 12 nodes. When the network grows, they buy another hub and connect the two hubs in a daisy chain. This growth pattern continues through the third hub, but if they try adding a fourth hub in this manner, they start getting collisions, runt (short) packets, and over-runs (long packets). The 10BaseT three-repeater rule essentially says that you can use only three repeaters between major LAN segments. If you add a fourth repeater, the timing of the packets can be impaired, and the CSMA/CD media-sharing scheme breaks down. Some companies have marketed hubs with tight timing so that you can have four repeaters, but the basic rule is a limit of three hubs. If you start buying ethernet network hubs without an expansion plan, you can run into problems.

There are two good ways to avoid conflicts with the three-repeater rule as your network grows. The first is to buy products that can integrate into what is called a *stackable hub*. The second is to buy a product called a *chassis hub*.

As the name implies, the parts of a stackable hub system physically stack, typically in some kind of frame or cabinet. But stacking is driven by more than physical convenience—it's an electrical necessity. The concept behind stacking hubs is to use a special high-speed connection, shown in Figure 4.5, between the hubs in the stack to reduce device delays. Because they intercommunicate over a separate high-speed connection, all the hubs in the "stack" act as one repeater for the ethernet rules.

The practical advantage of buying hubs with stacking capabilities is that you avoid the expansion trap. You can start with one hub, but if you expect growth, it will be a hub with "stacking" capability. As your network grows—perhaps you add a department of 6–18 people—you can add another hub. When the second hub fills, you can add a third. If you didn't buy stackable hubs, adding a fourth hub would create network problems. Without stackable hubs, you could have a network with fewer than 50 nodes that can't expand. With stackable hubs, you can expand one stack of hubs to connect to hundreds of nodes, but it is still only one ethernet repeater.

FIGURE 4.5
This stack of 10BaseT hubs appears as one ethernet repeater because the hubs in the stack communicate across a high-speed backbone cable rather than go through the ethernet connection. The speed of the backbone cable eliminates the ethernet delay. You can start by buying one hub and add more as your network grows. Each hub is shown with an expansion port for other types of ethernet connections.

A chassis hub is a little different product. As Figure 4.6 shows, this type of device is a large chassis with many expansion slots. The expansion slots are part of an electronic infrastructure called a *backplane*. A chassis hub takes add-in modules called *blades*, each of which is full of port connectors. The backplane has its own processor, and it moves data between the blades while also providing control and management. The chassis interconnects the connector strips across a very fast data bus, so adding more nodes doesn't upset the CSMA/CD timing. In other words, like the stackable hub, you can add more blades into the backplane of the chassis, and they still count as only one ethernet repeater.

Slide-in Modules

Many vendors make a variety of modules for their chassis hubs. You can select connection modules for any combination of cable and for any network architecture. Chassis hubs have various advantages:

- Nodes connected by ethernet over thick coax, ethernet over thin coax, and ethernet over UTP (10BaseT) can interoperate on the same network or on totally separate networks.

- Nodes connected by token-ring over UTP and by token-ring over STP can interoperate on the same network or on totally separate networks.

- Nodes connected by ARCnet over coaxial cable or by ARCnet over UTP can interoperate on the same network or on totally separate networks.

- Nodes using the same network communications protocols, such as IPX or IP, can exchange data through an internal router in the wiring hub, regardless of the type of cable or the network architecture they use.

- You can easily create new separate network segments as your system grows by changing a jumper or a switch.

These chassis hubs have other features such as dual power supplies for added fault tolerance. Some companies sell complete computers with Pentium processors and many megabytes of memory that slide into the chassis. The CPUs can run networking software, such as Linux and Novell's NetWare, and typically perform as communications servers or routers—they can even be file and print servers.

The only downside to backplane chassis hubs is that they are several times more expensive on a per-port basis than equivalent cabinet hubs.

The net effect of using either a stackable hub or a chassis hub is the same: You don't get trapped by the repeater rules. The stackable hub system enables you to start inexpensively and move up in increments. The chassis hub requires a large up-front cost for the chassis, but many blades and options are available. Today, most small to medium–size businesses want to start with stackable hubs. The chassis style hub is primarily for enterprises in which the capability to expand and manage the network has high importance.

Many people have been painfully caught unaware by the three-repeater rule. Small wiring hubs with a fixed number of ports are initially inexpensive, compared to stackable hubs or to hubs within a chassis with a data bus backplane. This is a classic case of "pay now or pay later." If you don't pay for the expansion capability in the beginning, you might have to throw away your investment and start from scratch later.

Because 100BaseT fast ethernet moves data faster, the timing changes. Because the timing changes, fast ethernet uses a different set of rules for repeaters and cable length. When the timing changes, nodes can't hear each other, and the collision problem emerges. Because the minimum packet size takes less time to traverse the network than regular ethernet, the length of the network links is shorter and fewer repeaters are allowed.

In fast ethernet, there are two classes of repeaters: Class I and Class II. Class I repeaters have an internal delay (termed *latency*) of .7 microseconds or less. This latency measurement means that it takes less than .7 microseconds to forward the incoming data to the outgoing side. Class II repeaters have a latency of .46 microseconds or less, so they're faster and, of course, more expensive. Because of the speed involved, the rules for 100BaseT networking say that you can have only one Class I repeater or two Class II repeaters on a LAN.

Table 4.2 shows the cable distance limitations for various types of fast ethernet with various types of cables.

Table 4.2 Cable Distance Limitations

Fast ethernet	Copper	Fiber
No repeaters	100 Meters	412 Meters
One Class I repeater	200 Meters	272 Meters
One Class II repeater	200 Meters	272 Meters
Two Class II repeaters	205 Meters	228 Meters

Most 100BaseT hubs are Class I devices. Basically, you have to know the type of repeater you have or plan to acquire when you plan the network.

Token-Ring

Token-Ring networking was designed by IBM for high reliability and guaranteed throughput. For a while, Token-Ring was very popular, particularly because IBM put up barriers to connecting with popular computers like its AS/400 line through ethernet. However, the lower cost and simplicity of ethernet eventually overcame the technical advantages of Token-Ring. The low cost and flexibility of ethernet won over Token-Ring, and good networking software includes plenty of error-control and delivery guarantees to overcome any perceived limitations of ethernet.

Like 10BaseT, the IEEE 802.5 token-ring system also uses a wiring hub as the center of the cable plan. The Token-Ring architecture was originally designed to operate with shielded twisted-pair cable, but

It's too complex— switch!

All this contention domain stuff is arcane and confusing. You can and should eliminate most of these concerns by using 10/100 switches instead of hubs. The market has reduced the cost of 10/100 switches to affordable levels. Don't buy hubs— switch!

LAN managers and designers quickly demanded UTP connections. IBM delivered a device that the company calls a *media filter*, which mates the STP connector on its network interface cards to UTP. Now IBM and many other companies market interface cards and wiring hubs designed for UTP.

SEE ALSO

➤ *To learn more about token-ring networks, see page 22.*

If you have only 4Mbps token-ring, you can run it over Category 3 UTP. You will see published specifications for running 16Mbps token-ring over Category 3 cable, but we don't recommend it. We think that 16Mbps token-ring requires an EIA/TIA-568 Category 5 UTP installation.

The number of active network nodes is a more important factor in token-ring than in any other networking scheme. Each time a token-ring node activates its network interface card, a voltage is imposed on a relay in the wiring hub. The relay in the hub pulls in and inserts the node's cable segment into the active ring, effectively changing the size of the overall network. In other networking schemes, the overall length of the cable stays the same when stations enter or leave the network, but as Figure 4.7 illustrates, activating a token-ring node automatically increases the overall active network cable length.

In this token-ring scheme, the maximum length of all STP cable is 1,312 feet at 4Mbps and 590 feet at 16Mbps. In a system that uses UTP cable, the maximum length of the total cable is 738 feet at 4Mbp and 328 feet at 16Mbps.

MTD = ECL + (Lobe Length * Nodes) + Loopback

There is a complex interaction between the cable length, the number of wiring hubs, the links between the wiring hubs, and the number of overall active nodes on a token-ring network. The picture is made even fuzzier by vendors who have introduced devices called *powered* wiring hubs, which they claim provide reliable operation at six times the distance of standard hubs. On the bottom line, it's difficult to give you hard-and-fast guidelines for maximum cable length because the manufacturers' specifications vary so widely. We suggest that you consult with the vendors of token-ring equipment before finalizing your token-ring cabling plan.

Don't be fooled by signaling speeds

Many token-ring users claim that 4Mbps token-ring has virtually the same performance as 10Mbps ethernet. The lack of contention and high probability of packet delivery make it very efficient. Advocates of 16Mbps token-ring claim that it has at least twice the usable throughput of standard 10Mbps ethernet. Similarly, a technology called *High Speed Token-Ring (HSTR)* is supposed to outperform 100Mbps fast ethernet. There might be a lot of life in your old Token-Ring LAN! However, the cost advantages of ethernet make new token-ring installations very rare.

FIGURE 4.7
A token-ring network is a complex arrangement of nodes, cables, and wiring hubs with active components. When a node activates its network interface card, it applies a voltage across the cable to a relay in the wiring hub. The relay activates, breaks the existing ring of cable, and inserts the added cable out to the new node. Every time a node activates, it increases the overall length of the network cable.

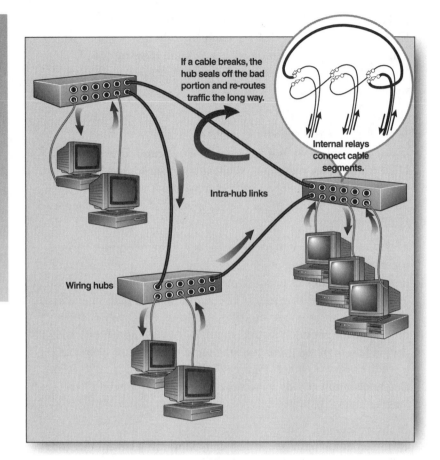

If a cable breaks, the hub seals off the bad portion and re-routes traffic the long way.

Internal relays connect cable segments.

Intra-hub links

Wiring hubs

Token-ring relies on the concept of *maximum total cable distance (MTD)*, which is used to describe the maximum amount of cable in the ring that you may use without employing powered, or *active*, hubs that regenerate the signals. The typical MTD for equipment using shielded twisted-pair wire is 1,312 feet (400 meters) at 4Mb and 590 feet (180 meters) at 16Mb. The MTD for Category 5 UTP is 738 feet (225 meters) at 4Mb and 328 feet (100 meters) at 16Mb.

The MTD includes all the actual physical cable and a factor called *equivalent cable length* (ECL) that represents the signal loss inside the wiring hub. Each manufacturer provides an ECL for the specific make and model of hub, but an average figure is 8 feet (2.5 meters) for STP hubs and 30 feet (8.5 meters) for UTP. You add the ECL factor into the MTD equation only one time for each hub; that is, you don't add an ECL for every active port.

The computation becomes complex if you consider every contingency involving multiple hubs. Token-ring has a self-healing feature that makes it possible for a hub to automatically loop back and create its own ring if a connection between hubs breaks. This loopback could theoretically almost double the active cable length because a hub sends frames back the long way around the ring. Planning for the worst case is prudent, but it requires careful study of a cable diagram, and it limits you to using very conservative cable lengths.

Here are some practical token-ring planning guidelines for shielded and unshielded twisted-pair cable. These guidelines are for 4Mbps token-ring systems. Generally, you will have to cut the maximum distance between the node and hub in half for 16Mbps token-ring. However, the specifications for some manufacturers' equipment will give you much greater distances.

- If you run 4Mbps token-ring on shielded twisted-pair wire, you can use as much as 150 feet (45 meters) of cable between each node and the wiring hub. Two wiring hubs can be separated by the same 150-foot distance, but the maximum overall length between wiring hubs can't exceed 400 feet (120 meters). An 8-foot adapter cable is allowed between the wall jack and the node. Theoretically, you can have as many as 260 nodes on the ring using shielded twisted-pair cable, but you will probably exceed the MTD before you exceed the node limit.

- On Category 5 unshielded twisted-pair, you are limited to a maximum of 132 nodes on the main ring. Limiting the number of nodes automatically limits the maximum amount of cable on the overall ring. However, the IEEE 802.5 standard for token-ring over UTP contains complex guidelines that require on-site measurement of signals between wire pairs, attenuation, and even temperature. In short, you will need a qualified and well-equipped installation team.

- The shielded twisted-pair wire originally suggested for the token-ring network architecture offers high-quality networking, but it also carries a steep price tag. In installations that won't suffer from much electrical noise, UTP makes sense.

ARCnet

ARCnet in commercial use

ARCnet was a favorite for installing point-of-sale (cash register/scanner) terminals and for general industrial use. You can still see it working in stores around the world. It is a rock-solid connection scheme with no foibles. Sure, it seems slow at 2.5Mbps, but that's still plenty of data-handling speed for many applications.

ARCnet evolved backwards. The original ARCnet plan, developed in the late 1960s, called for using wiring hubs with a dedicated run of coaxial cable between each node and the hub, which is now a key feature of the much newer ethernet and token-ring networks. In the 1980s, various companies delivered ARCnet adapters that could use both coaxial and unshielded twisted-pair wire in a station-to-station configuration like the linear bus configuration of the original thin ethernet.

SEE ALSO

➤ *Although you won't find new installations of ARCnet today, plenty of it is still around and works just fine for many applications; see page 20.*

ARCnet is a bad news/good news networking system. Its slow signaling speed of 2.5Mbps won't support a large number of high-powered PCs trying to run busy applications, but the slow signaling speed does facilitate using long cable runs and lower-quality UTP cable. Unlike 10BaseT or token-ring, you can use ARCnet on voice-grade telephone PBX cable that might already be in the walls of your building. An EIA/TIA Category 2 cable installation will work fine with ARCnet.

ARCnet often replaced 3270

Because ARCnet uses the same cable and topology as the old IBM 3270 cabling, companies often reused the same cable for a new LAN. It's likely 20 years old, so if you run into this kind of installation, it probably hasn't much of a future.

In its standard configuration (refer to Figure 4.6), ARCnet uses RG-62 coaxial cable, which is the same cable IBM used in its 3270 mainframe terminal system. You can have as much as 2,000 feet of coax between a node and its powered hub. Powered hubs in ARCnet systems are not expensive, as they are in token-ring networks, so they are commonly used. ARCnet allows for even lower-cost unpowered hubs, but the maximum cable run between a node and an unpowered hub is 100 feet. Because ARCnet doesn't depend on the CSMA/CD listen-before-talk techniques to regulate how the cable is shared, timing is not critical, and as Figure 4.8 illustrates, the maximum node-to-node distances can be as much as 20,000 feet. Under UTP, you can use as much as 400 feet of voice-grade cable between the node and wiring hub.

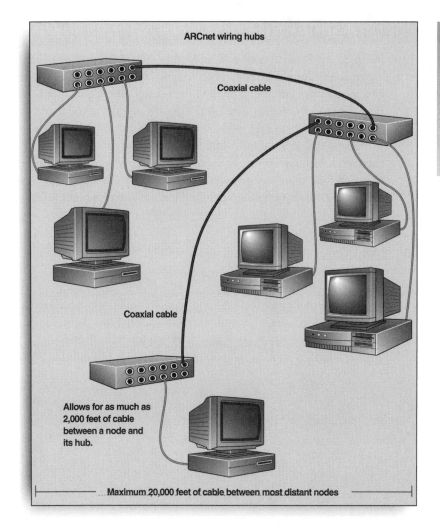

ARCnet wiring hubs

Coaxial cable

Coaxial cable

Allows for as much as
2,000 feet of cable
between a node and
its hub.

Maximum 20,000 feet of cable between most distant nodes

FIGURE 4.8
The classical ARCnet system uses wiring hubs with coaxial cable in a star physical topology. A few manufacturers sell interface cards that use UTP in a bus configuration.

Some specific brands and models of ARCnet adapters allow you to use either coax or UTP in a daisy chain or linear bus configuration. The overall length of the single coaxial cable span in linear bus is 1,000 feet, and the maximum overall length of UTP is 400 feet. However, because of the difficulty in matching overall impedance and signal levels, you can have only 10 nodes on the cable. Some companies suggest that you can connect a string of daisy-chained nodes to a wiring hub. However, we don't recommend it because we have found that these types of installations are often unreliable.

Newer Standards

Technology doesn't stand still, and many organizations have expressed needs for a networking system capable of signaling speeds of a gigabit and beyond. The old networking cable plans won't support those technologies. You need a good Category 5 cable system or (preferably) a fiber-optic cable system for gigabit ethernet. However, a 10Mbps thin ethernet network will allow its users to surf the Web through a common Internet connection, use line-of-business applications, and get a lot of work done. You won't do any new installations using these wiring schemes, but they can still carry a huge workload.

Managing Through the Hub

Management Plays   •

Network Management   •

Network Management Architectures   •

Network Management
and Troubleshooting   •

Management Plays

As the kicker's toe touched the ball to start the third quarter, Willy's beeper started to vibrate on his belt. After the runback, he read the message on the LCD screen asking him to call the network manager at one of OK Cable's clients, a local hospital. He considered using his cell phone there in the stands, but decided that it wasn't exactly the way to impress a client. He walked down the stadium's spiral ramp to the parking lot gate and negotiated a pass to get back in.

The cable service truck wasn't his idea of Sunday afternoon transportation, but it was his turn to be on emergency call, and driving the truck to the game was a good alternative to staying at home. He disarmed the truck's alarms, sat inside, and savored being out of the wind while the cellular phone woke up and negotiated with a local cell site. Then he called Janet Jackson at the hospital.

"Willy!" she exclaimed. "Thanks for calling so quickly. I can't get a hold of anybody else, and our network is down. The doctors can't enter patient records, the emergency room can't do billing, and I'm in hot water! I've checked everything on the server and clients. I think it's gotta be cable."

Willy winced. He was proud of the hospital's cabling system—he had designed it and supervised its installation. A fiber-optic backbone fed a series of wiring hubs that provided excellent physical isolation. "What about the hub management system? What's it showing?" he asked.

"I can't get into it, either. The management console can't talk to the hubs across the network to get any updated data."

"Janet, I'm going to call into the hub management system through the RS-232 modem connection. I'll call you back in a few minutes." Willy knew that Janet's management console didn't have a modem she could use to dial into the hub's serial port as a backdoor connection. It wasn't the cost of the modem that drove this decision, but rather the monthly recurring cost of the telephone line dedicated to a modem. Willy reflected that some forms of insurance seem awfully expensive until you need them.

He booted his laptop computer and connected a special interface cable from the laptop to a jack in the side of his truck's cellular phone. ("You'd think the thing was made of gold, considering what they charge for it," said Willy when he got the bill for the cable.) The resulting chain of cables and devices offended his sense of neatness, but he knew from experience that it worked.

The telephone number for the hospital's hub management system was in Willy's communications software. OK Cable paid for the phone line under the hospital's monthly maintenance plan. Actually, the hospital paid for the line through OK Cable, but it seemed to get through the budget that way.

Willy dialed the telephone number on the cellular handset, and when he heard the modem answer, he entered the command ATX0D on the laptop's keyboard to bring the modem online. The two modems negotiated a 9,600bps connection, the software's script sent the appropriate password, and he was in. The script had previously set up a long dropout time in the modem so that changes in the phone's cellular connection, which can take place even if you're standing still, didn't cause the modem to lose the carrier.

Willy's terminal emulation software didn't have the pretty windows or moving chart displays of the management console, but the network's problem was immediately apparent when he looked at the network traffic display. One adapter in the network was jabbering—it was constantly transmitting packets without listening. This caused what appeared to be a constant series of collisions, and all the other, well-behaved adapters were simply waiting for a clear channel. This hardware malfunction didn't have anything to do with Willy's cable, but he could fix it.

He entered the command mode in the wiring hub software and gave the command to partition or isolate the offending node. This caused the hub to literally disconnect that port from the rest of the network. Then he went back to the traffic monitor screen and saw the server start to announce its presence on the network. He was disconnecting the modem cables when his cellular phone rang.

"Everything is up!" Janet exclaimed. "You're magic."

"Magic is simply knowledge you don't have yet," Willy observed. "Go to the wiring hubs and see which port has a partition light lit. Then, change out the network interface card in the node connected to that port, and reset the port."

Willy entered the call in his service log (emergency calls on Sunday afternoon weren't in the hospital's maintenance contract), locked the truck, and headed back to the stadium. With luck, he'd see the whole fourth quarter.

Network Management

In this chapter, we're going to talk about network management. We're going to keep the discussion at the level of managing and troubleshooting the cabling. Because the cabling is part of an integrated and layered network, though, we also get into some of the network layers above the cabling. In this discussion, we use the term *wiring hubs*. In this context, we mean hubs and switches of all kinds, whether they use a closed cabinet or a backplane. We use the term *hubs* very generically as shorthand for all those combinations of things that sit at the center of the network traffic flow.

Wiring hubs are a critical part of a structured cabling system, and they provide the perfect pivot point for a network management system. The initial concept of a wiring hub has expanded and grown into modern network practices of switching and network segmentation. As these architectures have evolved, they've influenced another important technology: network management. This is important to us because network management software can give us the information we need to plan cable system expansion and can immediately help to pinpoint wiring problems.

Management for All

"How much management does a small business need?" That's a fair question. Network management systems can grow to look like something NASA would use to control a mission to the outer planets. At the same time, no business operation needs automated assistance more than the small business with a part-time computer systems staff and thin operating margins.

The fact is that today many network management tools are "free" or, at least, are included in the price of a product such as a hub or switch. You will pay more initially for a managed hub or switch. For example, a switch with no management features might be $20 per port, whereas a switch with management might be $40–60 per port (in part, because it also includes other features). However, the initial expense is probably offset by the benefits of better system planning and troubleshooting, even in a network of a few dozen PCs.

In Chapter 9, "Practical Home and Small Office Network Cabling," we look at practical cable schemes for very small offices and businesses. Every enterprise of every size can benefit from a structured cabling scheme.

The Network/PDS, Management Puzzle

In the late 1980s, Synoptics (now part of Nortel/Bay Networks) and Cabletron raised the wiring hub and its management to a new technological level. Now, dozens of companies compete in the hub business, but Cabletron, Cisco, Nortel/Bay Networks, 3Com, Hewlett-Packard, and Intel are leaders in the market for high-end products with internal management.

Modern managed hubs, switches, routers, network interface cards, and other devices contain internal processors that monitor several layers of network activity. They monitor the ethernet and token-ring packets, reduce the monitored information to statistics, compare the statistics to preset parameters, and then either take an action, such as sending an alert and shutting down a port, or simply store the statistics.

Figure 5.1 illustrates the relationship between the parts of the network system. It is a three-way merger between networking specifications, PDS specifications, and the features provided by the hub or switch manufacturers.

The networking specifications, like IEEE 802.3 (ethernet) and IEEE 802.5 (token-ring) described in Chapter 4, "LAN Combinations," supply the basic structure of the network. The various PDS companies, described in Chapter 3, "Standards: There Are So Many!," supply the products and detailed specifications for physical construction.

The hubs provide network functions and management/troubleshooting functions. In this combination, the wiring hub (or switch) assumes a central role.

- The networking specification defines the type of hub and details like cable length.

- The PDS specification defines the types of wall plates, patch panels, connectors, and jumpers used to interconnect the network cables and how they physically connect to the hub.

- The network specification limits the distances between network devices such as repeaters and the number of those devices.

- The PDS specification describes the cabinets, racks, and structures used to house those devices.

- The manufacturers of the hubs and switches give their products monitoring and management capabilities. They exercise these capabilities from their position as the center of network traffic.

FIGURE 5.1
This diagram shows a basic *premises distribution system* (PDS) that includes the "vertical" cabling between wiring closets, patch panels for the vertical cabling, both a chassis and a cabinet wiring hub, and a patch panel for the "horizontal" wiring going to the nodes.

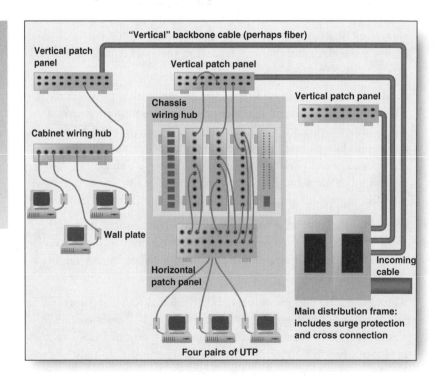

We aren't going to provide an exhaustive review of network management systems in this book on cabling. The information on cable testing and certification equipment in Chapter 9 is more important for cable installations than the larger topic of network management. However, network management systems are tied to and rely on cabling systems. They can also help you to uncover problems in the cabling system, so you should know a few of the facts and buzz words.

There are several reasons to choose a wiring hub, either a chassis style or a cabinet style, equipped with a network management system, but all the reasons hinge on gathering a baseline set of statistics that describe typical or normal performance and traffic load. This baseline of data allows you to quickly detect when and where things go wrong. If you first determine what is normal, it is easy to determine what is abnormal, and that's what a network management system is all about. The network monitoring and statistical reporting programs are like the level in the carpenter's toolbox—they indicate when operations are balanced correctly.

You can also use the set of baseline statistics to justify a budget for new equipment and software, to project personnel requirements, to bill clients and other departments for services, and to simply demonstrate the otherwise hidden role of the network in the organization's business. These statistics can help you make decisions about segmenting and augmenting the network based on the data gathered by the network management system.

Today's network management models define fault management, configuration management, performance management, security management, and accounting management as the primary management functions.

- *Fault management* includes detecting problems and taking steps to isolate them, and provides messages describing active connections and equipment.

- *Configuration management* is closely tied to fault management because changing configurations is the primary technique used to isolate network faults.

- *Performance management* includes counting things such as packets, disk access requests, and access to specific programs.

Looking for the abnormal

It's important to understand that most management systems operate by looking for the abnormal. You have to set "not-to-exceed" parameters (often called a *threshold)* for traffic levels, events, and operations in the statistical software. On the one hand, the only news you will hear from the management system will be bad. On the other hand, no news will be good news!

- *Security management* includes alerting managers to unauthorized access attempts at the cable, network, file-server, and resource levels.

- *Accounting management* involves billing people for what they use.

After you determine the baseline data for your system, you set up network management *console* software that watches for and reports deviations from the baseline. Network management console programs can make database entries, generate network messages, and even dial your pager when they detect specific variations from the baseline. When a management program responds to a specific condition, that response is called an *alert*.

An alert is nothing more than a preprogrammed value for some parameter being monitored by the program. When the parameter—for example, the number of packets on the cable—reaches the specified level (either abnormally high or low), the program notifies something or somebody about the deviation. You can elect to set alerts for a wide variety of monitored parameters, ranging from the percentage of packet collisions to the number of packets coming from a specific server within the past minute.

Modern methods of communications and flexible software give these products more ways to sound an alarm than simply sending a message to a console operator. Network management products can dispatch a message to any networked PC, originate email messages, or use a modem to dial the number of a pager service and enter specific error codes for the pager's display. Email and pager notifications, depending on the level of the problem, are the two techniques used in most situations. Monitoring programs can also execute other programs with their own scripted actions that can shut down processes and turn them on, and they can take a variety of other actions. In effect, you can monitor your network's problems from almost anywhere.

Network Management Architectures

In many modern organizations, the LAN carries the lifeblood of the operation and can often be as vital to production as the employees or the raw materials. Any downtime can have devastating consequences.

The LAN deserves the benefit of a strong suite of management tools, and the wiring hub provides an excellent central point for network management. In structured network management systems, specific devices called *agents* communicate with a management program that collects and displays data. Software in the management station, typically a computer running UNIX or Windows, regularly polls the agents for their data, and agents can send alerts when they detect specific deviations from preset conditions. The three main sets of network management system standards (from least to most popular) are NetView, the Common Management Information Protocol (CMIP), and the Simple Network Management Protocol (SNMP). Figure 5.2 shows the possible locations of the agents on the network.

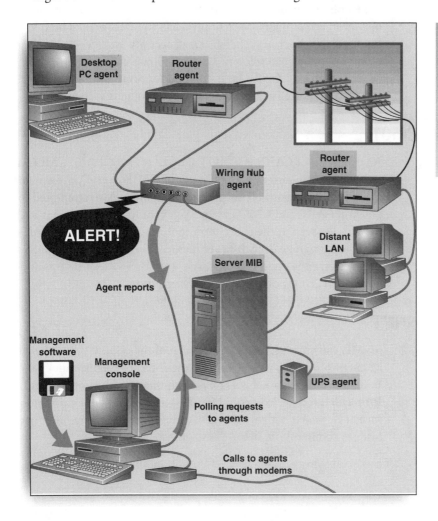

FIGURE 5.2
Network management agents, processors, and programs that collect statistical data are found in networked devices as varied as uninterruptible power supplies and routers.

Not the whole truth!

We're trying to simplify a complex subject here by sticking mainly to SNMP management. However, you should know that some vendors, such as 3Com, have been in the management business since before SNMP was easy to use and have developed excellent proprietary hub/switch management systems. 3Com's Transcend has always been and remains an excellent management system for 3Com wiring closet products. However, it's very difficult to keep a one-vendor network. Transcend can't see non-3Com products, and at some time you will probably install non-3Com products. In the end, SNMP wins.

Nod once and move on

We gave a nod in the direction of NetView, CMIP, and CMOT. Now, let's move on. If you can't stick with a one-vendor network and use a product like 3Com's Transcend, use SNMP.

NetView is a management product developed by IBM and 3Com and is generally the most expensive of the three systems to implement. This architecture requires extensive resources, including PCs and usually a mainframe, in order to operate. You will typically find NetView only in "true blue" organizations running IBM hardware.

CMIP

CMIP is an emerging "open" or widely published network management architecture that gained some attention in the mid-1990s. It was developed by the International Standards Organization (ISO) and was specified in U.S. federal government acquisitions. Because of the emphasis on an open architecture, CMIP offered the promise of operation across many types of products and networks. The CMIP standard also describes a full-featured security system—something lacking in other management systems. However, like many of the "open" standards, CMIP faces competition from older and proven standards that are backed by time-tested products such as SNMP.

CMOT

An evolution of CMIP is CMOT (CMIP over TCP/IP). CMOT is an Internet standard defining the use of CMIP over TCP for managing TCP/IP networks. The Internet Activities Board attempted to position CMIP and CMOT as "next-generation" management tools. SNMP was seen as the short-term tool, whereas CMIP and CMOT were going to take over. It never happened. Instead, SNMP kept getting better, easier, and less expensive until there was little room for CMIP or CMOT, or CMIP's other derivations.

SNMP

SNMP, the most used and well-known of the current network management protocols, was defined by the Internet Engineering Task Force for managing networks based on the Transmission Control Protocol/Internet Protocol (TCP/IP). SNMP provides a common format by which network devices such as routers, wiring hubs, and bridges communicate defined sets of management data.

SNMP was first released in 1988 by the Department of Defense and the commercial developers of TCP/IP in an attempt to manage the different network topologies of complex internetwork systems. Since then, SNMP has grown into a widely accepted network management protocol, not just for interconnected networks but also for smaller LANs using the same technology and topology. In May 1990, SNMP became a TCP/IP standard, which further increased its acceptance.

Agents and Consoles

All network management systems have basically the same architecture. Like ethernet and ARCnet, the popular network management architectures differ in how they communicate across the network, but the concepts are similar.

The SNMP and CMIP standards each define a set of network management variables, as well as the protocols or rules used to exchange network management information. In other words, each standard provides a common format for network devices and equipment such as bridges, concentrators, hubs, routers, and modems to send management data to the network management console software.

The agent typically consists of a special-purpose processor located in each SNMP-compatible or CMIP-compatible piece of equipment—although it can simply be a program running in a multitasking environment like a file server. The generic term *management module* describes either the slide-in card used in a chassis hub or a processor built in to a cabinet hub.

The management console software can run on a PC using Microsoft's Windows or on a UNIX-based workstation. The management console software polls each agent over the network cable for pertinent information regarding the individual nodes on the network, any error messages, and other statistics. It gathers the statistics from all agents on the network—there can be hundreds in a large LAN—and then presents the data in a useful format. Management console displays typically include multiple bar charts and graphs and can provide various levels of real-time and historical data.

When the management console polls and controls the agents across the network cable, it employs *in-band* signaling, a term carried over from telecommunications systems. Management console actions initiated through a separate RS-232C port are described as *out-of-band* signaling. This type of signaling usually occurs during setup and from a remote PC through a modem.

Management Information Base (MIB)

Each agent stores information in a virtual database called a *Management Information Base (MIB)*. The MIB stores all the information concerning traffic, equipment, and error logs. The MIB standard is constantly in evolution to increase the amount of available information and to further automate the management process. The agents can also send unsolicited information on high-priority alerts.

One problem inherent in any protocol implemented by many companies is compliance versus compatibility. Products can comply with a standard without being able to interoperate. Some vendors put proprietary information, called *extensions*, into the MIB. Software from other companies can't read these extensions, and errors result. Similarly, management software looking for proprietary extensions can't effectively display another vendor's agent equipment, so compatibility between agents and management console software from different companies is always a potential problem.

Management Software Suites

You can get a lot of information on the health of the network from many sources. The OpenView program, originated by Hewlett-Packard, is sold in slightly different forms by other companies. It is the basis on which all SNMP management console software is modeled.

Today, many companies have combined SNMP management capabilities with the capability to manage and receive special reports from their own hardware and software products. For example, Novell's ManageWise is a very complete hardware-independent software suite. It combines general network management, including SNMP, with reports from and control over Novell's NetWare file servers and other Novell products.

Management products from other software companies, including Intel's LANDesk Manager, Microsoft Systems Management Server, and Symantec's Norton Administrator for Networks, focus on the cost of ownership-related functions such as software distribution, inventory, and control, but they also include various network reporting functions.

All versions of the SNMP management station software for Windows allow you to use a program called *OVDRAW* to pick icons to create a diagram of the network. However, the icons have been customized for each company's products. A program called *OVADMIN* allows you to customize the diagram to include details such as ethernet addresses, concentrator names, and usernames.

All the programs display network traffic in the form of marching histograms and provide Windows boxes for error messages. You can set alarm levels for events, such as a certain number of collisions or bad packets, and set criteria for audit trails.

Hewlett-Packard enhanced OpenView by adding a program that automatically attempts to "discover" SNMP agents on the network. Although the company claims that OpenView works with any agent, our experience is that it can't always discover agents in hubs provided by other companies.

Device Setup

When you set up a hub, switch, or similar device with an SNMP MIB, it will pay you dividends to take a few minutes to enter some specific information in the device's memory. Typically, you will type the IP address of the device into a browser or use SNMP console software to connect to the device. There will usually be a Configure tab or button. In some products, you will find clearly labeled places to enter information. In other devices, you will see a rather terse and arcane list of labels. For example, the following commands are representative of the settings you can configure:

sysDescr—Shows the system description supplied by the hub's Management Agent software

sysObjectId—Shows the SNMP object identifier for the hub's Management Agent software sysUpTime—Shows the time that has elapsed since the last reset

sysContact—Provides a box for you to type the name of the person who can be contacted in the event of a problem with the hub

sysName—Provides a box for you to type the name of the hub

sysLocation—Provides a box for you to type the location of the hub

sysServices—Shows the services that the hub supports

Taking a few minutes to enter the information when you set up the devices can later save you many critical minutes during a system failure.

The newest evolution in all network management products is the browser front end. Whether it's an enterprise network or a single router, you can read its reports and reset critical aspects of its operation through your browser. Converting text-based reports and graphical images into HTML isn't difficult. The HTML format enables developers to take advantage of the wide availability of browsers on every type of computer to get out from under the burden of developing client software.

The browser interface also breaks down the line between products. As an end user, you don't care much whether the screen you see comes from an SNMP suite or a unique program running in the ROM of a LAN adapter. The commonality of the browser makes it easier to integrate software suites with the hardware-focused configuration and reporting programs that come with a lot of network equipment.

RMON—Listening on Distant Segments

In various places in this book, we discuss and praise the benefits of network segmentation. When you segment your network, you isolate and limit the effect of system failures, reduce contention, and simplify troubleshooting. At the same time, though, you make network management and monitoring much more difficult.

If all the network traffic passes all the points on a flat network, it is easy to monitor. However, on a segmented network, we split the traffic by using switching or by creating a bridge or router inside a server and installing multiple LAN adapters. In either case, the end result is that you have to gather management information at many points.

The Remote Network Monitoring (RMON) MIB was developed by the Internet Engineering Task Force to enable monitoring and protocol analysis in segments of ethernet and token-ring LANs that aren't directly connected to the SNMP management console. The standard for the MIB calls for RMON-compliant devices to include nonproprietary network fault diagnosis information and planning and performance–tuning features. It is an industry standard specification that provides much of the functionality offered by today's proprietary network analyzers and protocol analyzers.

Vendors can insert tiny special-purpose processors running RMON MIB firmware into a variety of devices that hang on the ends of networks, like racks of modems and even individual LAN adapter cards, in order to provide a comprehensive base of information. A small pocketsize device called an *RMON probe* can connect to a LAN cable and report back to a management station anywhere on the Internet.

With the RMON MIB, network managers can collect information from remote network segments for the purposes of troubleshooting and performance monitoring. The RMON MIB provides

- Current and historical traffic statistics for a network segment, for a specific host on a segment, and between hosts
- A versatile alarm and event mechanism for setting thresholds and notifying the network manager of changes in network behavior
- A powerful, flexible filter and packet capture facility that can be used to deliver a complete, distributed protocol analyzer

RMON is designed so that the remote probe devices do the data collection and processing. This reduces the SNMP traffic on the network and the processing load on the management station. Instead of continuous polling, information is transmitted to the management station only when required. Many RMON "client" applications (management stations) located in various parts of the network can simultaneously communicate with and get information from one RMON "server" in a hub, LAN adapter, or standalone probe. The information from a single RMON server can be used for many tasks,

---

A little RMON here and there

For people interested in cable problems, RMON provides an overall monitoring tool. The evolution of the RMON standard is pushing into the higher layers of network interconnectivity, not into the physical layer. However, the information on activity provided by RMON probes—combined with the information on link status and bad packets provided by hubs and switches—creates a powerful set of tools for cable troubleshooting and planning.

from troubleshooting and protocol analysis to performance monitoring and capacity planning.

An RMON probe provides valuable statistics on the whole network segment. Figure 5.3 shows an example of just one RMON reporting screen. The RMON probe information is different from other SNMP management products, which focus on monitoring and controlling a specific network device. Although device-specific management tools are important, they do not provide a picture of the health of the whole network segment and its cabling.

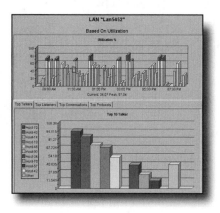

FIGURE 5.3
This screen shows an image of network activity based on the inputs from many RMON probes. The statistics show activity at specific times of day and activity by specific users. Other alternatives, available at a click, show you the most active stations, protocols, and activities. This information is useful for system and cable planning and for troubleshooting actions.

Through the reports from a system of RMON devices, a network manager can see the traffic on a LAN segment and identify trends, bottlenecks, and hotspots. When a problem arises, RMON includes a protocol analyzer so that the network manager has distributed troubleshooting tools immediately at hand. Because the RMON device is permanently attached to the network segment, it's already collecting data about the remote LAN and is ready to transmit it to a central network management station whenever required. This network monitoring and troubleshooting can be done without the time and travel required to send expensive network experts with "lug-able" protocol analyzers to the remote site.

An improvement to the original RMON specification, called *RMON2*, extends the degree of monitoring. The original RMON, now called *RMON1*, provides traffic statistics at the MAC layer of the protocol. RMON2 adds insight to those traffic statistics by specifying the protocol and applications that make up that traffic. This protocol-specific and application-specific knowledge is crucial to deploying and troubleshooting today's client/server environments. As a result, this raises RMON from the "segment view" provided by RMON1 to the "enterprise view" provided by RMON2.

RMON2 devices show the network manager which nodes are exchanging data and which application(s) they are using. With this detailed knowledge of traffic patterns in the network and how the traffic from client/server applications is growing and changing, the network manager can ensure that users, servers, communications links, and cable resources are placed in the correct network location to optimize performance and reduce costs.

Network Management and Troubleshooting

When the automated network management console reports an alert, the human troubleshooting sequence begins. The more information you have regarding normal operation, the quicker you can solve the problem of abnormal operation. If you know what the normal pattern of traffic and connections looks like, you can quickly spot problems. If you suspect that the cable system is at fault, a wiring hub helps you to troubleshoot the problem by reporting stations with abnormally low traffic counts or with high levels of bad data. We describe more troubleshooting tips in Chapter 10, "Fiber-Optic Cable," but the basic technique is no mystery to anyone who has ever tried to find the bad bulb in a string of Christmas lights: Replace a suspect item with one known to be good. In the next chapter, we describe the wiring closet, patch panels, and other devices that help you troubleshoot and substitute cable segments.

The Structured Cable System: Wiring Closets and Cross-Connections

Wiring at the Core   •

More Than Just Skeletons in That Closet   •

Conduits and Cable Trays   •

Up the Backbone   •

In the Closet   •

Wiring at the Core

The scout ship lurched violently and popped out of hyperspace too close to a star. "What have you done and why are we here?" Wirejack asked the ship.

"There is a malfunction in my central wiring core," the ship's voice replied in what was programmed to be an efficient and soothing manner. "I detected a discontinuity in the wiring core and dropped into normal space."

"Yeah, but it's too darn hot here," Wirejack moaned. "We're practically in the corona of that star. Get us out of here."

"I cannot access the normal space drive until the wiring discontinuity is repaired," the ship replied.

"Open the wiring core," Wirejack ordered.

The wiring core was the convergence of tens of thousands of individual meson beams sent by transceivers inside each discrete logic node in the ship. The transceivers twisted space and time so that the intersection was a fifth-dimension hole in the heart of the ship. In response to Wirejack's order, the ship created a normal-space portal into the fifth-dimension hole, and Wirejack gingerly inserted his head and one arm into the hole. His vision extended only a few inches, and he felt as though he was pushing his hand through spider webs as it crossed the beams.

Then his fingers touched something solid. A worker at the last spaceport had left an alignment tool inside the hole, and it was floating around and interrupting the path of the beams. When his fingers brushed against it, the tool drifted away. Wirejack was reaching as far as he could into the hole, and his breath was coming in gasps. His consciousness was fading as he tried over and over to grab the floating object.

"Willy? Willy? Are you okay?" Bill asked. Willy's hand brushed Bill's face and grabbed it. Bill yelled, which startled Willy into letting go and simultaneously gasping in a deep breath of cool, conditioned air.

"Huh? What happened?" Willy asked.

"The heat in that darn wiring closet got to you," Bill replied. "It must be 120 degrees in there, and you were practically standing on your head trying to fish out that screwdriver I dropped into the cabinet. I had to pull you out."

The wiring closet in this job was poorly planned. It was the old broom closet of a remodeled building, but the remodeling hadn't included adding conduits to the walls or providing the wiring closet with air conditioning. The closet's only redeeming quality was its central location. The closet contained a wiring hub for 128 ports, a large, horizontal patch panel, a vertical patch panel, and an uninterruptible power supply for the hub. It was crowded and hot.

"Let's get a couple of fans," Willy said in a still shaky voice. "We'll blow some air in there until we get those meson beams aligned."

Bill gave him a strange look while Willy drank some water and went back to find the dropped screwdriver.

More Than Just Skeletons in That Closet

Each wiring closet is a pulse point for a major network's cabling system, although many successful networks don't have even one wiring closet. In a small office, the total extent of the cable system can be a wiring hub hanging from the back of a desk, with the cables running directly to the LAN adapters in each node. But in an installation of more than a dozen nodes, you will want the flexibility of a wiring closet like the one shown in Figure 6.1. The equipment in a wiring closet typically includes patch panels for the vertical wiring, patch panels for the horizontal wiring, the wiring hubs, and other devices such as uninterruptible power supplies.

A wiring closet might be as big as a broom closet, or it might be part of a larger equipment room. On the one hand, a wiring closet should be easily accessible, but on the other hand, it is a vulnerable point in the network and should be well secured. A disgruntled employee or someone intent on mischief can disable your entire network during a few seconds' work in the wiring closet. Whether a wiring closet is a true closet or a part of someone's office, it should be physically secured.

Security is no platitude!

Competition among telecommunications carriers is fierce. Because your outside cables typically come into at least one of your wiring closets, various communications service providers and their subcontractors will have access at different times. Sabotage and mischief have been known to happen. Keep control of the access to your wiring closets, log who goes in and out, and protect your assets!

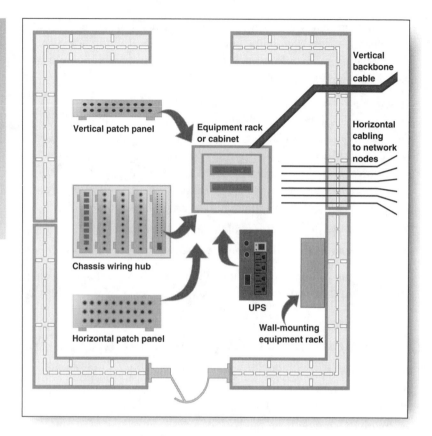

In the ideal installation, each wiring closet is connected to a main cross-connect point—a series of panels with plug-in jumpers. Usually, these wiring closets contain all cabling for voice, data, and video. For the purposes of this technical position, there are two types of wiring closets to be considered:

- *Intermediate Distribution Frames (IDFs)*—These wiring closets are strategically placed throughout the building and provide the connections to end devices. For a multistory building, there is usually at least one IDF per floor. Larger floor layouts might require multiple IDFs to provide connections for all end devices while remaining within the distance limitations of the chosen LAN standards, typically a 100-meter radius or less.

- *Main Distribution Frame (MDF)*—The MDF is the main concentration point for an entire building or campus cable plant.

Importantly, it's the place where the inside cable plant meets the outside world's connectivity. The termination points for incoming services are in the same room as the MDF and lead to the MDF. Typically, all IDFs throughout a building are connected to the MDF in a rough star topology. For campus locations, one building typically houses the MDF, and each individual building has its own concentration point, or Building Distribution Frame (BDF), connecting the building's own IDFs.

The MDF is often part of a larger server room containing communications servers, file servers, and perhaps even the desks of the people in the network management and support team.

Of course, in many installations the main cross-connection is also the only wiring closet.

In this chapter, we describe the relationship of the wiring closets to the rest of a structured wiring plan, how to plan for the location and determine the size of a wiring closet, and the equipment inside the closet and their functions. We provide details of the various options associated with different network cabling schemes. Although most installations superficially look alike, they vary considerably in their specifics.

The cable plant within a building or campus is a long-term investment. The investment in building wiring can and should last 10 years or more, as compared to the 3 to 5 years associated with network electronics. Because the cable plant is a long-term investment, it must be able to support existing business needs and provide for future growth. This translates into LAN technologies that range from 10Mbps ethernet, to 622Mbps ATM and gigabit ethernet today, and potentially greater speeds in the future.

Because many enterprise sites house multiple departments or divisions with a variety of data communications requirements, the cabling infrastructure must be flexible. As individuals and devices move throughout the building or campus, the cable plant should meet the necessary data networking requirements without the need for recabling (although the network electronics at either end of the cable may change). In general, building or campus wiring typically outlives multiple organizational structures and tenants.

Generally, we also add some practical insights and observations to the recommendations made in three EIA/TIA standards:

- EIA/TIA-568—Commercial Building
- EIA/TIA-569—Commercial Building Standard for Telecommunication Pathways and Spaces
- EIA/TIA-570—Residential and Light Commercial Telecommunications Wiring Standard

Note that TIA (http://www.tiaonline.org/) is planning to replace and amend these documents through its standards process. For example, TIA Standards Proposal 4195-B (called *SP 4195-B*), Additional Transmission Performance Specification for 4-Pair Enhanced Category 5 Cabling, specifies new testing criteria for an enhanced level of Cat 5 cable. The SP series of documents are important in the development of new standards. However, catalogs, specifications, and people will recognize the older descriptions and documentation for many years.

These standards are valuable additions to your technical library. You can obtain copies of these standards from

Global Engineering Documents
15 Inverness Way East
Englewood, CO 80112
800-854-7179 or 303-267-1470

Be tough

If your installer isn't familiar with these standards, get another installer.

There is a substantial charge (approximately $50 to $100) for these documents. As the name implies, Global Engineering Documents (http://global.ihs.com/) has offices around the world.

A comprehensive structured cable system provides a description of every inch of cable, every connector, and every additional piece of equipment in the cabling system. A structured cabling system begins with the cable connecting the wall jack to the LAN adapter. The wall-jack system (known in stuffier descriptions as the *telecommunications outlets*) is an important part of the installation because it must provide the correct electrical characteristics and be reliable through thousands of connections and disconnections. In addition to these requirements, it must also provide modularity so that you can change between different cable options as your system evolves.

The cable that runs between each wall jack and the associated wiring closet is called the *horizontal wiring*, mainly to differentiate it from the so-called vertical wiring that forms the backbone between the wiring closets and the main cross-connect point in the building. Of course, these are only general terms; the vertical wiring might actually be as horizontal as all the rest of the cabling, when compared to the horizon. The horizontal wiring is typically copper cable, whereas the vertical backbone wiring is often fiber-optic cable.

The equipment inside the wiring closet must meet the requirements of the specific type of network architecture such as ethernet, ARCnet, token-ring, telephone PBX, IBM 3270, or any of several wiring plans from other companies.

Of backbones and horizontal runs

How the terms fly around! The term *backbone* is typically a network architecture or topology term. Physically, the network backbone traffic typically rides over the horizontal wiring. One is physical and the other is kind of metaphysical.

Conduits and Cable Trays

If you are fortunate enough to work in a building that was designed to accommodate a network, you probably have conduit (typically plastic pipes) going from each wall plate to the wiring closet and between the wiring closets. This conduit is both a blessing and a curse. On the positive side, if there is space left in the conduit, it should take you only a few minutes to pull a new cable, as a replacement for a bad one or for added capacity. New conduit should have a piece of string inside that an installer can use to pull the cable, and thoughtful installers find a way to get the string back into the conduit after a cable is pulled. A piece of equipment called a *fish tape*— a standard part of any installer's toolbox—consists of a reel of wire stiff enough to push its way through the conduit. The fish tape makes it easy to pull a cable.

On the negative side, no conduit ever has enough space. As needs evolve and installations grow, the number of cables usually grows to fill all the space in the conduit. The need to make the available space last as long as possible is a powerful argument in favor of unshielded twisted-pair and fiber-optic cable and a real mark against shielded twisted-pair.

The ideal way to provide for large cable systems is with a *cable tray*. As Figure 6.2 shows, a cable tray is a wire rack designed to carry the weight of the cables. Cable trays are common in modern wiring closets and in building infrastructure spaces such as basements, air-shafts, and ceilings. Some open offices even expose the raceways as an interesting design element.

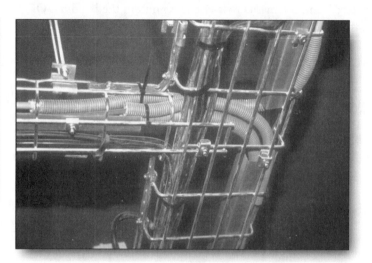

FIGURE 6.2
A cable tray is a wire rack. Cable tray systems, like this EZTray from Cablofil, Inc., include an ingenious assortment of hangers, clips, and supports so that they can hang or stand at any angle and conform to building spaces.

Inside the wire closet, cable trays control the heavy cascade of cables and help to distribute them to the patch panels. As Figure 6.3 shows, cable trays keep things neat and solve the mechanical problem of how to handle the cable.

SEE ALSO

➤ *UTP is much thinner and takes up less room in a conduit than does STP; see page 37 and page 40.*

When planning for conduits and cable trays, you have to consider that the volume of cable between the endpoints should be adequate for all communication requirements, not just data networking. By volume of cable, voice media may take up the most space in vertical wiring conduits because every voice user in the building can potentially be represented by a dedicated cable segment from desktop to the PBX (through a punch-down block or two along the way). This is unlike data media, which is usually terminated at a hub or switch in the nearest wiring closet (IDF), with vertical cabling used to extend LANs from the IDF, to provide uplinks to the backbone network. Additional cabling may be required for circuit-switched or broadcast video, but with the trend of migrating video to IP-based transport, video applications will increasingly utilize the same network infrastructure as other data traffic.

FIGURE 6.3
Wiring closets aren't plush, but they should be neat. Careful installation promotes high signal quality and makes it easier to reconfigure the system in the future.

Even if you are fortunate enough to have conduits in your walls and cable trays in your ceilings, you will still have cables running outside those neat structures. When you plan the cable runs inside ceilings and walls, here are a few rules to keep in mind:

- Always plan the cable arrangements so that copper data cables cross power lines at right angles. This approach limits the energy absorption and therefore the electrical noise on the data cable.

- Never run copper data cables parallel to 120-volt power lines at distances of less than 6 to 8 inches. Keep data cables at least several feet away from higher voltage power lines.

- Keep each copper data cable as far away as possible from sources of electrical noise, including fluorescent lights, motors, elevator relays, radio transmitters, microwave transmitters for burglar alarms, and anything else that consumes electrical power.

- Run the data cables by the most direct route. Every extra foot of cable used in a horizontal link to a wall plate can reduce the cable available for other horizontal links.

- If you have false ceilings, use cable hangers (there are many types of hooks, loops, and trays) to keep the weight off the ceiling tiles.

- Don't run UTP wires inside the same cable sheath for both data wires and voice telephone wires. The voice system will create spikes and crosstalk that disrupt the data system.

- Similarly, keep wires carrying data and those carrying voices on separate punch-down blocks.

- Don't bend cable tighter than a radius ten times the diameter of the cable.

- Patch cables pick up electronic noise, so keep the patch cables as short as possible.

- Strip off as little of the outside cable jacket as possible. If you strip off the outside jacket, particularly where wires enter conduit, the conductors can lie too close together and generate crosstalk.

In some solidly constructed buildings, you might not be able to run the cables inside the walls or ceilings. Panduit Electrical Group and other companies market products called *surface raceways* that house cables in a neat and rugged metal external duct. Panduit also offers a series of data cables designed to run under carpeting.

Up the Backbone

Each wiring closet contains patch and cross-connect panels that connect to the horizontal wiring and to the vertical wiring, also known as the *backbone* wiring. In data installations, the wiring closet also houses one or more wiring hubs for the appropriate network architecture.

Vertical or backbone wiring, regardless of its actual orientation to the horizon, links each wiring closet to a main distribution frame (MDF), or cross-connect point. A separate cable runs between each closet and the main cross-connection. The function of the MDF is primarily to distribute circuits coming in from outside the building. The cross-connect panel in the MDF provides a testing and connection point for outside circuits and backbone wiring. The MDF cross-connect panel has terminations for the vertical cabling (which is often fiber-optic cable) that goes between wiring closets on different floors or in different work areas. Technically, the term *backbone* can include cabling between buildings.

The EIA/TIA standards specify that the backbone system should be a star configuration, with separate backbone cables going from the main cross-connect point to each wiring closet. Although such a configuration is useful and expandable to a point, it eventually forces you into impractical scenarios, such as connecting a hub in a wiring closet on the fifteenth floor to a hub in a wiring closet on the fourteenth floor through the single cross-connect panel in the basement.

The standards allow for a second level of cross-connect points on the backbone. In the example just cited, you might put the second-level cross-connection on the tenth floor. More importantly, the standards also allow for whatever separate direct connections are necessary between each wiring closet. Technically, the direct connections between wiring closets are adjuncts to the backbone, but in practical installations these intercloset connections are primary communications links.

Locating the Closets

As you plan for one or more wiring closets, you have to think in several dimensions. The parameters of your planning are defined by the maximum backbone cable lengths between each closet and the main cross-connection, by the maximum horizontal cable lengths between each closet and each wall jack, and by the maximum distances between wiring closets. It's like setting up a three-dimensional chess game with pieces of string. In this game, string of various lengths is tied to each chess piece and limits its position.

The game has other limitations, too, because each specific distance depends on the type of cable used in the cable span. On the backbone, for example, you get the best distance, as much as 6,560 feet (2,000 meters), from fiber-optic cable. Unshielded twisted-pair cable

Plan on 250 to 1

As a rule of thumb, plan on providing at least 1 square foot of wiring closet floor space for every 250 square feet of usable office floor space.

offers a maximum length of 2,624 feet (800 meters), and more complex rules apply to shielded twisted-pair and to the older, thick ethernet coaxial cable.

Figures 6.4 through 6.7 provide graphical examples of various cable combinations and how they affect the location of the wiring closets and cross-connect points. Use caution when examining these figures; the maximum cable lengths shown there are from the EIA/TIA standard. All the ethernet and token-ring specifications and limitations detailed in Chapter 4, "LAN Combinations," still apply, and particularly in the case of token-ring, they are probably more limiting than the EIA/TIA standard.

FIGURE 6.4
This diagram shows the maximum cable lengths allowed under the EIA/TIA-568 standard for four types of cable. The most common combination uses STP for both the horizontal and backbone wiring, but fiber-optic cable is being used increasingly for the backbone. Note that fast ethernet or gigabit ethernet might impose tighter limitations on maximum cable lengths.

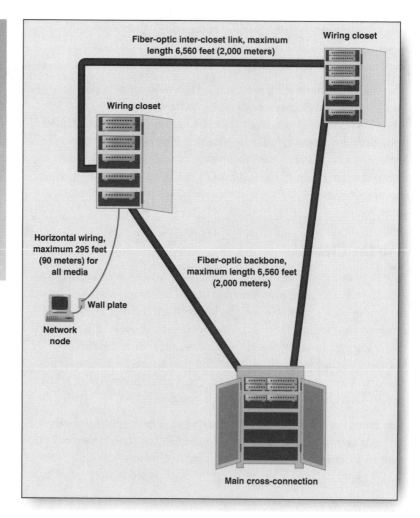

128

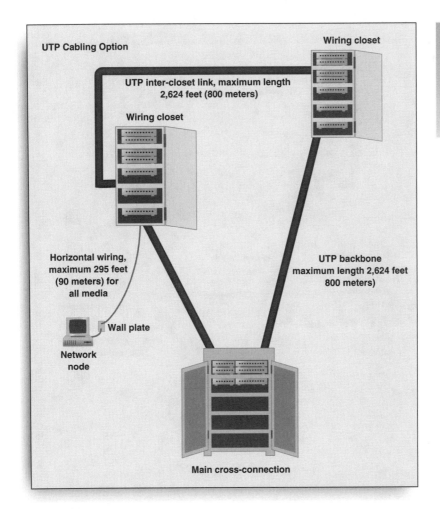

UTP Cabling Option

Wiring closet

UTP inter-closet link, maximum length
2,624 feet (800 meters)

Wiring closet

Horizontal wiring,
maximum 295 feet
(90 meters) for
all media

UTP backbone
maximum length 2,624 feet
800 meters)

Wall plate

Network
node

Main cross-connection

FIGURE 6.5
This diagram shows how
using UTP cabling
affects placement of
your wiring closet and
cross-connect points.

The illustrations of the intermediate cross-connect points in these diagrams can also be misleading. Where the diagram shows that inserting intermediate cross-connections provides longer runs, those intermediate cross-connect points would require repeaters or other devices to keep the entire system within the limitations of ethernet or token-ring.

FIGURE 6.6
This diagram shows how using STP cabling affects placement of your wiring closet and cross-connect points.

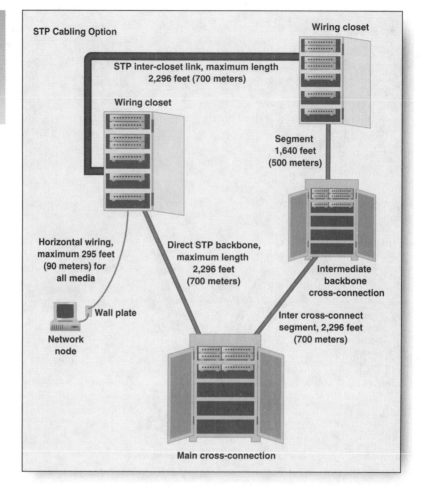

FIGURE 6.6
This diagram shows how using STP cabling affects placement of your wiring closet and cross-connect points.

Finally, as you're planning the data cables, don't forget that the wiring closets and cross-connection points will need 120-volt AC power and good electrical grounds, too. Proper lighting, adequate heating, ventilation, and cooling should also be part of the plan.

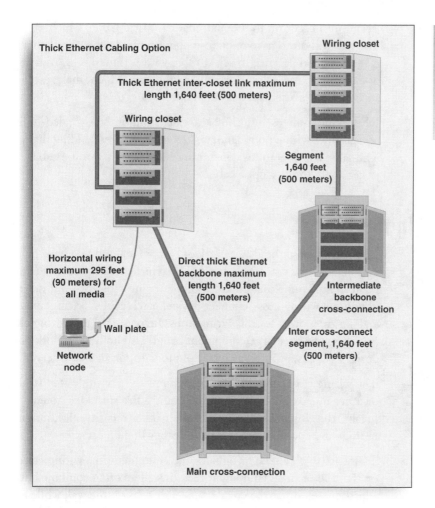

FIGURE 6.7
This diagram shows how using thick Ethernet affects placement of your wiring closet and cross-connect points.

The Backbone Cable

Modern installations will typically use UTP or fiber-optic cable for the backbone. When the backbone is UTP, designers often select multipair cables. These cables are typically 25 pairs of 24AWG wire. Each pair must have a different wire twist rate from all the other pairs in the cable to reduce the crosstalk between the pairs. As explained in Chapter 3, "Standards: There Are So Many!," the cable jacket must conform to the National Electrical Code, which means that you will often have to choose plenum-rated cable. We believe that it's a good practice to select cable with UL markings. A variety of companies, including Lucent, Anixter, and Belden, make cable appropriate for use in the backbone.

Fiber-optic cable used in the backbone is multimode, graded-index optical fiber with a nominal 62.5/125 micron core/cladding diameter. The same considerations concerning the fire rating of the cable jacket apply to fiber-optic cable.

In the Closet

The wiring closet holds a variety of equipment, and you have many options for how you configure it. The typical major pieces of equipment in a wiring closet are a backbone wiring cross-connect device, a horizontal wiring cross-connect device, patch cables, wiring hubs, and backup power for the wiring hubs. Increasingly, the wiring closet (which might be a large equipment room) also houses network portal devices such as a router, a cluster of modems, or an access server.

The wiring closet should never contain pipes carrying water, steam, or other liquids, the sole exception being a fire sprinkler system. Ideally, the closet shouldn't be used for other security, elevator, or heating and cooling purposes or for other building services.

There are two general layouts for the equipment in a wiring closet: on the wall or in an equipment rack. Installers often combine both approaches and put the cross-connect devices on the wall while keeping wiring hubs and other devices in an equipment rack. The best finish for the walls inside a wiring closet is 3/4-inch marine-grade plywood, instead of plasterboard. The plywood should be sanded, free of dust, and painted with a latex paint in a light color.

Keep it neat!

Unlike plasterboard, plywood walls hold screws securely, so you can easily attach the necessary hangers, clips, and other cable management gear. Light colors show the dirt that shouldn't be there.

Cross-Connect Devices

People frequently change desks and offices, and their needs for connectivity evolve. Accommodating moves and changes is a major part of a network manager's job. Cross-connect devices make it easy to reconfigure the horizontal and backbone wiring to add network connections and to substitute for bad wire pairs.

A cross-connect device terminates a cable or a group of cables and makes the terminations available for interconnection to other cables. In typical data networks, one small cross-connect device will terminate the backbone cable and make it available for connection to a wiring hub. On the other side of the wiring hub, a larger cross-connect device will terminate the horizontal wiring before it enters the hub. These cross-connect devices enable you to easily adapt your cabling system to growth and, more importantly, to the moves and changes in your organization.

For about 30 years, the major type of cross-connection used in telephone systems was a *Type-66 block*, shown in Figure 6.8. This type of device, also known generically as a *telco splice block* or a *punch-down block*, is still used, but it is in direct competition with modern alternatives that use RJ-45 modular telephone jack connections.

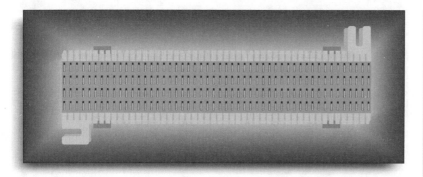

The use of punch-down blocks for data connections is controversial. Some manufacturers claim that their punch-down blocks meet all criteria for impedance, attenuation, and crosstalk in data systems, but other experts express doubts that the mechanical connections will hold their quality over a long period of time.

A punch-down block contains rows of terminals configured in a 10-by-3.44-inch or 1.25-inch-thick nylon or plastic package. Installers use a device called a *punch-down tool* to insert wires into the jaws of the terminals. The terminals pierce the insulation of the wire to make a connection. Typically, one 25-pair cable or a group of cables, such as the horizontal wiring, terminates on each punch-down block, and separate jumpers, often called *fly leads*, link the punch-down blocks. As needs and conditions change, installers can

FIGURE 6.8
The Type-66M punch-down block can terminate 50 pairs of wire. Each wire is "punched" into the jaws of a contact. The contact pierces the insulation to make the connection. Jumper wires placed between each contact make it easy to change connections to each network node. Note, however, that the typical-66 block will not pass the crosstalk tests for Category 5 cable.

vary the jumpers to change the interconnections. Some punch-down blocks come prewired with a short, 25-pair cable and connector. The prewired connector is particularly useful for connections to a wiring hub.

The jumpers used between punch-down blocks present another set of problems. Installers must be careful to keep the leads twisted on the jumpers and to carefully dress the leads away from sources of electrical noise. Finally, the punch-down tool is a mechanical device that can cost $50 to $80, and installers need training and the patience to work with fine wires in this technical environment. Because of these drawbacks, alternatives to the punch-down block, such as the patch panel shown in Figure 6.9, are flourishing.

FIGURE 6.9
Moves and changes make life difficult for a network administrator. A patch panel provides a flexible and fast method of changing connections and adding services. For example, one strip of connectors might connect to the wiring hub through a 25-pair cable, whereas the other strip terminates the horizontal cables. Patch cables make the final link between the horizontal cable and the hub.

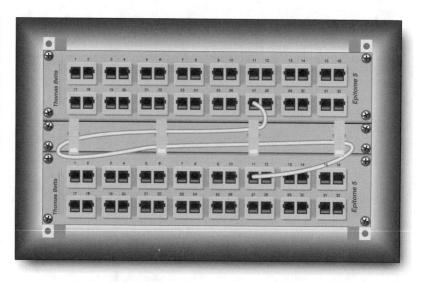

Krone, Inc., of Englewood, Colorado, markets a series of patch panels that terminate cable pairs in RJ-45 telephone jacks with four wire pairs per jack. The patch panel system is certified for Category 5 cable installations, and it can be mounted on a hinged wall mount or in a cable cabinet. One 19-by-7-inch panel can terminate as many as 96 connections. Preconfigured patch cables with RJ-45 connectors make it easy to alter configurations as needs change.

Lucent markets many versions of the Lucent 110 Connector System. The 110 Jack Panel System consists of 8-conductor RJ-45 jacks, mounted in a holder and wired to a block with terminating connectors. Panels are available in configurations with 12, 36, or 108 jacks, and you can combine panels to make huge installations. Similarly, Amp and other companies market cross-connect systems for practically any size network and any configuration. Lucent also offers PC software called the *110 Connector System Configurator* that guides your planning for a single wiring closet or a complete building by posing a series of questions for you to work through. Figure 6.10 provides a reference for the wiring sequence of punch-down blocks, patch panels, and 50-pin connectors.

Jack panel systems often connect to large wiring hubs (particularly the chassis type described in Chapter 4) using a 50-pin connector generically called a *telco connector*. These connectors use a 25-pair cable to make a neat short link between equipment.

SEE ALSO

➤ Tip *and* ring *are old terms that refer to the two wires that connect to the end of a switchboard telephone plug (the tip) or to the back portion of the plug's connecting surface (the ring); see* page 171.

An Octopus with a Harmonica

You will find some strange things in the wiring closet, including an octopus attached to a harmonica. These odd devices connect various pieces of equipment. One common means of connection is the telco connector, or *50-position modular jack*, that terminates a 25-pair cable. In some cases, devices such as punch-down blocks and cross-connect panels come prewired with a telco connector and 6 feet of cable. In other cases, a 25-pair cable might break out into eight separate male RJ-45 plugs, a configuration known as an *octopus*. In other cases, the cable can terminate in a group of eight RJ-45 female jacks, a device known as a *harmonica*. Figure 6.11 shows a hub with telco connectors.

A bad patch cable can kill your LAN

We're not sure why, but it seems that patch cables cause more trouble than any other piece of wire in the entire installation. Maybe it's because they get more physical handling or maybe it's because they're made out of stranded unshielded twisted-pair wire. Remember, the connectors for stranded and solid wire are not the same. When in doubt, check your patch cable first.

Confusing patch panel standards

Some patch panels have RJ-45 connectors wired according to the AT&T/Lucent 258A standards, and others are wired according to the EIA/TIA-568 standards. Be sure that you know how your panels are wired and what kind of patch cord you have.

FIGURE 6.10
This chart provides a reference for the wiring sequence of punch-down blocks, patch panels, and 50-pin connectors. The first color stated is the major color. A white/blue wire is primarily white with blue tracing. The top wire listed in each pair is the *tip* and the bottom wire is the *ring*.

66 and 110 Block Wiring

Wire/Color Code	Pair Number	50 Pin Cable Positions	66 or 110 Block Positions
White/Blue		26	1
Blue/White	Pair 1	1	2
White/Orange		27	3
Orange/White	Pair 2	2	4
White/Green		28	5
Green/White	Pair 3	3	6
White/Brown		29	7
Brown/White	Pair 4	4	8
White/Slate		30	9
Slate/White	Pair 5	5	10
Red/Blue		31	11
Blue/Red	Pair 6	6	12
Red/Orange		32	13
Orange/Red	Pair 7	7	14
Red/Green		33	15
Green/Red	Pair 8	8	16
Red/Brown		34	17
Brown/Red	Pair 9	9	18
Red/Slate		35	19
Slate/Red	Pair 10	10	20
Black/Blue		36	21
Blue/Black	Pair 11	11	22
Black/Orange		37	23
Orange/Black	Pair 12	12	24
Black/Green		38	25
Green/Black	Pair 13	13	26
Black/Brown		39	27
Brown/Black	Pair 14	14	28
Black/Slate		40	29
Slate/Black	Pair 15	15	30
Yellow/Blue		41	31
Blue/Yellow	Pair 16	16	32
Yellow/Orange		42	33
Orange/Yellow	Pair 17	17	34
Yellow/Green		43	35
Green/Yellow	Pair 18	18	36
Yellow/Brown		44	37
Brown/Yellow	Pair 19	19	38
Yellow/Slate		45	39
Slate/Yellow	Pair 20	20	40
Violet/Blue		46	41
Blue/Violet	Pair 21	21	42
Violet/Orange		47	43
Orange/Violet	Pair 22	22	44
Violet/Green		48	45
Green/Violet	Pair 23	23	46
Violet/Brown		49	47
Brown/Violet	Pair 24	24	48
Violet/Slate		50	49
Slate/Violet	Pair 25	25	50

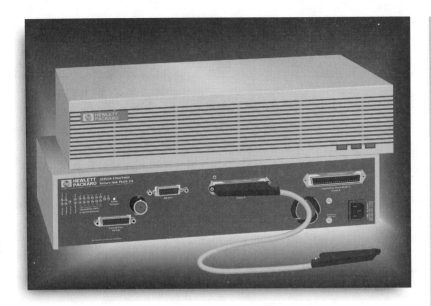

When you configure your wiring closet, you will be faced with a variety of options concerning the use of octopus cables, harmonicas, double-ended telco extension cables, and devices such as wiring hubs and cross-connect panels equipped with telco jacks. It pays to draw a diagram and to create a list of parts so that you can be sure of having the right kinds of cables and connectors on hand to finish the job.

Because the various manufacturers of wiring hubs and computer equipment offer models with different specifications, it also pays to know exactly what the manufacturers require and provide. For exam- ple, some manufacturers use female telco chassis jacks on their equip- ment, and others use male telco chassis plugs. Obviously, you must have the correct type of mating connector on the cable you use to link the equipment. To make matters worse, these 25-pair cable sets are typically prewired, and they are expensive. If you can't get advance information from individual manufacturers, Mod-Tap (now Molex Premise Systems) maintains a library of publications that document the exact installation recommendations of dozens of manufacturers.

Cabinets and Racks

Inside the wiring closet, patch panels and wiring hubs can mount on the wall in brackets, stand in racks, or reside in full cabinets that are racks with doors. Since the 1940s, electronic equipment has come in chassis with 19-inch–wide front panels, and cabling equipment is no exception. The mounting holes in these cabinets, spaced from 5/8 inch to 2 inches apart, match the holes in the front panels of the equipment. The popularity of this configuration means that you can choose from cabinets and mounting brackets made by many companies. A few companies are marketing 23-inch–wide products, but we recommend staying with 19-inch–wide racks.

If you have a small installation, you should consider mounting the patch panels and wiring hubs on the wall using hinged wall brackets. These brackets are available in heights of 3 1/2 to 14 inches high. A hinge on one side allows the assembly to swing out so that you can work on the back side. This type of mounting uses space economically, but you must allow 19 inches for the panel to swing out from the wall. Some brackets come with a locking cover to deter tampering.

A distribution rack, like the one shown in Figure 6.12, is a simple skeletal frame, typically between 39 and 74 inches high, that holds 19-inch–wide equipment panels. The skeleton frame makes it easy to work on the front and back of the equipment. When you plan the closet, you should allow a 6-inch depth for the equipment and then another 12 to 18 inches minimum for physical access. Typically, a floor plate with a depth of about 22 inches provides stability and determines the minimum distance of the rack from the wall. You typically need a 1/2-inch socket wrench and an adjustable wrench to assemble a rack, and you should secure the rack to the floor in some way.

A full equipment cabinet, shown in Figure 6.13, is much more expensive than a distribution rack, but it offers the advantage of security because you can lock the cabinet doors. A typical equipment cabinet is 72 inches high, 29 inches wide, and 26 inches deep. A cabinet requires at least 30 inches of clearance in front to allow the door to swing open. Some fancy cabinets have Plexiglass doors through which the lights of modems and other devices are visible.

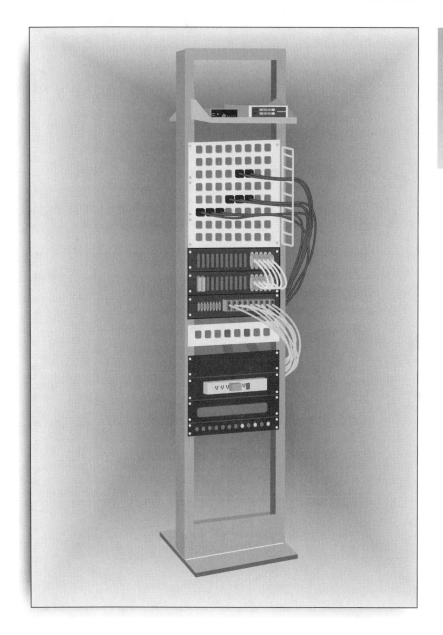

FIGURE 6.12
A distribution rack is a simple frame that holds equipment with a standard 19-inch front panel width. Racks provide flexibility and are only moderately expensive.

FIGURE 6.13
An equipment cabinet provides added security, but it requires more space, including room for the door to swing open.

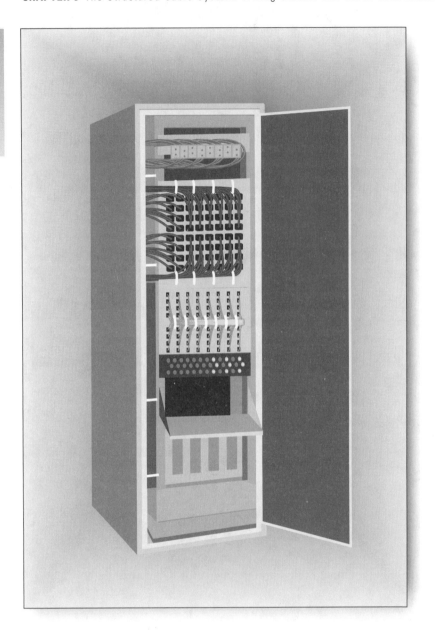

South Hills Datacomm and Newton Instrument Company are retailers of wiring closet brackets, racks, and cabinets that offer a wide inventory of products.

Neat Cables

Neatness counts! You are judged by how your wiring closet looks, and for good reason. The cables emerging from the conduits or racks must be arranged neatly to avoid damage to cable pairs and to simplify adding cables and troubleshooting. Before the 1970s, cables were bound together using waxed twine. The ability to neatly sew cables together with twine and a needle was highly prized among cable installers. Replacing a cable, however, often meant discarding many feet of neatly sewn twine.

During the 1970s, several companies made available self-locking cable ties, shown in Figure 6.14. These ties come in many sizes and materials. Installers can quickly whip a tie around a group of cables and lock them tightly together. Best of all, if you have to make repairs, you can quickly snip off the necessary cable ties.

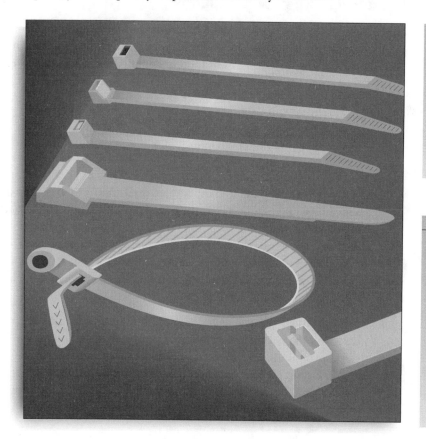

FIGURE 6.14
Cable ties are an installer's best friend. Plastic cable ties hold cables securely and speed installation. In addition, they easily break apart for additions and repairs.

You can never have enough cable ties

Buy them by the dozens in big sizes—you can always cut off the excess. Some cable ties come with screw mounts, so you can secure them to a wall. Companies also offer special adhesive mounts with a hole for the wire tie. One of the later developments is Velcro wire ties.

Easy on those cable ties

Don't make the wire ties too tight. Never tighten the wire tie so much that it deforms the cable. You will spoil the beneficial electrical effect of all that good twisting and self-shielding! Be gentle and resist the urge to crank the wire ties down tight!

In addition to being neat, your cables should also be clearly identified. You can buy identification tags for the cable ties or use separate slip-on or adhesive labels for the cables. EIA/TIA standard 606 (Administration Standard for the Telecommunications Infrastructure of Commercial Buildings) describes a method of numbering and labeling cabling, pathways, and spaces. The 606 standard recommends specifically colored tags for different types of cables. For example, network connections are green, backbone cables are white, and horizontal cables are blue.

Frankly, few installations require the complex specifications of the standard, but you should have some reasonable method of identifying each cable pair and piece of equipment. At least, every cable should be labeled at each end.

Uninterruptible Power Supplies

Your wiring closet needs an uninterruptible power supply (UPS). It does no good to equip network file servers with backup power and then to allow the wiring hubs to go without power during a power failure. Wiring hubs don't require much power, but if you have other devices in the closet, such as a router or access server, you will need more capacity. You must base the UPS selection on the power requirements of the equipment in the wiring closet.

Product features in the UPS market are often obscured by marketing techno-babble. For example, some vendors rate the capacity of their units in volt amps (VA), and others rate their units in watts. The difference between ratings in volt amps and in watts is as much a matter of marketing as of technology. In a marketing sense, a small UPS device can be said to put out more VA than watts. In a technical sense, the VA system is more accurate because the true maximum output of the UPS is limited by its output current capacity, which is directly related to the VA rating.

In resistive devices, such as light bulbs, the voltage and current are in phase, and the device makes full use of power applied. But when devices show an inductive or capacitive component to the power line—and most electrical devices do—the voltage and current get out of phase, and the devices don't make the most efficient use of the applied power. A number called the *power factor* describes the phase relationship. The power supplies in PCs typically have a power factor of about 0.6.

To further complicate the math, a PC's power supply is only about 75% efficient. It loses about 25% in heat and fan noise. The power supply wattage number that you will find in the typical documentation for a PC shows the power supply output, not its input. The required input is considerably higher.

Here is an example applying the 75% efficiency and 0.6 power factor to a PC showing a 200-watt power supply. The bottom line demonstrates the method of finding the appropriate VA rating of a UPS:

```
PC Watts = 200 watts (manufacturer specification)
PC Input Watts = 200 ÷ 75% efficiency = 267 watts
PC Input VA = 267 ÷ 0.6 power factor = 445 VA
```

Connections Up and Down the Line

Although a wiring closet might not always be a closet, it will always be one of the most important parts of the network. The patch panels and cross-connect points in the wiring closet make it easier for you to expand and reconfigure the network and can save many times their initial cost in the wall wrecking, rebuilding, and reconstruction you will otherwise have to do later. It costs more to do it right the first time, but when your business depends on its network connections, it pays to install it correctly the first time.

VA = lotsa watts

As a quick rule of thumb, you should choose your UPS with a VA rating at least two times the combined wattage ratings of all the power supplies that the UPS will support.

chapter

7

Power Wiring and Grounding

Killing Power •

What You Don't Know Could Kill You •

Where Problems Can Begin •

What Is a Ground? •

Grounding Problems •

Normal Mode and Common
Mode Power Problems •

Surge Suppressors •

Uninterruptible Power Supplies •

Killing Power

"Let's get started!" The woman calling the meeting to order wasn't here to socialize. As the men sitting around the table fell silent, all of them felt a cold icicle of doubt. Each man was sure his part of the system was working right, yet somehow glitches kept occurring. This was a big job, and there was a lot of money—invisible but vulnerable—on the table.

"I've never been involved in such a finger-pointing game!" Cheryl Hudson exclaimed. "According to each of you, nothing's wrong, yet nothing works. I've held up final payment on the master contract, and none of you gets another dime until this computer system works. Now who wants to start?"

A large man dressed in a T-shirt and sitting at the end of the table spoke up first. "Well, I know it's not my program. That's proven code! I demonstrated it for you at our offices and it works fine."

"The problem acts like a software bug," Cheryl replied, "but yes, the software does seem to work in demonstrations on different computers in different places. So, is the problem in the computer hardware?"

This raised the hackles of a smaller man in a shiny suit. "No way! We've run the software on those same computers we fabricated in our gara…umm… I mean in our offices and it works fine. The problems start when the computers are brought into this building."

"Willy, does it come down to the cabling?" Cheryl asked the man dressed in a white shirt with "OK Cable" stenciled on the left pocket.

"I'd still be out there checking if I wasn't so certain," Willy responded. "But I've got attenuation, spectrum noise, and crosstalk readings on every LAN cable in your building. After you reported the first problems, we went back and checked everything twice. This is a great cable installation." He waved his hand for emphasis at the pile of printouts showing graphs and tables of numbers. "But I'll admit," he continued, "that it's really curious how the hardware and software stop working when they come together in this building. I'd say you're missing two people in this meeting—a priest and an electrician."

Cheryl eyed him like he'd spent too long smelling the fumes from hot solder, while the others seemed vaguely relieved that the guilt might splatter on someone, anyone, else.

"Either this place is haunted or it has a power problem," Willy continued. "If you want to eliminate all of the options, you need to look into both of those possibilities, too. But, uh, I think the power problem is more likely."

The others were silent, but Cheryl said, "Wait a minute. This is a new building, the lights don't blink, and everything seems to run fine. How could we have a problem with the power?"

"You can have many kinds of power problems in new and old buildings. There is one kind of power problem called third-order harmonics that can affect a computer system despite filters on the power supply. It can cause intermittent outages that look like software problems. You have a big building fed by several separate transformers, which creates the potential for a couple of different types of power problems."

The meeting broke up after Willy gave Cheryl the telephone number of a consulting engineer who specialized in analyzing commercial power systems. He kept the priest's telephone number in his pocket.

Cheryl never called back, and Willy figured that no news was good news. Three weeks later, when the final check for the cable installation work arrived in the mail, he called her. "We had another one of those tense meetings in that same room," she explained, "but this time it was between the engineer you recommended, the power company, and the electrical contractor. I didn't understand a word they said beyond 'neutral to ground connection.' The electrician didn't admit to anything, but there was a crew working on the power panels the next morning, and after they left at noon the computer system ran just fine."

"Yeah, Cheryl," Willy replied with a smile in his voice, "but the full moon is this week. That will be the real test."

What You Don't Know Could Kill You

There are only a few things you need to know about power and grounding, but they are important enough to merit their own chapter because *what you don't know could kill you*. If you become involved in network cabling and ignore grounding, you could set up situations in which lethal voltages exist between different pieces of computer equipment. In less dramatic circumstances, you could create installations in which the network is subject to frustrating, intermittent, and mysterious failures due to AC power and grounding problems. These problems fall into several categories, but they all occur because of bad design or bad connections.

Where Problems Can Begin

AC power-line noise is everywhere inside buildings. Any first-year engineering student quickly learns that you can wave an oscilloscope probe in the air and pick up AC power line noise. Engineers design computer data buses to siphon AC line noise to a neutral ground, but a designer can only do so much while also trying to accommodate low-power, fast data signals. In some instances, AC line noise coupled from a nearby video monitor or hard disk drive can create errors in a computer system, because the interference caused by the line noise overwhelms the data signals used internally by the computer. The problem is compounded if the computer has a poor ground connection.

Other problems related to power and grounding result from electrostatic discharge, the arc that jumps from your fingertips when you walk over a wool carpet in cool dry air. A static discharge can shoot through your computer like a bullet, destroying semiconductors and data in a seemingly random manner. Good grounding can eliminate the threat from electrostatic discharge.

What Is a Ground?

In both alternating current and direct current systems, electrons flow from the negative source, such as a battery or generator, to the positive source. A complete circuit with two conductors is required to carry the flow of electrons. In earlier commercial power systems, the earth was one half of the circuit. At the beginning of the twentieth century, electrical power was delivered to homes and offices over just one wire (see Figure 7.1). The return path was through the earth itself, which acted as an electrical ground. Copper poles driven into the ground at the power transmitting station and at the home or business grounded the negative side of the circuit. The electrons moved through the moisture of the soil.

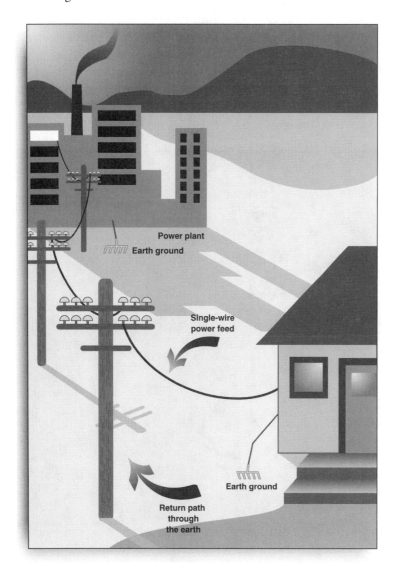

FIGURE 7.1
Early electrical power delivery used one wire and grounded the current in the soil.

However, the earth has a high resistance to electrical flow, and as the consumption of power increases, the loss of power in the earth makes the one-wire system impractical. The one-wire power system quickly gave way to one that delivered power using two copper wires. This system, still used in some countries, is more efficient, but a problematic current path often still exists through the earth between the device using the electricity and either the generating plant or its nearest electrical supply point, typically an electrical transformer.

All modern electrical distribution systems send power across open spaces and across towns at high voltages. A transformer, shown in Figure 7.2, reduces the high transmission voltages to the 120 or 240 volts used in consumer electronic equipment. The transformer can have several windings that feed separate legs of the electrical system. The transformer is your computer's interface to the commercial power grid.

FIGURE 7.2
A power transformer reduces the high voltages used to overcome distance to voltages appropriate for electrical service. Transformers can have multiple secondary stages used to feed several homes or offices. Equipment on the same secondary stage can create electrical interference even though it is in a different building.

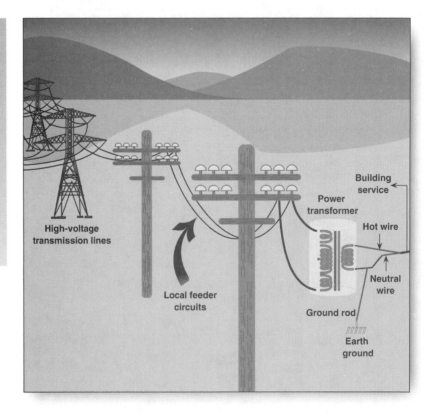

The difference in the resistances between the copper wire path and the earth path can cause a voltage difference to exist between the cabinet or case of an electrical device and the earth ground. This voltage difference can become lethal if one wire going back to the power transformer has a poor connection and the earth ground provides a connection with a lower resistance. The voltage difference can create an electrical shock in extreme cases, and can cause other damage such as galvanic corrosion in less serious situations. Because an earth ground can be something as simple as a wet floor or a water pipe, it's too easy for people to touch the case of a piece of electrical equipment and receive a shock if the equipment is fed with a two-wire electrical system.

Modern power systems use three wires. The two wires that come from the transformer are called the "hot" wire (usually black) and the "neutral" wire (usually white). The neutral wire is connected to an earth ground at the power plant and at the local transformer. In North America, the neutral wire is connected to the longer vertical slot (shown in Figure 7.3) in the AC power socket, and the hot wire is connected to the shorter vertical slot. The third wire (green or bare copper) in the AC power system, which is accessed through the round hole in North American power sockets, connects to a local earth ground for the building. The power plug connects this wire to the outside case of electrical equipment to ensure that no voltage potential exists between the case and the earth ground.

Unfortunately, a large building typically requires more than one so-called earth ground, and the earth ground is almost never the same between two buildings. If the ground wires in two separate locations have slightly different potentials to the common and hot leads, then there will be a voltage difference between the chassis of the equipment in the two locations. This usually isn't a problem, because someone would need very long arms to reach between devices with different ground connections. However, a network cable can connect such devices.

If a system works correctly, there should be no voltage difference between a network cable and the chassis of a computer. The IEEE 802.X committees were careful to create standards that isolate the LAN cable connections from the power connections. Unfortunately, things don't always work as planned.

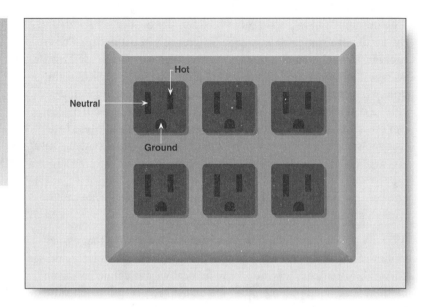

Hands off!

The outer case of a coaxial ethernet BNC connector is connected directly to the outer shield of the coaxial cable. It's possible for the connector to have a potentially dangerous voltage on it. The voltage may not become apparent until you disconnect the cable from a PC with one hand on the cable and the other on the PC Chassis. Always use caution when handling BNC cables.

If a building has faulty wiring—particularly a faulty ground wire connection to an outlet—lethal voltages can exist between the LAN cable and the chassis of a piece of equipment. Even plugging the LAN cable into the network interface card doesn't solve the problem because, according to the standard, the interface card's connection is isolated from the chassis power ground. Putting your hand on the computer's chassis and touching a coaxial Ethernet T-connector can result in a dangerous shock if the AC wiring has a problem. Similarly, dangerous voltages on RS-232 or parallel printer cables can occur if the pieces of equipment on either end are plugged into power circuits with different ground connections.

Because electricity doesn't travel over glass, we strongly recommend using fiber-optic cables to link buildings as well as wiring closets on different floors, particularly if different power transformers feed the buildings or floors. Also, fiber-optic cables don't carry lightning strikes between buildings, which commonly cause damage on campuswide networks.

Grounding Problems

Engineers designing digital systems need what is called a *signal reference ground* to establish the reference point for the 3- or 5-volt data signals inside the computer and to drain off leaked AC power. This signal reference ground must be close to the digital circuits, so engineers design a *ground plane*, typically a large area of conductive material, into circuit boards and use the computer equipment cabinet as a common point of connection for the circuit board ground planes to establish the signal reference ground.

In an ideal world, the signal reference ground would be completely isolated from the electrical ground. In the massive computer rooms installed in the 1960s, the signal ground system was an elaborate web of conductors under an elevated floor supporting the equipment. An isolated signal ground keeps AC power leakage and voltage spikes off the electrical ground. But in the real world of engineering, computer design, and compromise, the chassis of an electronic computing device serves as both the signal reference ground and the AC power line ground. It isn't practical to design modern PCs and other devices with a signal reference ground that is insulated from the power ground.

This link between the signal reference ground and the power ground means that problems with the power ground can interfere with the data system. Power grounding problems fall into two categories: an open or high resistance ground, or an abnormal pulse or condition between power conductors. But signal grounding problems are more complex.

Open or highly resistive power grounds occur primarily because of poor installation, vibrations that loosen connectors, or corrosion. These are simple, but potentially dangerous, problems that can be detected by a relatively low-cost AC circuit tester, such as the one shown in Figure 7.4, which measures the voltage difference between the neutral wire and the ground wire at an electrical socket. Typically, a set of lights on these devices indicates proper connections. A tester like this is a good investment in safety for anyone with wiring and cabling responsibilities.

Search and destroy

The world's best power wiring system is no good at all if someone plugs a sub-standard—or even worse, an ungrounded— extension cord or outlet strip into the system. Be on the look-out for extension cords and outlet strips that have had the ground pin removed. When you find one, toss it before it causes damage or hurts someone. When testing a suspect outlet that has a power strip connected to it, test each outlet in the power strip, too. We've seen new 6-outlet strips with bad ground connections on one or more outlets.

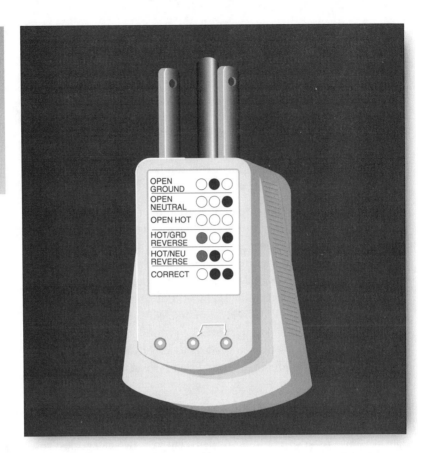

Temporary insanity

Power tools, especially circular saws, produce some of the nastiest electrical interference imaginable. If you're having construction or remodeling work done in your building, provide a separate power feed for the construction crew to use.

But these testers do not uncover signal ground problems. Electrical contractors typically don't care about the length of the neutral and ground wires feeding each power outlet, but these long wires act as an antenna for electrical noise that interferes with higher frequency data signals. The safety provided by the AC ground wire connected to the chassis is a critically important factor, and it can lead to problems with more sensitive data signals.

Generally, the best advice we can provide is to work closely with your electrical contractor and the power company to get the best and shortest electrical ground you can afford, as illustrated in Figure 7.5. In a small network installation, you can investigate the costs of getting a single power transformer dedicated to your office. If you have your own transformer, you can control the attachment of other devices, such as large motors or high-current electrical heaters that can generate electrical noises.

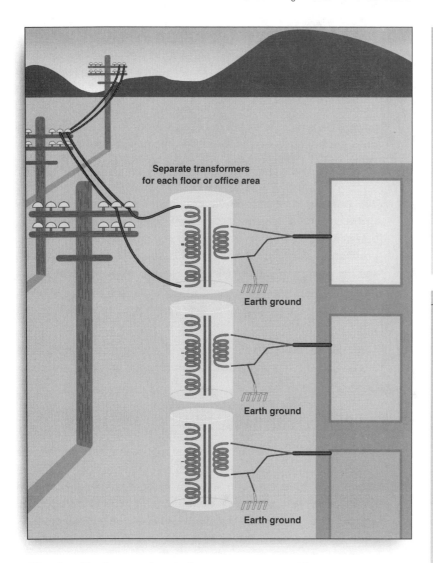

Separate transformers
for each floor or office area

Earth ground

Earth ground

Earth ground

FIGURE 7.5
If you have your own power transformer, you can control the devices connected to your leg of the power circuit. Installing individual power distribution panels for every cluster of computers increases the up-front cost of power wiring, but it reduces the length of the ground wires and can limit several kinds of disruptive electrical noise.

You should ask your electrical contractor to provide separate power distribution panels, normally known as *breaker boxes*, for each office area. The neutral wires and the ground wires from each outlet come together in the breaker box, so you have a better chance of shortening the effective length of the signal ground if each office or group of offices has its own breaker box.

Things aren't always what they seem

It's not uncommon—especially in older buildings—to encounter three-prong outlets that appear to be properly grounded. But all too often, the third (ground) pin isn't connected to anything. This happens when someone remodels a home or office and replaces old-style two-prong outlets with the more modern three-prong outlets. Because the older outlets didn't have a ground connection, there is no ground wire to connect to the third prong on the outlet. The only solution to this problem is to have a qualified electrician run new cable from the circuit breaker panel to the outlet. This is one of many problems that you can easily locate with an inexpensive outlet tester.

Normal Mode and Common Mode Power Problems

Open or highly resistive ground connections can cause serious safety problems and difficult data problems, but other conditions on the power line can cause additional categories of mischief. These conditions can be shorts between wires on the power line or power fluctuations called surges, spikes, or sags that appear between the power conductors.

The power cable has three wires, and power problems can be classified according to which wires they affect. If a condition exists between the hot and neutral conductors, it is called a *normal mode* problem. If a condition involves either the hot or neutral conductors and the ground, it is referred to as a *common mode* problem.

Normal mode problems are usually intercepted by a computer's power supply, an uninterruptable power supply, or an AC power-line filter. Because common mode problems can go directly to the computer chassis without an intervening filter, they can do more insidious damage to data signals than normal mode problems and they are harder to detect.

Spikes, Surges, and Sags

The most typical problems coming across power lines are the voltage surges, sags, and spikes. Each type of power surge or loss has its own name based on its characteristics: the amount of voltage it imposes on the power lines and its duration. Most of these events appear as normal mode problems—they enter between the hot and neutral lines. But incorrectly connected wiring or the physical failure of connectors or equipment can cause them to appear as common mode problems—usually with more disastrous results.

A *spike* or impulse refers to an overvoltage, superimposed on the desired line voltage waveform, lasting between 0.5 and 100 microseconds and possessing an amplitude over 100 percent of peak line voltage. In simpler terms, this means your power line has been struck with a short-duration but powerful hit of at least 240 volts.

You have a *surge* on the power line when the voltage reaches above 110 percent of the nominal value. A surge typically lasts only seconds, but this type of disturbance accounts for nearly all hardware damage experienced by users of small computers. Most computer power supplies running at 120 volts cannot handle 260 volts for any length of time.

Other possible power disturbances include sags and oscillations. A *sag*, or brownout, occurs when the power-line voltage falls below 80 percent of the nominal value and lasts several seconds. An *oscillation*, also referred to as harmonics or noise, is a secondary signal on top of the 60-Hz waveform with a magnitude ranging from 15 to 100 percent of the nominal line voltage. Complex building wiring systems, particularly those that load many different legs onto power transformers, and unwanted interconnections between the neutral and ground wires, are common causes of oscillation.

Oscillation is best cured by rewiring to get the cleanest and most direct power and ground connections you can afford. Sags and complete power outages are handled by uninterruptable power supply systems. Spikes and surges are caught by surge suppressors.

Surge Suppressors

The typical surge suppressors that mount on a wall power socket or are built into protected outlet strips have circuitry designed to protect the connected computer system from spikes and surges. The most common method used is a *metal oxide varistor* (MOV). This device protects the equipment by diverting excess voltages to a ground. However, recent research at the National Institute of Standards and Technology indicates that the commonly used divert-to-ground scheme can still result in damage to data and equipment. Because it's the common reference point for data going into and out of the computer, dumping spikes and surges into the power-line ground close to the computer can create problems. Although the diversion to the power-line ground can avoid damage to the power supply, it can still garble the data.

Surge suppressors that dump large quantities of voltage onto the common ground can create a large voltage differential between the nodes on the network, which can result in data loss or fried input circuits on the computers and printers exposed to the redirected surge. Another limitation stems from the MOV's limited in-service lifetime, which depends on heat, usage, and other factors.

We suggest that you work with your electrical contractor to install commercial-quality surge protection at each power distribution panel, as shown in Figure 7.6, instead of buying consumer-grade individual surge protectors for each networked device. Placing the surge protector at the office power panel doesn't reduce its effectiveness, but it does reduce the impact of voltage surges and spikes that are routed to the ground circuit.

FIGURE 7.6
When you install separate power distribution panels for each office or cluster of computers, you should also install surge protection devices at the power panels.

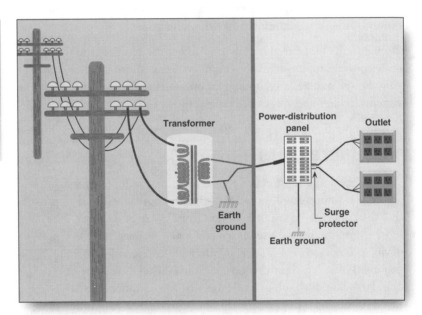

Uninterruptible Power Supplies

Low-voltage conditions (sags) and voltage interruptions are cured by uninterruptible power supplies. In their marketing literature, the UPS companies bury you in brownouts, whip you with waveforms, and petrify you with power factors. Many people who need an uninterruptible power supply are frightened off by the conflicting buzz of technical phrases, claims, and concepts that UPS vendors wrap around their products. No other part of the computer market seems to threaten you with such total disaster if you don't select the right product. Fortunately, the truth is much simpler.

Local area networks need the support of uninterruptible power supplies; every network file server absolutely requires power backup. If you use powered wiring hubs, you must also provide backup power for the wiring hubs. Extended networks with bridges and routers need power backup to avoid systemic failures. Smart network administrators also know they must supply backup power for LAN client stations, because it does users little good to have an operational server and wiring system if their computers go down before they can save their spreadsheets and word processing files onto the file server.

Today's desktop computers have robust and durable power supplies able to survive an amazing gauntlet of brownouts and interruptions. The electricity provided by your power company is a pure sine wave, alternating at 60 cycles per second. The power produced by UPS supplies isn't as pure because it's difficult to create a pure AC sine wave from the DC power provided by the UPS batteries. Many UPS companies expend a lot of effort convincing you that pure sine wave power works better for computer power supplies than other waveforms. Some devices with older-technology power supplies or motors running directly from the AC line do run better on sine waves, but modern desktop computers thrive on square waves, trapezoidal waves, or any other kind of alternating current waves you feed them. However, if you plan to back up printers with a UPS, the circuitry in many printers clearly prefers pure sine waves to their more jagged cousins.

Frankly, while most of the claims and specifications broadcast by UPS vendors are important to purists, they shouldn't concern someone who wants backup power for network devices. Buyers need to know two things: First, will the UPS provide power to the network devices through most outages? And, second, will the UPS tell the servers it's about to run out of juice and initiate an orderly shutdown of the system?

Two separate studies conducted by IBM and Bell Laboratories investigated the type and nature of power disturbances. The studies revealed that more than half of all power disturbances last less than six seconds; they also found that power disturbances occur on the average of twice a week for most commercial sites.

Power outages fall into two categories: a few minutes and a few hours. Outages lasting a few minutes take place when something—a lightning strike, an unfortunate squirrel, or a wayward Mylar balloon—creates a power-line overload that trips a circuit breaker. Because these circuit breakers possess automatic reset capabilities, they can work from the surrounding power grid into the source of the short to reestablish power within seconds or minutes.

Outages of several hours' duration take place when something—a car crashing into a power pole, a fire, or high winds—physically disrupts the power transmission system. This kind of outage typically lasts for hours or even days until repair crews can restore service.

If you require absolutely uninterrupted power, even during outages of several hours, then you need a generator to supplement your UPS, rather than an extremely large UPS. But if you just want to survive the typical short-duration interruption and have time to gracefully shut down the system when short outages become long outages, then you only need a few minutes of UPS power. Almost all the UPS units on the market support a heavily equipped server for more than ten minutes.

The typical UPS consists of a set of batteries, a battery charger, and a power inverter. The inverter does the job of converting the relatively low, direct-current voltage of the batteries into the typical 117 volts of alternating current normally supplied by the power line. It's difficult to produce pure sine-wave power from an inverter, because an inverter creates alternating current by switching the direct current from the batteries on and off quickly, resulting in a square, not sine, waveform. Changing these square pulses into pure sine waves takes a lot of circuitry. The battery charger keeps the batteries in peak condition during normal operation from the power line.

Simply stated, big batteries let UPS systems provide more power for a longer period of time. The amount of output power and the output duration increase or decrease in an inverse ratio. All modern UPS products use sealed, maintenance-free batteries. Like ordinary automobile batteries, the batteries are all based on some form of lead-acid technology, often incorporating a jelled electrolyte for added safety so that the active chemical agent doesn't spill or vent hazardous fumes.

UPS products differ primarily in the power storage capacity of the batteries, the power delivery capability of the inverter, the waveform output of the inverter, and whether the inverter operates all the time or only when the input voltage reaches a specific low or high level. Full-time systems require robust components and designs, and therefore cost more money. Minor differences between products include the indicators they provide to signal the status of battery life and power load, and the aural and visual alarms they use to alert you to problems.

Not all UPS products work identically. Most of the low-cost products act as standby power systems (SPSs). They monitor the power line and, if a problem occurs, switch in the inverter, powered by their batteries. The time needed to switch from power line to battery-supplied power, called the *transfer time*, can be just a few milliseconds. Meanwhile, the power supplies in modern desktop computers can coast for at least a hundred millisecondswithout causing a system failure.

The online UPS design, typically more expensive, constantly supplies power from the inverter while the batteries continue charging from the AC power line. No spikes or noise pulses from the power line reach the supported PC, because the inverter supplies freshly generated alternating current. When the AC line faults, the battery smoothly supplies power to the inverter. The protected device never experiences a millisecond of outage, and the transfer time is nil.

Some products appear to be online systems because they can adjust to low voltages without switching to battery backup, but, like SPSs, they don't run their inverters all the time. These devices use a ferroresonant transformer design that regenerates the sine wave for a more stable voltage and an output free of distortions. Products with ferroresonant designs offer excellent line-filtering capability with virtually no switching time. These systems fall into a hybrid UPS category.

This is only a test

Even if you've carefully selected and installed a UPS system for your critical machines, there's no guarantee that the system will actually work when you need it to. Like any electronic device, UPS systems are subject to failure. It's a good idea to test your UPS system on a regular schedule to make sure it will deliver power when you need it. Do your testing after hours or on a weekend so that you won't create a disaster if the UPS doesn't work as planned. Make sure you run the UPS for at least 50 percent of its rated runtime.

The UPS supporting a network server must communicate with the server and warn it to close files and shut down when its battery power nears its end. Most UPS-to-LAN interface programs also report when the server starts to run on battery power and notify any network client stations fortunate enough to be up and running after the outage.

Apart from the necessary power cord connection, the method of connecting the UPS to the server varies. Most vendors supply you with an appropriate interconnecting cable and software on request so that you can monitor the UPS. However, you must carefully decide what kind of cable and software you need for your hardware and operating system combinations.

Underwriters Laboratory (UL) has a safety standard covering uninterruptible power supply equipment. In Canada, the Canadian Standards Association (CSA) performs the same function. UL standard 1778 describes exactly what a UPS is and does. UL testing stresses the safety of products, and only products that pass specific UL testing procedures can carry the UL seal. Many state and federal agencies and private corporations require products they buy to carry UL approval. We believe that UL or CSA approval should be an important consideration when you buy a UPS.

UPS protection, combined with the other power and grounding recommendations illustrated in Figure 7.7, will keep your network safe and reliable. Power wiring is just as critical to good network performance as the network cable—in the end, both safety and the performance of the computer system are at stake.

You should buy UPS protection for every network server, wiring hub, and bridge or router on the network. Because you don't need to buy excessively large and expensive products, you can afford to back up many networked desktop computers, too. Relying on a few criteria such as UL approval, the right network interface, and appropriate sizing, you can confidently ignore the technobabble and choose from among many fine products on the market.

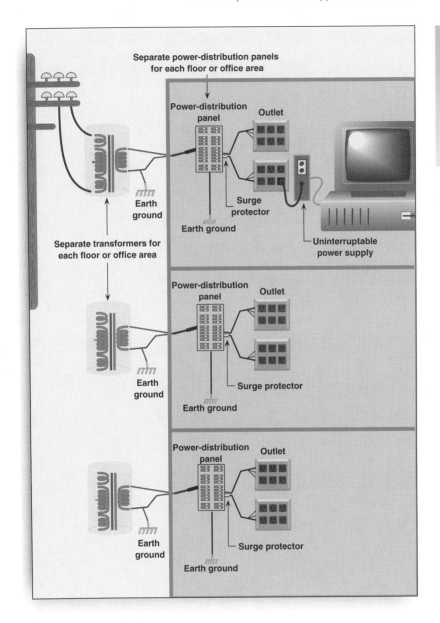

Separate power-distribution panels
for each floor or office area

Power-distribution
panel

Outlet

Earth
ground

Separate transformers for
each floor or office area

Surge
protector

Earth ground

Uninterruptable
power supply

Power-distribution
panel

Outlet

Earth
ground

Surge protector

Earth ground

Power-distribution
panel

Outlet

Earth
ground

Surge protector

Earth ground

FIGURE 7.7
Using dedicated power
transformers, separate
power-distribution pan-
els, surge protection,
and uninterruptable
power supplies in a dis-
tributed network.

163

chapter

8

From the Wall to the Desktop

Cable Crimps •

The Weak Link •

Information Outlets •

The Station Cable •

Cable Connectors •

Cable Crimps

"We went a full year without a single major problem. Now, within the last 30 days, we've got a rash of what seem to be cabling problems, but they're intermittent. I'm stumped, Willy."

"Okay, Margaret, let's see what we can find." Willy intended to plug a cable analyzer into the wall jack to measure the noise and crosstalk on the cable segment between the wall and the wiring closet. But when he disconnected the station cable running from the desktop to the wall jack, something didn't feel right. "This RJ-45 jack is kinda sloppy. OK Cable didn't make up your station cables, did we?"

"No, our maintenance staff made those cables after you were done with the installation job," Margaret replied.

"Hmmmm. Let's talk to them," suggested Willy.

Willy and Margaret met with the maintenance supervisor and asked to see his supply of RJ-45 connectors and crimping tool. "Do you recollect what you paid for this crimping tool?" Willy asked.

"Yeah," the supervisor replied, "$40—it was the best deal I could find." Willy sighed. "I think it was the worst deal you ever made. Good crimping tools cost well over $100. This tool doesn't let you position the plug properly, and you'd need a grip of iron to exert enough force to get good compression on the connector. Look here, these jaws bend out of alignment when you squeeze the handle." Willy didn't want to sound critical, but settling for cheap tools was one of his pet peeves. Then he examined the supply of RJ-45 plugs in the box with the crimping tool.

"Oh-oh," he said. "These connectors are for solid wire, but you've got stranded wire in your station cables. See here, these connectors only have two prongs per wire, and these prongs are supposed to trap and hold the solid wire. After a while, the stranded wire squishes away from the prongs. It happens whether you touch the station cable or not, but it happens faster when the cable gets yanked and moved during cleaning and other daily activities. Connectors for stranded wire have a single, wide serrated conductor that grabs and traps the wire strands, but they won't work on solid wire."

"So the connectors we have on every cable going to every PC are little time bombs waiting to go off," Margaret said. "Willy, can I get OK Cable to replace them all?"

Willy was already flipping open his case and reaching for the industrial-grade crimping tool that would be more than adequate for the job.

The Weak Link

Like a chain, a network cabling system is only as strong as its weakest link. The weakest link in a cabling system is often the station cable, which runs from the wall to the desktop. A first-class cabling installation deserves high-quality connectors. Otherwise, that excellent system will perform as badly as a third-class system—or worse.

In a structured cabling system, the link between the wiring closet and the network node is typically unshielded twisted-pair wire, although it can also be fiber-optic cable. This configuration, and the physically similar IBM Wiring Plan, lend themselves to using information outlets, connectors, and separate cables between the wall plates and the network nodes. Even if you use a thin ethernet system with coaxial cable running from node to node, a wall plate adds reliability and security, but an information outlet and the associated cable connectors can also be a source of electrical noise, high resistance, and crosstalk. Exercise care to ensure that you retain the quality of your installation.

The three pieces of the final link that are most frequent sources of serious problems are the connector on the information outlet, the connectors on the station cable, and the station cable itself. Because people move and change their desks and equipment, that cable and those connectors are subject to more wear and tear than any other portion of the network. This abuse makes them quite prone to failure. In addition, the connection between copper wires and a metal connector must comply with strict installation steps; if it doesn't, the weakest link will be doubly fragile. This chapter addresses the three pieces of the final link in the network, and suggests strategies for avoiding trouble.

Information Outlets

You'll typically use wall plates as the point of connection between the horizontal wiring and the station cable extending to the node. But wall plates are just one alternative among various "information outlets." These products include so-called "monument" outlets that stick up from the floor, outlets buried in the floor, and even outlets that pop up out of desktops.

Information outlets are a two-edged sword. On the one hand, you need them because they protect the horizontal wiring from the physical handling that cables receive when employees clean around desks and move computer equipment. They also keep the installation neat and eliminate the unsightly snake pit of unused cables coiled on the floor. However, information outlets introduce two additional connectors (one on the outlet and one on the mating station cable) to a cable that would otherwise run unbroken from the wiring closet to the node or from node to node, and every connector is a potential source of network problems. You need information outlets, but they *must* be carefully installed.

The latest buzzword in information outlets is "modular." Several companies, including Amp and Molex Premise Networks, sell outlets that can hold a variety of connectors ranging from the common RJ-45 phone and LAN connectors to more exotic token-ring and fiber-optic attachments. You can also find modules with coaxial BNC connectors (see "The BNC Coaxial Connector" later in this chapter for more details). These modular units snap in and out of the outlet frame, so you can configure and modify outlets to meet your organization's needs. When you use a modular connector, it doesn't matter if you use unshielded twisted-pair, shielded twisted-pair, or coaxial cable in your wiring scheme, and it doesn't matter if the cable is in a star configuration or a daisy-chain; there is an information outlet for you.

The connection at the back side of the information outlet (the side toward the wiring closet in a star-wired system) has an easy life because it typically isn't subject to movement or strain. Connecting unshielded twisted-pair wire to modular RJ-45 jacks is the simplest process—another plus for UTP. With a typical modular jack, the wires press into slots in the back of the jack, as shown in Figure 8.1.

A slotted plastic "keeper" snaps over the slots to hold the wires firmly in place. Metal fingers in the slots pierce the insulation of the wires to make the electrical connec-tion. There is no wire stripping and very little untwisting required to make the connection.

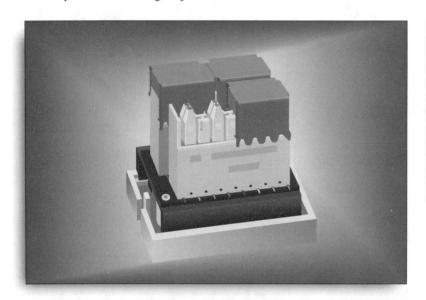

FIGURE 8.1
This Molex Premise Networks system makes it easy to attach unshielded twisted-pair cable to two RJ-45 jacks. The ends of the module are color-coded to indicate which wire pair matches each pair of connections.

Information outlet connections on the back side of shielded twisted-pair and coaxial cable modular connectors are practically identical to the connections for the station cable.

Keep it twisted

Whenever you use UTP or STP, keep the wire twisted just as much as it was originally. Untwist the smallest amount possible when making a connection. The twisting shields against crosstalk, so don't sacrifice even an inch of that protection!

The Station Cable

The *station cable*, sometimes confusingly called the patch cable (a term that should be reserved for patch cables used in wiring closets), runs between the information outlet and the network node, that is, between the wall and the desktop. Station cables, with the exception of thin Ethernet, use stranded wire to improve the flexibility of the cable and its resistance to breaks caused by metal fatigue.

While you might think of the station cable as a simple piece of wire, some configurations make it an active part of the network. For example, many companies sell cables specially configured with "media filters" that allow you to connect a token-ring network interface card designed for shielded twisted-pair cable to unshielded twisted-pair horizontal wiring. Figure 8.2 shows a cable equipped with a media filter. You can also buy cables equipped with devices called *baluns* that allow you to connect thin ethernet (10Base2) network interface cards designed for coaxial cable to a UTP system. These specialized station cables let you use the network interface cards you already own even when you install a new structured wiring system.

FIGURE 8.2
A station cable equipped with a media filter connects a network interface card and an unshielded twisted-pair horizontal wiring system. With this type of cable, you can continue to use your old interface cards even with a new wiring system.

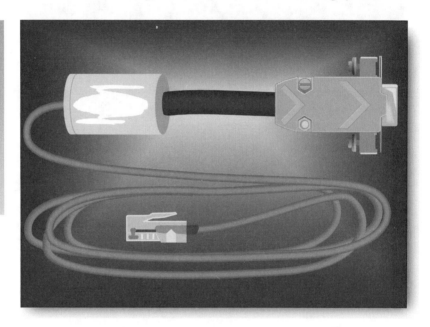

The connectors on the station cable are often a point of failure in network systems, so they deserve special attention.

Cable Connectors

We'll focus on three types of cable connectors in this chapter: RJ-45, BNC, and token-ring data connectors. RJ-45 connectors are used in ethernet, token-ring, and ARCnet installations. BNC connectors are small coaxial cable connectors used in thin ethernet and ARCnet installations. However, ethernet and ARCnet cables each have a different outside diameter; the connectors and tools are also slightly different. Token-ring data connectors, despite their imposing appearance, are actually the easiest to install properly.

The RJ-45 Connector

The 8-wire RJ-45 connector is the joy of UTP cabling systems. The positive click of an RJ-45 practically guarantees a good connection between the plug and the socket. This connector is small, inexpensive, and, if you have the right tools, easy to install.

When is an RJ-45 connector not an RJ-45 connector? When it's a WEW8. Actually, a WEW8 and an RJ-45 are the same thing. Similarly, the smaller six-wire RJ-11 commonly used in telephone systems connector is a WEW6, but the naming schemes originated with different companies. The WE designations were part of the old Western Electric nomenclature, but they are still used in the industry.

Telephone wiring installers use the term *polarization* to describe the physical form and configuration of the connectors, and you'll often hear the phrase "polarization and sequence." Sequence refers to the order of the wire pairs in the connectors, so taken together, these terms describe the connectors and how they attach to the cable.

Both RJ-45 and BNC connectors depend on force, typically applied by a crimping tool, to make a secure mechanical connection. An RJ-45 crimping tool, shown in Figure 8.3, is often called a plug presser because of its pressing action. When you connect the plug to the cable, you place a plastic connector in a die in the jaw of the crimping tool, carefully dress and insert the wires into the open connector, and then close the handles of the crimping tool to force the connector together.

Because of the force required, the crimping tool must have a sturdy frame and broad handles. A good crimping tool will more than pay for itself, while a cheap one will only lead to headaches—and lots of them. Companies like Amp, General Machine Products, and Molex Premise Networks make excellent tools. The Molex Premise Networks Modular Crimping Tool has a handy set of wire cutters in the handle that make the whole job fast and easy.

Which Wire Is Which?

Examine a piece of UTP cable, and you'll notice that each strand of wire inside the cable has a unique color code. The color coding makes it easier for the installer to identify each wire or pair of wires

For posterity's sake…

The common use of the terms RJ-45 and RJ-11 is not strictly correct. The device we call an RJ-45 is technically an eight-position plug or jack, and the RJ-11 is a six-position plug or jack. The letters "RJ" stand for registered jack and are supposed to connote a specific wiring sequence. We would prefer not to perpetuate this incorrect usage, but if you ask a supplier or installer for an eight-position jack, you'll probably get a blank stare, while everyone understands RJ-45.

in the cable. While the colors used in UTP cabling are fairly well standardized, the way the pairs of wires are connected is not.

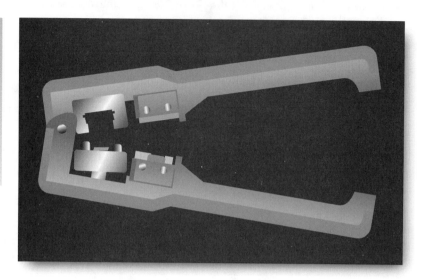

FIGURE 8.3
A good crimping tool is invaluable when you make RJ-45 connections. This Molex Premise Networks Modular Crimping Tool has a sturdy frame, broad handles, a wire stripper, and strong jaws.

If you are involved in cabling, at some time you will hear the terms *tip* and *ring*. These terms harken back to the earliest days of the telephone industry and refer to each of the two wires that connect to the end of a switchboard telephone plug (the tip) or to the back portion of the plug's connecting surface (the ring). Using the terms tip and ring is like saying the plus wire and the minus wire. Although modern telecommunications connectors don't resemble switchboard plugs in any way, we still use the terms tip and ring to designate the polarity of each wire in a cable pair. Similarly, each pair of wires has a name—a sort of shorthand that makes it easy to identify each pair of wires in the cable. The wires in the first pair in a cable or a connector are designated as T1 and R1, the second pair is T2 and R2, and so on.

In UTP horizontal wiring, there is general agreement on how to color-code the wires in a cable. In a four-pair cable, the tip conductors (T1 through T4) in each pair are white with a stripe of a secondary color that designates the pair. The ring conductors (R1 through R4) have jackets of the secondary color with a white stripe.

The secondary colors used in a 4-pair cable are blue, orange, green, and brown. The color slate is also assigned as a secondary color in cables with more wire pairs. So in UTP connections, wire T1 is white with a blue stripe, while its partner R1 is blue with a white stripe. Wire T2 is white with an orange stripe, and R2 is orange with a white stripe, and so on. Some cables, like those connecting the 50-pin telco connectors used in wiring closets, need more pairs, so red, black, yellow, and violet are assigned as other primary colors. Used together, the five primary and five secondary colors identify all pairs in a 25-pair cable.

If only the rest were so simple. It would seem that it should be easy to agree on which wire pairs connect to which pins on a plug. Unfortunately, there isn't one set of agreements but rather at least eight agreed-upon (by various companies and associations) sequences for mating UTP wires and connectors, five of which are widely used. Here is a short list and description of each.

- USOC. The Universal Service Order Code (USOC) is the oldest specification (see Figure 8.4). It is derived from original Bell System specifications, so it is widely used by telephone companies. Note that the USOC system arranges the pair sequences from the center out. Specifically notice that pins 1 and 2 are not a part of the same pair as they are in the other common configurations. The USOC wiring pattern doesn't conform to the 10Base-T network specifications, but then a USOC-wired installation probably doesn't meet the data service requirements for crosstalk or noise either. Caution: Don't use USOC for data.

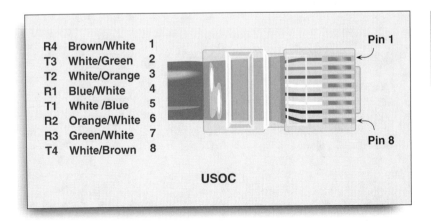

R4	Brown/White	1
T3	White/Green	2
T2	White/Orange	3
R1	Blue/White	4
T1	White /Blue	5
R2	Orange/White	6
R3	Green/White	7
T4	White/Brown	8

Pin 1

Pin 8

USOC

FIGURE 8.4
Universal Service Order Code (USOC).

- EIA Preferred Commercial Building Specification. Despite its imposing title, this isn't the sequence we prefer (see Figure 8.5). However, you won't go wrong using this sequence, as long as everyone who works on the cabling knows that your building is "EIA-standard."

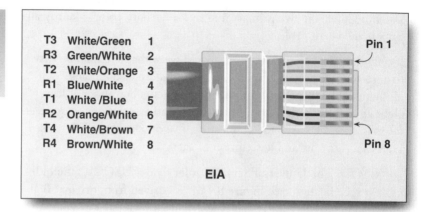

FIGURE 8.5
EIA Preferred Commercial Building Specification.

- AT&T 258A. This is the configuration we recommend and the one used by most installers (see Figure 8.6). Pairs T2/R2 and T3/R3 carry the data. You should never simultaneously use pairs T1/R1 or T4/R4 for voice; instead, use those pairs for spares or for future high-speed data requirements that might demand more than two pairs. In some installations, pins 7 and 8 are left open; this configuration is designated as AT&T 356A.

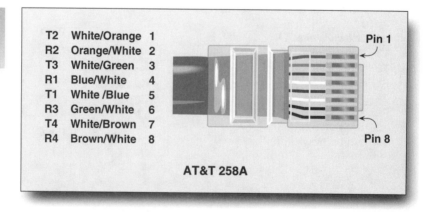

FIGURE 8.6
AT&T 258A.

- IEEE 10Base-T. The IEEE simply took the AT&T standard and stripped out the pairs normally used for voice (see Figure 8.7). We think you will find the R1/T1 pair useful as a spare.

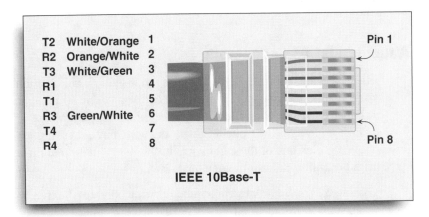

T2	White/Orange	1
R2	Orange/White	2
T3	White/Green	3
R1		4
T1		5
R3	Green/White	6
T4		7
R4		8

Pin 1 ... Pin 8

IEEE 10Base-T

- Rolm and Digital. Not only do Rolm and Digital Equipment Corporation have their own wiring sequences, but Digital also sometimes uses different plugs and jacks. Older Digital Equipment installations use a particularly obnoxious proprietary plug (the modified modular plug or MMJ) with a small, plastic, locking tab offset to the side instead of in the center.

The fundamental connection concepts for the Digital and Rolm systems are exactly the same as the other sequence schemes, and Digital's Open DECconnect is compatible with AT&T 258A and the 10Base-T specification, except that Digital leaves T4/R4 as a spare and keeps T1/R1 (pins 4 and 5) open.

While the wiring and color-coding scheme described here works for horizontal cables, patch cables have their own color-coding scheme. The wires inside the patch cables use solid colors in the following sequence:

T1 Green

R1 Red

T2 Black

R2 Yellow

T3 Blue

R3 Orange

T4 Brown

R4 White

Attaching RJ-45 Connectors

RJ-45 connectors are exceptionally easy to install. As we mentioned earlier, you'll need a good pair of wire cutters, a cable stripper, and a crimper tool. Many installers forego the cable stripper and use a pocket knife or cutting pliers to strip the wire, but either of these tools can nick one of the eight wires inside the cable, which can lead to cable failure months or even years later.

Although each brand of stripper and crimper operates differently, the basic steps to install an RJ-45 connector are the same:

1. Using a cable stripper, remove about 1" of the outer jacket from the cable (see Figures 8.8 and 8.9).

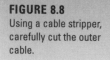

FIGURE 8.8
Using a cable stripper, carefully cut the outer cable.

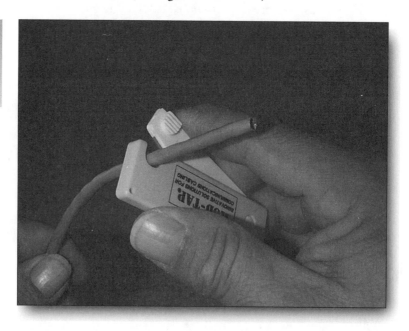

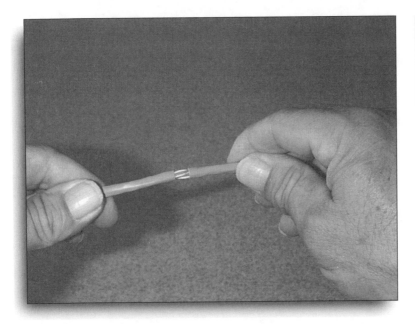

FIGURE 8.9
Once the jacket is cut, slide it away to expose the cable pairs inside.

2. Most UTP cable has a polyester fiber bundled in with the wires. This fiber keeps the cable from stretching and must be removed before you attach the connector. Clip the fiber off, and check each strand of wire to make sure that there are no nicks or cuts (see Figures 8.10 and 8.11).

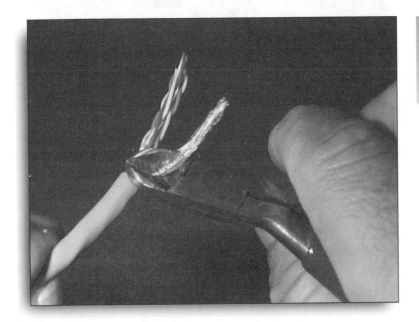

FIGURE 8.10
Remove the polyester fiber with a pair of wire cutters.

177

FIGURE 8.11
Inspect the wire pairs to
ensure that there are no
nicks or cuts in the
cable.

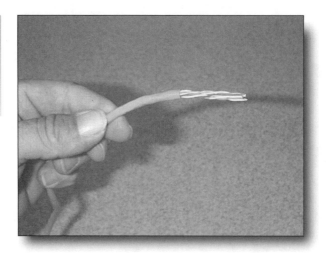

3. Separate the four twisted pairs of wires and then untwist each
   pair of wires, smoothing the wires out as you go (see Figures
   8.12 and 8.13).

FIGURE 8.12
Separate the four
twisted pairs.

FIGURE 8.13
Untwist each wire pair so that you have eight individual wires.

4. Arrange the wires in the correct order according to your chosen wiring plan. It helps to hold the arranged wires between the thumb and index finger of one hand while you arrange them with the other. Once you've arranged the wires, double-check that they are in the correct order (see Figure 8.14).

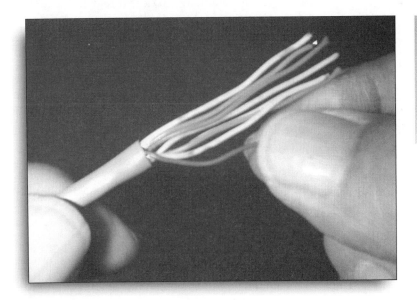

FIGURE 8.14
Arrange the wires in the order in which they will fit into the RJ-45 connector. See "Which Wire Is Which?" earlier in this chapter for help.

5. Using a sharp wire cutter, trim the wires so that they extend 5/8"
   from the end of the cable jacket. Be sure to keep the cutter blade
   perpendicular to the cable so that the trimmed wires are all the
   same length (see Figure 8.15).

FIGURE 8.15
Trim the wires so that
they extend 5/8" from
the end of the cable
jacket.

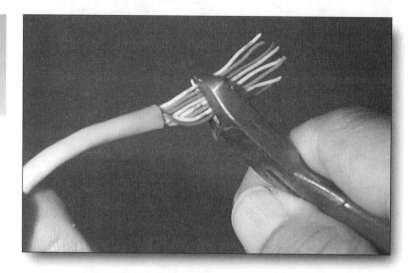

6. Place the connector over the wires, making sure that the wires
   remain in the correct order. Check that each wire extends as far
   as possible into the connector (see Figure 8.16).

FIGURE 8.16
Place the RJ-45 con-
necter over the wires so
that the wires stay in the
correct order.

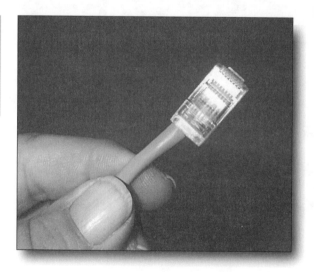

7. Carefully insert the connector into the crimping tool, being careful not to pull any of the wires back out of the connector. Squeeze the crimper firmly to attach the connector, then squeeze it again to make sure you have a good connection (see Figures 8.17 and 8.18).

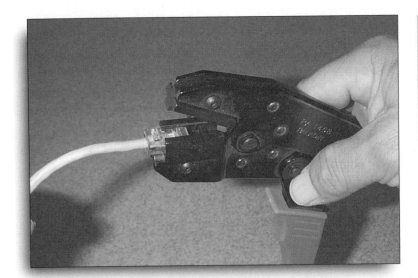

FIGURE 8.17
Insert the connector into the crimping tool and check to be sure that none of the wires have slipped out of the connector.

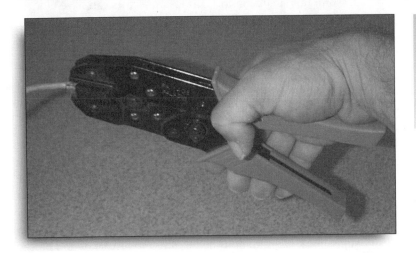

FIGURE 8.18
Squeeze the crimper firmly to attach the connector and then squeeze a second time for good measure.

Beware of role reversal

Some telephone systems use patch cables that reverse the sequence of the wires from end to end. Patch cables designed for data applications have the connectors on each end wired in the same sequence. Keep reversed patch cables away from your data patch panels. Better still, use distinctive colors for each type of patch cable.

If you're using RJ-45 connectors in your system, we suggest that you keep in mind the following considerations:

- Carefully count the number of RJ-45 connectors you think you'll need, and then add 50 percent more to the order. Your needs will grow faster than you can imagine.

- If you ever put the wires in the wrong order or suspect that one wire isn't properly seated in the RJ-45 connector, cut the connector off and start over. Don't try to open or reseal the connector because it will fail to work correctly in the long run.

- Different connectors are sold for stranded wire and for solid wire. Be sure to use the appropriate connectors in every case.

- Carefully match the tip and ring pairs. Improperly connecting the wires in a pair so that they are not part of the same circuit (a condition called *split pairs*) is the major source of twisted-pair wiring problems.

The BNC Coaxial Connector

BNC connectors make a neat-looking connection, and the male connectors lock on to the female connectors with a reassuring snap. Despite this small comfort, BNC connectors can have hidden, intermittent short circuits that frustrate attempts at troubleshooting because they disappear when you touch them.

You can buy several types of BNC connectors, but we strongly suggest avoid-ing the so-called "crimpless" connectors. Crimpless connectors use screw-on sections to hold the pieces together, and in our hard-won experience, they are not as reliable as a connector with a good crimp.

The previously proffered advice about buying a good quality tools is triple in importance with BNC connectors. The cable stripper should remove the outer jacket and braid without nicking or cutting into the center insulation. Most coaxial cable strippers allow you to adjust each blade's cutting depth independently, which allows you to adjust for small variations between different brands and batches of cable. The handle and jaws of the crimping tool should ratchet—You should be able to give it one squeeze to get it tight and then another good squeeze to really make the crimp. The jaws of the crimper should be wide enough to cover the entire crimped sleeve at one time. When you use a tool with a narrow jaw, you'll have to make several crimps on the sleeve, they won't be uniform, and the cable can eventually flow out from the crimps. Anything less than a tool with a wide and strong ratcheting jaw is simply unacceptable.

Figure 8.19 shows the correct dimensions of a piece of cable stripped and prepared for a BNC connector. Careful preparation of the cable is critical to making a connection that doesn't short between the tip and the ring of the connector and that doesn't have an open circuit between the ring of the connector and the copper braid of the cable.

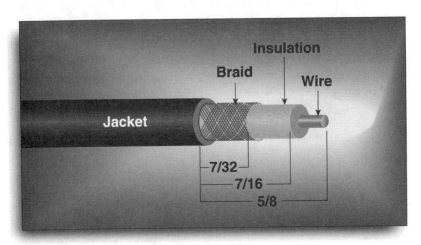

FIGURE 8.19
The two keys to making a good BNC connection are proper preparation of the cable and a good crimp. Many crimping tools have a life-size diagram on the stripped cable on the handle. Follow the dimensions carefully.

The assembly sequence for every connector is usually shown on the packaging for the connector. Don't forget to crimp the silver or gold tip before you insert it into the body of the connector.

Dress the braid carefully so it is completely under, but not over, the crimp-down collar. A good, professionally installed connector, shown in Figure 8.20, might have just a hint of braid showing at the shoulder of the crimp.

The Token-Ring Data Connector

What is ugly, expensive, and easy to use? A token-ring data connector. Although there are fancy tools available, you really only need a knife or wire stripper and a pair of pliers to install a token-ring data connector on the end of a shielded twisted-pair cable.

FIGURE 8.20
A good crimp on the sleeve of the BNC connector is critical to a good connection. The jaws of the crimping tool should span most of the sleeve, and copper braid should not be dressed back over the sleeve.

The process is easier to perform than to read about. See Figure 8.21 and follow these steps:

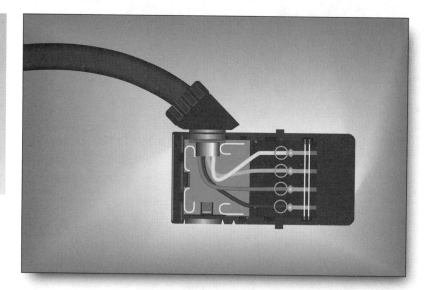

FIGURE 8.21
The token-ring connector literally snaps together. With the shielding removed, the wires fit into special barrel connectors, and a plastic keeper forces the wires into slots that cut the insulation and make the connection.

1. Strip 1 1/8 inches of the outer jacket off the cable.
2. Cut off 1 inch of the copper braid and the same amount of the foil surrounding each pair.
3. Fit the cable through the threaded sleeve of the connector.
4. Fold the braid against the connector's metal frame.
5. Slide each wire into its own connection-barrel connector.
6. Put the plastic retainer on top of the posts, and squeeze it down with the pliers. A special tool is available to do this, but we don't

think you'll need one. The post pierces the insulation and makes a positive electrical contact. The plastic post even shows you the correct wire sequence: red, green, orange, black. The red and green wires are the first pair, and the orange and black wires are the second pair.

7. Snap the cover on the open side of the plug.

Wall plates for data connectors follow the same process. It is important but not difficult to ensure that the braid makes solid contact with the metal interior of the plug. From the point of view of the installer, the data connectors are the best thing about the IBM cable plan.

Connectors are *so* important. Take the time and make the investment to install them properly.

chapter

9

Practical Home and Small Office Network Cabling

Home Sweet LAN   •

Networking Your Home   •

Ethernet: Still the Speed Champ   •

Alternatives to Ethernet   •

Home Sweet LAN

The employees of OK Cable had never seen Willy so angry. At least not since one of the ex-employees crimped an entire building's worth of solid Category 5 UTP cable with RJ-45 plugs meant for stranded cable. Something different had set Willy steaming this time. Whatever it was happened as he opened the mail. Employees tip-toed past his office door as he muttered, mumbled, searched his bookshelf, and started Internet searches that never finished.

After an hour of this, Willy called in his three lead installers from the field. It was late in the day when they gathered and he asked, "What do you guys know about power line networking and who have you told?" His question drew two blank stares, but it caused one face to flash wide-eyed panic. "Stewart," Willy asked the guilty face, "who did you talk to at Direct Data?"

"Uh, I met Sharon at the post office and we talked for a while. I think she asked me if I knew anything about using the power lines in a house for a network."

"Let me guess," Willy said. "You really didn't know what to tell her so you made it up as you went along in order to be able to talk to her for a while, right?"

"Uhhh, well..." Stew said.

"And somehow she got the idea that power line networking was a good idea? Willy asked. "Let me tell you how I know. This is an RFP we got from Direct Data. They want somebody to help their 200 work-at-home employees to set up home networks. This is a great idea. It could be a start on a whole new line of business for us. But the RFP gives preference to what it calls 'easily installed' alternatives such as wireless and power line networking. A nice note from Janet clipped to this copy of the RFP thanks me for the help my guys provided."

"Well, I set up one of those power line networking things for my sister and it worked." Stew replied.

Willy pushed back from his desk and started to pace. As he walked across the tile in front of his desk, he said, "Well, that's a big part of the problem. Often it does work, but often it has problems. Power line networking pushes radio waves over copper power wires. But the power wires are a radio nightmare. Any high-current motor, a sparking hair dryer, an elevator motor, or other electrical device can raise the noise level and reduce performance. But you never know where or when it will happen. Tech support would be a nightmare. I don't want a thing to do with this."

"Well, what can we do, Willy?" Stew asked.

"Research!" Willy replied without hesitation. "I'm going to work with you, and we are going to reply to the RFP with research. There's nothing better than good data-grade cable for any network, and we're going to prove it. "

Their work paid off two months later. It was a similar meeting with a happier group. "Well," Willy began, "we have a challenge in front of us. We have two weeks to figure out how to help the first group of Direct Data employees with their home networks. It's time for more research."

Networking Your Home

Home Networks—once a badge of honor for the truly nerdish—are now a mainstream item. Walk into any computer superstore and you'll likely find an aisle devoted to home networking kits. As the price of PCs has come crashing down, many users have discovered that it's often cheaper to buy a new PC than it is to upgrade an old one. When people buy new PCs, they often give the old one to the kids or keep it as a second PC. It doesn't take multi-PC home users long to figure out that they need a network. Just as in the office, home networks allow users to share files, printers, and—most importantly—an Internet connection among two or more PCs. A new generation of multi-player games—with each player on his or her own PC—has also increased the demand for home LANs.

Since home users are doing many of the same things with their LANs as their office counterparts, it seems logical that they'd use the same networking technologies—although on a smaller scale—as office LANs. But aesthetics are much more important in a home environment than in the office. Most companies won't hesitate to drill holes or install in-the-wall wiring when needed, but home users aren't as willing to pick up the drill and punch a hole in the wall or floor. It may be perfectly acceptable to have a tangle of wires under your office desk, but that high-tech look is out of place in your den.

If all of your PCs reside in the same room, you can easily install an ethernet LAN using many of the same techniques we've described for office LANs. But if you want to scatter your home PCs around the house, you'll need to consider several alternatives. We'll examine the ethernet options first, since they're the least expensive and offer the highest performance. If ethernet cabling isn't an option in your home, we'll also discuss ways to connect your PCs using phone lines, radio waves, and even the AC power wiring.

Ethernet: Still the Speed Champ

Do a quick survey of mail-order and computer superstore catalogs, and you'll find 10/100 ethernet starter kits for about $99. These kits—from well-known vendors like 3Com, Intel, D-Link, and Linksys—typically include two ethernet network interface cards (NICs), a small 4- or 5-port hub, and two 25-foot ethernet cables.

Ethernet offers the best performance (up to 100Mbps) at the lowest cost of any of the home networking alternatives. Other home networking technologies are limited to speeds of about 2Mbps. While 2Mbps is fast enough for casual file and printer sharing, it may not be fast enough if you have a high-speed Internet access device like a cable or DSL modem. Figure 9.1 shows an example of how an ethernet network might be used to share several computers, printers and a modem in your home.

As with office PCs, you'll need to open the case of the PC to install the NIC cards. Most of the ethernet vendors provide excellent installation instructions and self-installing driver software, but there's always a risk of messing something up when you install a new card in a PC—especially in today's resource-crowded multimedia PCs.

We prefer PCI network cards because they offer higher performance and easier installation than the older ISA cards. We also prefer 100Mbps Fast ethernet to the older, slower 10Mbps standard ethernet because it offers ten times the speed for only a nominal increase in cost.

PCI versus ISA/EISA

Virtually all new PCs come with one or more open expansion slots. There are two types of slots: ISA and PCI. PCI expansion cards typically offer higher performance and fewer installation hassles than the older ISA cards. When shopping for a home network kit, check your PC to see what type of expansion slots you have available before you buy your network kit. Both slots look the same from the outside of the PC, so you'll have to remove the cover and take a look inside. PCI slot sockets are smaller than ISA slots and are almost always white. ISA slots are larger and are usually brown or black.

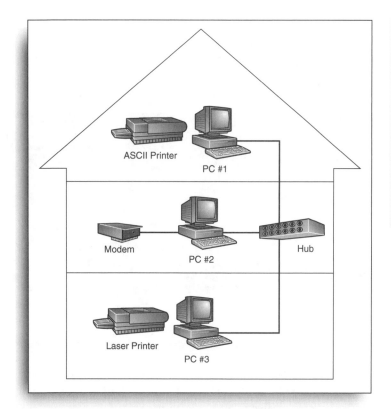

ASCII Printer

PC #1

Modem

PC #2

Hub

Laser Printer

PC #3

FIGURE 9.1
A typical home ethernet
LAN allows users to
share files, printers, and
an Internet connection
over the LAN. As you
can see from this dia-
gram, a home LAN is
much like a small office
ethernet LAN; it uses a
centrally located hub
and UTB cabling to con-
nect each PC to the hub.

Most of the hubs provided with home networking kits have four or
five ports, and are switchable between 10 and 100Mbps. It's important to note that when you use a switchable hub, all the devices on
the LAN must operate at the same speed. In most home environments, you'll simply set the hub to operate at 100Mbps and forget
about it. But if you ever need to connect a 10Mbps device (like an
older laptop with a 10Mbps ethernet card) to the LAN, you'll need
to slow the entire LAN down to 10Mbps. A few hubs offer 10/100
auto-switching operation, which allows each port to operate at either
speed, independently of the other ports. These hubs are often more
expensive than switchable hubs, but they provide more flexibility.

The most obvious shortcoming of ethernet home networking kits is
the cable itself. Most networking kits include two 25- to 30-foot
CAT 5 cables, with connectors already attached. If your PCs are in
the same room, you can usually hide the cable along the baseboard
or under the carpet. But some kits include bright yellow or blue

cable that sticks out like a sore thumb, so you'd be wise to check the color of the cable when shopping for a network kit.

Figure 9.2 shows a typical ethernet kit (also commonly called "a network in a box").

FIGURE 9.2
Many manufacturers offer ethernet kits specifically designed for home networking. This kit from D-Link includes two PCI network cards, two 25-foot cables, a 5-port 10/00 switching hub, and a copy of MidPoint Gateway Internet connection sharing software. Photo used by permission of D-Link.

If your computers aren't in the same room, you'll need to run ethernet cable from the hub location to each PC on your home LAN. Unless you live in a very small house, the 25-foot cables provided with most network kits probably won't be long enough. You can buy ready-made 50- and 100-foot ethernet cables with the connectors already attached, but they're usually expensive, and the pre-attached connectors make it difficult to pull the cable through tight spaces. Thanks to the popularity of home LANs, many residential electrical and alarm contractors are ethernet-savvy, so you may want to consider farming out the cable-pulling to a professional.

No matter how you run the cable, you'll want as neat an installation as possible. While it's tempting to simply pull a cable to each PC and attach a connector, you may want to consider using one of the modular wall outlet systems we mentioned in Chapter 8, "From the Wall to the Desktop." These outlet systems let you mix and match several ethernet, telephone, and cable TV connectors on a single wall plate. If you already have a TV or phone outlet, you can usually pull an ethernet cable to the same outlet and then use a modular connector plate to neatly connect your PC, phone, and TV.

Alternatives to Ethernet

While ethernet offers the best bang for the buck, there are circumstances where it's too difficult or even impossible to run ethernet cabling. Fortunately, there are three "no new wires" networking technologies that allow you to connect two or more PCs into a LAN without running an inch of wire.

True wireless systems use two-way radio signals—mounted on an ISA, PCI, or PC Card—to transmit data among the PCs on a LAN. These systems offer 2Mbps of throughput at a reasonable cost. 11Mbps wireless systems are also available, but they are much more expensive and are targeted at business users. See Chapter 12, "Wireless Communications," for more information on business wireless systems.

Phone line networking products like Intel's AnyPoint use your home's existing phone wiring to carry data at 1 or 10Mbps. These systems typically connect to your PC via the parallel port, so they have the added benefit of being simple to install. The downside is that they require a telephone outlet near the PC.

Power line networking systems are similar to phone line networking, but they use your home's existing AC power wiring to carry data that is modulated onto a weak radio signal carried over the wires. Most power line products also connect via the parallel port, but power line LANs run significantly slower than phone line LANs. Most homes have several power outlets in each room, so they're slightly more flexible than phone line systems. Unfortunately, our experience with power line systems has been erratic at best.

Wireless LANs

Wireless systems offer the best flexibility of the three ethernet alternatives for home networking. Unfortunately, they're also the most expensive of the three, weighing in at about $200 to $400 per PC. Wireless networks are most appropriate for notebook PCs, because they allow you to stay connected to the network while you move your notebook around the house. Some wireless systems also are well-suited for medium-speed Internet sharing and multi-player game duty in multi-story homes, apartment buildings and college dorms (see Figure 9.3).

193

FIGURE 9.3

FIGURE 9.3
Wireless networks provide excellent flexibility and mobility. There's no cable required, and you don't need to have a phone line or power outlet near each computer as you do with phone line and power line networks. Wireless LANs are especially useful with notebook PCs, since they allow you to move the notebook around the house while remaining connected to the LAN.

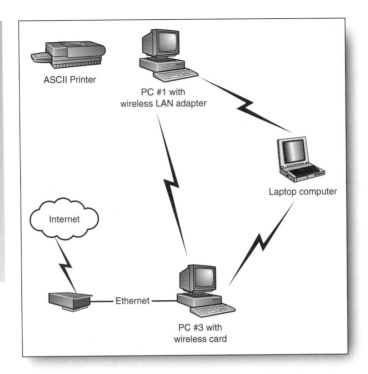

A typical wireless network consists of one or more desktop PCs with a wireless network card installed, and one or more notebook PCs with a wireless PC Card. Desktop wireless cards come in ISA and PCI formats, so you'll need to purchase the appropriate type for your PC. Most desktop wireless cards include an external antenna with 6 to 8 feet of cable. Although it's tempting to hide the antenna in that tangle of wires behind your PC, you'll experience better range and more reliable connections if you position the antenna clear of other objects and as high up as possible.

Notebook wireless cards usually have a built-in antenna contained in a small plastic cover that is permanently attached to the end of the PC Card (see Figure 9.4). The antenna sticks out of the PC Card socket by an inch or so. Software installation for both the desktop and PC Cards is similar to conventional ethernet cards.

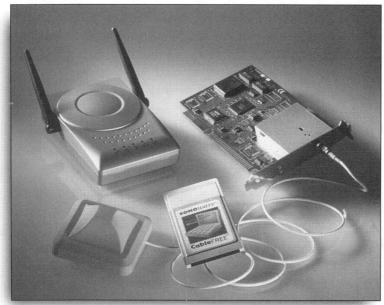

FIGURE 9.4
NDC's SOHOWare wireless networking kit is one of several wireless LAN kits designed specifically for the home market. This picture shows a SOHOWare internal ISA card, and a PC Card for notebook computers. The silver box with the two antennas is an ethernet bridge that allows you to add wireless connectivity to an existing ethernet LAN. Photo used by permission of NDC.

Be sure to use the same type of wireless gear

There is an IEEE standard (IEEE 802.11) for wireless networking systems, but you can't always mix 802.11-compatible products from different vendors in the same LAN. If you want to bring your 802.11-equipped laptop home from the office and use it on a wireless LAN at home, you'll probably want to purchase the same brand of wireless gear for your home as you use at the office. Also, you should know that there are two different "802.11" specifications. Older 802.11 products operate at 2Mbps; newer 802.11HR (high rate) products operate at 11Mbps but can also operate at 2Mbps to maintain compatibility with older 802.11 products.

Range is always an issue with wireless systems. Most vendors claim an effective indoor range of 150 feet between units, but we've found that figure to be wildly optimistic. Radio waves don't carry well through metal-reinforced walls and floors. The radio signals used by these systems are extremely low in power, so it doesn't take much of an obstacle to completely block the signal. Fortunately, moving one of the antennas an inch or two usually cures any signal blockage problems. Most wireless vendors provide a signal-level checking program that lets you see the strength of the radio signal; this is especially useful on portable PCs.

Virtually all wireless LAN systems offer security features to keep unauthorized users from connecting to your wireless LAN. In most cases, one PC is designated as the security master, and other PCs can't connect to the LAN until the security master verifies their identity. Given the short range of most wireless LANs, it's highly unlikely that anyone will try to access your LAN, but security can be a problem in multi-unit homes and apartment buildings. We recommend that you use whatever security features your wireless LAN offers.

Phone Line Networks

Second on our list of ethernet alternatives, phone line networks offer adequate performance at a much lower cost than wireless systems. Phone line adapters cost about $75 to $100 per PC, but there's no hub or wiring costs as with ethernet products. The current standard for phone line networking provides 1Mbps of throughput, but a faster version is on the drawing boards. Figure 9.5 shows a typical phone line network.

FIGURE 9.5
Phone line networks operate much like ethernet LANS, but they use your existing home phone wiring to carry data from one PC to another. They provide the same services—file, printer, and Internet sharing—as conventional ethernet LANs but are much easier to install. The original phone line LAN products operated at 1Mbps, but newer HomePNA 2.0-compatible products operate at 10Mbps. Note that the dotted line in this illustration represents the existing house phone wiring.

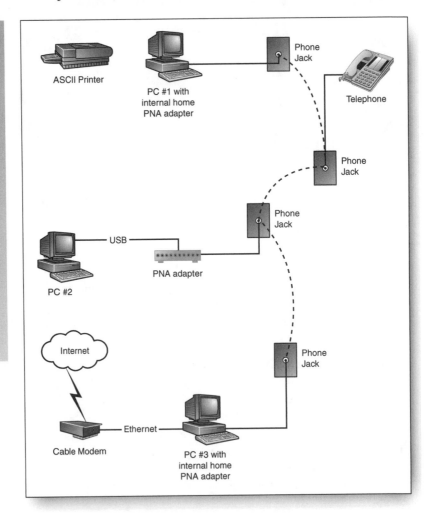

While phone line LANs use your existing phone wiring, they do not interfere with normal operation of the phone. The LAN and telephone signals travel over the same copper pair, but they are electrically distinct and completely invisible to each other.

Phone line LAN adapters come in internal (ISA and PCI) and external (parallel) versions. The parallel units don't require you to open your PC, and most provide a printer pass-through port that allows your PC's parallel port to connect to the LAN adapter and printer at the same time.

Figure 9.6 shows a typical phone line network adapter.

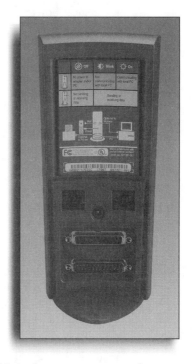

FIGURE 9.6
Intel's AnyPoint phone line network offers a full line of adapters, including internal PCI bus cards and external parallel and USB-connected adapters. This external parallel adapter has a parallel pass-through port that allows you to connect the AnyPoint and a printer to a single parallel port. Photo used by permission of Intel.

The big advantage of phone line LANs is that you can network two or more PCs located anywhere there is a phone jack—with one important caveat: Each PC on a phone line network must be connected to the same phone line. If you have multiple phone lines in your home, you'll need to connect all of your network adapters to the same phone line.

We like phone line networks for their simplicity and ease of use, and they're fine if you already have phone jacks in every room. But if you don't have phone jacks and are going to run new cable, you may as well install ethernet and get 100 times the speed for less money.

Power Line Networking

As you can tell from our story at the beginning of the chapter, Willy doesn't like power line networks, and we don't either. The power line products we've tested offer barely acceptable performance of 350Kbps when they work properly—which isn't all that often.

At first glance, power line networking products appear to be very similar to phone line networks. Both typically attach to your PC through the parallel port, and both use existing wiring to carry networking data around the house.

Unfortunately, power wiring makes a less-than-ideal carrier for network data. The weak radio signal used to carry data over the wiring is easily overwhelmed by interference from a variety of sources including elevators, washing machines, and even vacuum cleaners. This means that your power line network may work fine one moment, then inexplicably slow down or even stop working a few seconds later.

To further complicate matters, the signal from power line networks can't pass through transformers. This can be a problem in modern homes that are wired for 220-volt service. The power company delivers 220 volts to residential customers by providing two 110-volt feeds from the neighborhood step-down transformer. Some of the outlets will be fed by one of the 110-volt lines, and the rest by the other. But the two 110-volt lines aren't electrically connected to one another, so there's no path for the power line LAN to follow. The end result is that power line LANs may not work in every room if you have 220-volt service.

chapter

10

Fiber-Optic Cable

Looking Through Glass ●

The Skinny on Fiber ●

Light Through the Tunnel ●

Single-Mode and Multimode ●

Ordering Options ●

Signaling and Connection Standards ●

Practical Installations ●

Looking Through Glass

Willy had mixed feelings about thunderstorms. The destructive tornadoes they often spawned were terrifying, but the lightning strikes were good for business. The morning after a thunderstorm, he would receive plenty of cries for help—particularly from organizations with multiple buildings connected by copper cables. Early this morning, a thunderstorm had crossed the city, and about an hour after the spectacular lightning departed, the phone began ringing. Willy had already dispatched three crews on emergency calls and was trying to reschedule the day's new installations and routine maintenance when the phone rang again.

"Hi, I'm calling from the Broadview Country Club and we have a problem with our computers." Willy could hear the problem in the background. The exclusive country club was 30 miles out of town, and apparently the caller was right under the traveling lightning storm. The circuit crackled as thunder boomed.

"Get off the phone and I'll be out there in time for lunch," Willy promptly replied.

Over lunch with the club manager, Willy learned that the country club's far-flung pro shop, restaurant, pool, and maintenance facilities were connected by a mile of buried multipair cable that was used for both voice and data. Devices called line drivers—similar to high-powered modems—were used to move data over the cable. Every time there was a lightning storm in the area, one or more line drivers "popped," the club manager's word for what Willy saw as a smoking ruin of wires and plastic.

"You'll have this problem until you lay fiber-optic cables," Willy explained. "For you, the most important benefit of fiber is the complete freedom from worry about lightning or other electrical problems. But you'll also benefit from higher speeds between the three facilities. You should get rid of those 9,600-bit-per-second line drivers, use wiring hubs with ports for both the fiber and for regular copper unshielded twisted-pair wire, and have a high-speed network that covers the whole club."

Willy walked the manager through the details of the installation. In some areas, the club already had a buried conduit, and Willy's crew could use a commercial vacuum cleaner to suck a string, taped to a little plastic ball, through the conduit. Using the string, his crew would pull through the only slightly larger dual fiber. In other places, including a run across a fairway, the fiber would have to be directly buried, but Willy explained that this would require only a small slit, not a wide trench. The club would need three new wiring hubs with fiber ports to use the new cables. Willy promised to fax a proposal the next day.

As Willy walked toward his truck, he noticed how unusually green the grass was and how healthy the trees looked. "Yes," he thought, "a little lightning can sometimes do some good."

The Skinny on Fiber

Fiber-optic cable is wonderful stuff. It offers freedom from electrical grounding and lightning problems, and transmission speeds in the range of hundreds of megabits per second. Because it is free of crosstalk and interference from outside noise sources, you can use it to connect over much longer distances than is possible with copper cables. It would certainly replace copper cables for every data application if it weren't so expensive.

The rule of thumb is that labor is the most expensive part of any cable installation. The exception to that rule is fiber-optic installations. On a per-foot basis, fiber is about three times as expensive as thin ethernet coaxial cable and about seven times as expensive as high quality 3- or 4-pair UTP. The cost of the fiber-optic cable itself exceeds the cost of labor in many geographical regions.

On a per-connection basis, fiber-optic cable connectors are less expensive than the IBM data connectors used on STP in IBM Token-Ring installations, but hundreds of times more expensive than RJ-45 connectors. However, the real cost of fiber lies in the training, practice, and tools needed to make a good fiber-optic connection.

On the bottom line, our best advice is to use fiber-optic cables where they make the most sense, particularly between buildings and often between wiring closets within buildings. Until recently, organizations in very special situations, perhaps those with long cable runs, high bandwidth requirements, or those operating in electrically noisy or explosive environments, could cost-justify running fiber-optic cable to desktops.

An emerging class of low-cost fiber-optic products, however, may make us change our minds—as soon as the industry agrees on a standard. When you need to add fiber to your installation, you can either hire an outside contractor with a proven track record or send some of your own people to school to learn how to install connectors. Without the proper training and tools, installing fiber is not a do-it-yourself project.

Light Through the Tunnel

A piece of commercial fiber-optic cable contains two pipes for light. Each pipe, or glass strand, carries light in one direction, so a cable for digital communications requires two separate strands in the cable. A light source, typically a laser at one end of each glass strand, generates a beam of light that is turned off and on very quickly. These light pulses represent the zeros and ones of a digital signal. A receiver at the end of the cable opposite the light source decodes the signals.

Fiber-optic cable is so effective because the light is tightly contained inside the fiber. Light can't get in or out, so unlike electrical pulses in copper cables, the light pulses are completely isolated from the outside environment. You can run fiber with impunity next to high-voltage power lines, radio transmitters, welding machines, and in other environments that would disrupt signals in copper cables.

DANGER!
Never look into the end of a fiber when optical power is applied. The infrared light used in fiber-optic systems is invisible, but it can cause serious injury to the eye. You'll want to look, but don't do it!

The center of each glass strand, called the *core*, is the conduit for the light. Light from a diode or laser enters the core at one end and is trapped by the shiny walls of the core—a phenomenon called *total internal reflection*. The core is surrounded by a glass or plastic coating, called the *cladding*, that has a different optical density than the core. The boundary between the cladding and the core reflects the light back into the core.

Single-Mode and Multimode

This discussion could quickly become overly complex, so we are going to avoid wading in very far and instead tell you what you need to know to be safe. In commercial use, you'll find two categories of fiber cables: *single-mode* and *multimode*. These categories are defined by how light moves inside the cable—that's the aspect we are going to avoid.

The practical difference between these types of fibers is that single-mode fiber will carry signals farther and faster than multimode, but it is more expensive to buy and more difficult to install. The single-mode fiber is also thinner than the multimode fiber, which makes it even more difficult to work with. In commercial use, single-mode fiber is typically installed in very long distance runs. If you aren't thinking in terms of tens of miles, then you can and should use multimode cable. If you do need to cover these types of distances, check with your local telephone or cable television companies to subcontract for an experienced installation team.

Multimode fiber-optic cable is commonly used in LANs and campus-wide installations. You will find that multimode cable is available in catalogs in two different core sizes: 62.5 microns and 100 microns. The 100-micron material is now used only in a few instances such as in IBM Token-Ring installations, while the 62.5-micron material is the most widely used. With the smaller core size, the physical size of the fiber itself is about 0.002 inches, and the cladding typically is 125 or 140 microns thick—about 0.003 inches. So the fiber you'll probably use will be listed in the catalog as multimode, graded-index, optical-fiber waveguide with a nominal 62.5/125 micron core/cladding diameter.

Ordering Options

When you order fiber, you face other practical considerations. The same factors that apply to copper cable concerning the fire rating of the cable jacket also apply to fiber-optic cable. Always use plenum-rated cable if you can foresee that it might be needed. Fiber-optic

Want to learn more?

If you want to delve into the physics and the math, we suggest reading *A Technician's Guide to Fiber Optics*, written by Donald J. Sterling, Jr., and published by Delmar Publishers. Amp and other cable companies may make this book available to commercial installers.

Also, we recommend that you pick up a copy of *Upgrading and Repairing Networks, Second Edition*, published by Que.

cable products come in versions with reinforced jackets designed for direct burial, and in multifiber versions. Unlike UTP, there are no operational drawbacks to including multiple fibers within the same outer jacket. If you go to the expense of installing fiber between buildings, it makes sense to buy cables that contain more fibers than you have immediate use for to meet future requirements.

Connectors

No book can teach you how to attach fiber-optic connectors. 3M, Amp, Lucent, Molex Premise Networks, and other companies offer formal courses, typically one or two days long, in which you can learn the skills. The courses cover methods of "cleaving" (cutting) the cable and various polishing techniques to reduce loss of light through the "window" at the end of the cable. Most of the class time is devoted to hands-on practice, so there is a relatively high cost for class materials.

All fiber-optic connectors attempt to transmit light in the most efficient manner. To do so, the ends of the fibers must be cleaved at a perfect right angle, polished thoroughly to remove scratches, and then attached so the plug and jack meet in perfect alignment. That is tricky and painstaking work requiring physical dexterity and patience.

If you hire an outside contractor, you'll want an installer who is quite experienced at putting connectors on fiber cables. Let this person learn and practice on someone else's time; you should buy experience. If you are training your own installers, provide them with incentives to stay with your company after the training and be prepared to pay well over $1,000 for the equipment needed by each trainee. In addition, investing several thousand dollars more in devices such as curing ovens and inspection microscopes can speed the work of an installation team.

There are at least eight types of fiber-optic connectors in common use, but only four are widely used: the ST, SMA, MIC, and SC. In addition to these four, several vendors, including 3M, AMP, Lucent, and Panduit, have developed smaller, lower-cost connectors that are easier (and therefore less expensive) to install. These new connectors—coupled with rapidly falling desktop fiber NIC prices—provide a way to bring fiber to desktop PCs without breaking the bank.

Avoid intervendor complications

Whenever possible, order related products from the same manufacturer. If you can, buy your LAN adapters and cable hubs from the same company, purchase your cables and connectors from the same company, and get your connectors and tools from the same company. Things just work better that way.

The devil is in the details

Almost all recent ethernet installations use Cat 5 (or higher) UTP cable with RJ-45 connectors. Thanks to a well-defined and widely adopted set of standards, network planners don't have to worry about interoperability when choosing 10 and 100Mbps ethernet products. That's not true with fiber-optic products. Although there are only a few basic types of fiber cable, there are at least a dozen different—and incompatible—types of connectors currently in use, so it's important to choose carefully.

The ST connector, shown in an exploded view in Figure 10.1, is the most commonly used connector in commercial installations. Originally designed by AT&T, it has been adopted by many companies. Most courses teach the techniques of installing ST connectors.

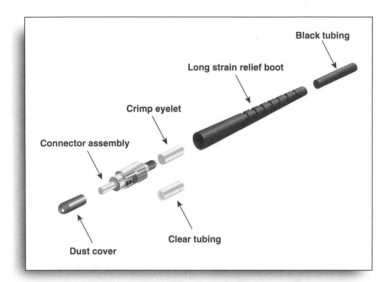

Black tubing

Long strain relief boot

Crimp eyelet

Connector assembly

Dust cover

Clear tubing

The center of the ST connector is a ceramic sleeve, or ferrule, 2.5 mm in size, that is glued to the fiber. The fiber itself appears at the end of the ferrule. To transmit the greatest amount of light, it must be polished by hand or by machine until it is free of scratches. The outer shell of the ST connector is similar to the shell of the BNC coaxial connector in that the plug locks on to the jack with a quarter twist. ST connectors work well in commercial and office environments.

Some equipment, particularly equipment from European manufacturers, uses a connector called the SMA that looks similar to the ST but uses a threaded outer shell (see Figure 10.2). This type of connection is more rugged, particularly under the stress of vibrations. The SMA connector, developed by Amp, has been standardized by NATO and the United States military. There are two styles of the SMA connector, one with a blunt tip like the ST connector and another with a stepped-down tip for better alignment. If you have equipment that uses these connectors, make sure your installer knows exactly which style of SMA plug is required.

Fiber mix and match
While most fiber-optic distribution equipment uses ST connectors, it's possible to mix and match equipment with different connectors—as long as the equipment at both ends of the cable uses the same signaling protocol. You'll need to make or order special adapter cables, and you should make sure you have a spare of each type of mixed-connector adapter cable on hand.

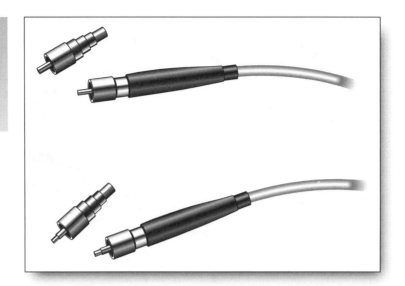

As we explained earlier, fiber-optic cables use two fiber strands, each of which carries light in one direction. The two strands are connected together in a manner that makes the fiber-optic cable look something like the power cord for a lamp. The ST and SMA connector systems use a single connector on each strand. Although the outer jacket of one fiber in each pair carries a stripe or other specific marking, most problems during installations, moves, and changes result from the wrong fiber being plugged into the wrong jack.

The Medium Interface Connector (MIC), adopted by the American National Standards Institute as a part of the Fiber Distributed Data Interface (FDDI) architecture, eliminates that problem. Unlike the ST and SMA connectors, a single MIC connector, shown in Figure 10.3, holds two fibers and is keyed so the plug and socket can only attach one way. MIC connectors are used in many brands of wiring hubs and LAN adapters, in addition to FDDI systems.

In some applications, you might find a connector called the SC (for "Small Connector") style connector. As the name implies, the SC connector is smaller than the more common ST and SMA connectors and is about the same size as an RJ-45 UTP connector. SC connectors provide a very strong "pull proof" connection that is sometimes used in cable splices. Like the SMA, the SC connector can handle two fibers and ensures that they connect properly. It is, however, a difficult connector to install. Our best advice is to avoid splices whenever possible.

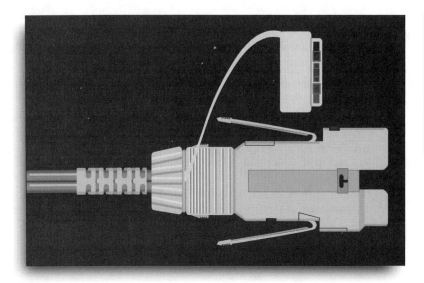

FIGURE 10.3
The MIC connector, typically associated with FDDI, holds two fibers and is keyed to insure proper polarity between the male and female plugs.

There is one significant drawback to the dual-cable connection scheme in the MIC and SC connectors: If the installer makes one good connection but then makes a bad cut or does a sloppy job of gluing the second connection, the good connection is wasted because the installer must cut off both connections to start over again. This drawback explains the popularity of the single ST and SMA connectors and drives the need for particularly experienced and careful installers if you use MIC or SC connectors. While it is very likely that new equipment you order will be equipped with ST connectors, it always pays to check. You can intermix equipment with other connectors in an installation—the connectors at one end of the cable don't dictate what connectors must be at the other end of the cable—but your installer must know what to expect. The MIC connectors are growing in popularity, and you should consider using them, particularly if the installer quotes a flat rate for the job.

Low-Cost Connectors

As we mentioned earlier, several vendors have recently introduced smaller, less expensive fiber connectors that are designed for the fiber-to-the-desktop marketplace. Besides being cheaper to buy, these new connectors are easier to install and are physically smaller than the SC and ST connectors they replace.

3M's VF-45 connector is typical of this new breed of small connectors. Like the ST and SC connectors, the VF-45 cabling system uses two fiber strands in a single jacket. 3M claims that a trained technician can install a VF-45 connector in about a minute, and we witnessed a trade show demonstration where a 3M technician beat a 60-second countdown clock by a few seconds. The VF-45 connectors snap on to a prepared fiber cable with no glue or screws, and the installation kit includes cutting, polishing, and inspection tools that are designed to work together.

The small size of the VF-45 and other small fiber connectors means that you can install more connectors in a smaller space than with conventional SMA or ST connectors. The VF-45 is about two-thirds the size of a standard RJ-45 UTP connector, making it ideal for patch panels, distribution frames, and other high-density applications.

Signaling and Connection Standards

You should be familiar with three standards for signaling over fiber and for making fiber-optic cable connections: FDDI, the fiber-optic inter repeater link (FOIRL), and the 10Base-F standard that is part of the IEEE 802.3 (Ethernet) specifications. Primarily, you must know about these standards to make sure you order equipment that can work together. Beyond that, the operation of the equipment conforming to these standards is invisible to you.

FDDI

FDDI is complex. The full specification includes two rings of fiber-optic cable that send frames of data in opposite directions. If one cable is broken in the primary ring, data completes its trip in the secondary ring. FDDI equipment is highly reliable and fast, using 100Mbps signaling. An extension to FDDI, called FDDI-2, allows a single fiber cable to carry voice and video signals in addition to data. FDDI-2 provides speeds up to 200Mbps.

But few companies need all of the features of FDDI, and we predict that it will be bypassed in the rush of technology toward other schemes such as Asynchronous Transfer Mode—an emerging technology for fast signaling that can use high-grade UTP cable plants. Due to this and other stresses, the original concept of FDDI is changing rapidly.

Even the word "fiber" in the acronym FDDI is misleading. Under the latest definition of the American National Standards Institute, the term FDDI can include fiber-optic, shielded twisted-pair, or unshielded twisted-pair cable—so the term FDDI no longer necessarily implies fiber.

FDDI is a networking scheme that gains high reliability through redundancy and sophisticated data-handling protocols. The fiber-optic cable alternative in FDDI provides signaling out to 2 kilometers, but the higher cost of fiber has limited its popularity. The FDDI protocols can run over copper cable to a maximum distance of 100 meters and require a Level 5 UTP installation.

An ANSI committee has approved a plan for signaling using two pairs of Level 5 UTP. This plan uses a transmission scheme called Multi-Level Transmission-3 (MLT-3), which randomizes data to reduce emissions, and also specifies a method of equalizing signal levels.

At the same time, IBM and other vendors are pushing for the use of FDDI protocols over shielded twisted-pair wire, a proposal that goes by the name of SDDI. IBM, Network Peripherals, and Nortel Networks are among the companies shipping SDDI modules for their chassis-based wiring hubs.

Cisco Systems uses the term Copper Distributed Data Interface (CDDI) to describe its products that use the FDDI techniques over unshielded twisted-pair. Other companies like Network Peripherals use the term FDDI over UTP to describe their products that conform to the ANSI draft standard.

FOIRL and 10Base-F

While FDDI took advantage of the quality of the signal traveling over a fiber-optic link to increase the signaling speed to 100Mbps, other standards are content (for now at least) to only extend the distance or operational capability.

The fiber-optic interrepeater link (FOIRL) specification was created to describe how ethernet repeaters should communicate over fiber-optic cable. The goal of the FOIRL design is to integrate fiber into certain critical points in an ethernet network in order to extend the distance of operation or to allow operation in environments with high levels of electrical noise.

FOIRL is an old specification, but many transceivers (external devices that connect to the AUI port on an Ethernet adapter) follow the FOIRL standard. The FOIRL standard allows connection of repeaters over at least 2 kilometers of cable. FOIRL devices typically use ST connectors.

The only trick to employing FOIRL is making sure you have compatible devices on both ends of the link. Wiring hubs might have FOIRL ports to link to other hubs, but the connections to the desktop LAN adapters typically use a different scheme. FOIRL is designed to extend copper cable, not to replace it.

The strategy for replacing copper cable with fiber cable is described in a newer standard called 10Base-F. This standard, which includes two variations called 10Base-FB and 10Base-FL, are products of the same IEEE committee process that delivered 10Base-T. 10Base-FL describes the connections between LAN nodes and a cable hub, while 10Base-FB describes a backbone connection between cable hubs. The difference between the two lies in the signaling, and both standards allow for cable runs of up to 2 kilometers.

While products conforming to these standards typically stay with ethernet's 100Mbps signaling, there is a new standard on the horizon. After several false starts, the IEEE Ethernet committee ratified a standard for Gigabit Ethernet in 1998. As you might expect, gigabit products are expensive, so they're best suited to backbone and inter-building use. But like everything else, the prices will fall rapidly over the next few years.

Practical Installations

Overall, the use of multimode fiber-optic cable can be just as simple as we've presented it here—order the right equipment and connectors, keep distances down to 2 kilometers or less, and they should work together. Longer installations require the use of calculators to work out "power budgets" (the amount of light that must enter the cable to be detectable at the receiver) and other factors, so we suggest leaving them to experienced professionals.

Here are a few hints gained from experience:

- Because fiber-optic cable is so small and flexible, it's easy to forget that there is a piece of glass inside. Be particularly careful of the bend radius of the cable when it goes around walls and in other tight places. As a practical rule, never bend a cable in a circle with a radius of less than 2 inches and, if there is any force on the cable, keep the bend radius to 6 inches or more.

- Because fiber-optic cable is small and flexible, it's easy to snake it into conduits with other cables. Electrically, this isn't a problem, but the weight of heavy copper cables can crush the cladding on the fiber-optic cable and cause the cable to leak light. Keep heavy weights off the fiber.

- Even small bends, called *microbends*, can cause light to leak into the jacket. Avoid using a great deal of force to pull a fiber, because it might cause a microbend that will ruin a section of cable.

- Avoid splicing cable whenever possible. New cable installations should never use spliced cables. If a cable must be spliced to restore service, the installer should choose an appropriate splice kit from any of several on the market. The type of splice kit is not driven by the type of connectors used on the ends of the cable. Cleaving, gluing, and polishing the ends of the cable in the splice kit while working inside a wall or in a hot crawl space is no fun.

- Use fiber to extend copper cable networks where it makes sense. A good UTP cable installation can carry a lot of data and is less costly, so use both UTP and fiber cables to their best advantage.

chapter 111

Cable Testing and Certification

The Best Test ●

Nobody Knows the Troubles... ●

What Cable Testers Measure ●

Testing Fiber ●

Baseline and Certification ●

The Best Test

"This room wasn't here before! It's not on our plans," exclaimed Willy, looking over the top of the plans he was holding and fixing the network manager with a glare. "What did you do with the cables that were in this space when you built the room?" he asked.

"We put them in the false ceiling. We didn't disconnect anything, so they should be OK," the manager replied. Willy stopped himself from adding, "Then why am I here?" The client had a problem and he was here to fix it even if the problem resulted from the client's careless actions.

Willy got a short ladder from his truck, removed a ceiling tile, and poked his head into the false ceiling space. The high-quality Level 5 cables coming from the wiring closet were there, but instead of lying in the hangers his crew had installed, they were bent sharply around metal ceiling brackets, stretched directly over the new fluorescent lights, and crisscrossed over AC power cables at every angle.

"Look," Willy explained, "the connectors are important, but it's what happens to the cables in between the connections that counts. We'll have to do a new profile on each wire pair in each cable your people moved—then we'll know what we've got."

The network manager seemed interested, so Willy explained the process as he removed a device about the size of a paperback James Michener novel from its case. He unpacked a small printer, connected the two with a cable, and then moved the whole system to a wall jack. "This is a Microtest Penta Scanner. We'll take it from jack to jack, where it will scan each wire pair, check the level of electrical noise in several frequency bands, measure crosstalk between pairs, and compare the results to the published standards."

Then he removed a thick printout from his soft-sided satchel and thumped it down on a desk. "We'll compare this profile from the initial installation with the results we get today, and then we'll know what we need to do."

Willy used a low-power walkie-talkie to coordinate with an assistant standing at the patch panel in the wiring closet. The assistant moved the Penta Scanner's signal source from cable to cable so the scanner could measure against a known signal. It took longer for the printer to produce each report than it did for the Microtest scanner to perform its tests.

A few minutes later Willy had the printouts spread in front of him on the network manager's desk. "Well, across the board these cables have higher levels of low-frequency noise than they had before. That noise comes from the power wiring and lights, but it only exceeds the standard on these two cables. The near-end crosstalk is very high on this cable, so I imagine it has a pretty good kink in it, probably around a metal bracket. Looks like a couple hours of work overall. Without the scanner, we'd have spent the entire day replacing all the cables."

As Willy walked out to the parking lot, he reflected that as a result of investing a few thousand dollars in a modern cable tester, he had a happy customer but a shorter billable day. He hoped this customer's long-term business would make up for the hours he had saved this time. "Oh well," he reflected, "I'd rather be fixing things for real than spinning my wheels in frustration."

Nobody Knows the Troubles...

Your network can't be better than its cables, but how good are those cables? That's the most important question you can ask during installation and troubleshooting. Even if you use the best quality cable, connectors, patch panels, jumpers, and hubs, sloppy installation or a hostile electrical environment can prevent your network from operating at peak potential. To diagnose the electrical environment that the LAN adapter's signals pass through in the cable, you must test the entire installation in place.

Once a good cable system is installed, what do you do when problems arise? Unfortunately, network cable problems can closely mimic network software problems. Network cables can pick up electrical noise and interference from electric motors, light dimmers, fluorescent lights, and any of a thousand other sources. If the noise is strong enough, it can overwhelm the "good" signal on the cable, causing retransmissions or complete failure. UTP cable is often its own worst enemy, since the signals on the two pairs of wires within the same cable often interfere with each other, a phenomenon called *crosstalk*. Recent studies show that closely spaced Cat 6 cables can interfere with each other, introducing a problem dubbed "alien crosstalk."

If a network cable has high noise or high near-end crosstalk, the networking software might respond by working overtime sending extra frames of data to push the message through. If the software reaches an impasse, it can generate an error message like NetWare's all-too-familiar "Server Not Found." Dozens of types of problems can cause that message to appear, so you must troubleshoot the problem to find the true source.

Whether you're troubleshooting problems with your kitchen toaster or the internal navigation system on a Boeing 747, you will follow the same procedure:

- Logically break the system into functional elements.
- Based on the symptoms, determine the most likely dysfunctional element.
- Use testing or substitution to determine if the suspect element is in fact bad.
- If the suspect element is not bad, move to the next likely suspect.
- When, through testing or substitution you find the dysfunctional element, repair or replace it.

Substituting one cable for another to test for a dysfunctional element does not offer certain proof of anything, because a common problem can affect all cables. Your best bet is to compare recorded measurements taken when the system was working properly against current measurements. This amounts to testing against an established baseline, and it's as important in cable testing as in medicine and aerospace.

Several companies, notably Datacom Technologies, John Fluke Manufacturing, and Microtest Corporation, market handheld cable testers with a variety of features, including the ability to certify that a cable meets specific IEEE or EIA/TIA standards. These devices can operate across several different cable types, providing various functions for each type of cable. Figure 11.1 shows a Microtest cable scanner.

FIGURE 11.1
This Microtest Pentatest cable scanner has options for several different types of cable, performs an automated series of tests, and can compare the test results against standards, including IEEE 10Base-T and EIA/TIA 568.

These devices can create either a printout or, when attached to a PC, a data file that you can keep as a baseline for future reference. You can use this record to check a cable's characteristics against a fixed standard and against measurements taken previously. This comparison makes it easy to spot specific problems and to track degradation caused by aging, weather, or other factors. A printout showing the evaluation of a cable against EIA/TIA 568 Level 5 standards is shown in Figure 11.2.

In previous chapters, we told you that installing fiber-optic cable connectors was not a do-it-yourself project and that you need a good electrician to help you with grounding problems. But these handheld cable checkers can be used by any knowledgeable network manager or installer with little or no special training. While they usually come with excellent manuals, the units have simple controls and explanations of their operation that appear on LCD screens. Perhaps the most important tip we can offer regarding these cable scanners is to remember to keep them charged. While they do have external power adapters, these portable cable scanners are much easier to use with full batteries.

FIGURE 11.2
This printout compares the test results of a specific cable's attenuation, noise, and near-end crosstalk against the published standards.

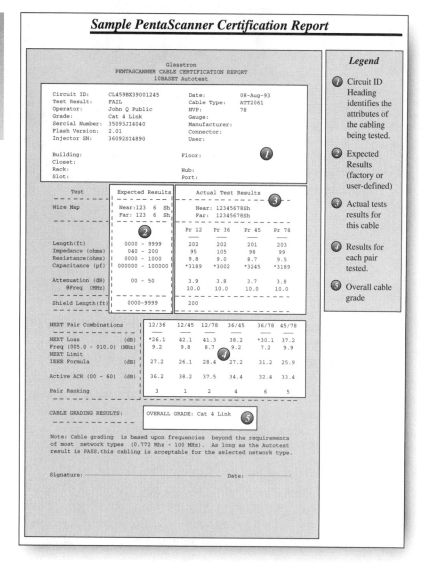

Sample PentaScanner Certification Report

What Cable Testers Measure

Cable testers come with a variety of capabilities. Because the companies change their models, prices, and features at least every year and a half, we don't try to associate a set of features with a specific product in this book. Instead, we list the features you'll generally find in these devices and let you select the product that meets your needs.

Cable Distance

The various IEEE networking standards specify maximum cable lengths. In the case of IEEE 802.3 (ethernet), the overall length directly affects the ability of network nodes to share the cable; a cable that is too long degrades the system.

Cable scanners measure the distance to an open-ended or shorted cable by sending a pulse down the cable and then timing its reflection back from the end of the cable, a technique called *time-domain reflectometry* (TDR). Companies like Hewlett-Packard sell very precise and expensive TDR devices for use on long cable runs. The TDR capabilities available in handheld cable checkers is less precise, but good enough for most work. You can expect distance readings to be accurate to about two feet.

When you measure a cable with an electrical pulse instead of a tape measure, the pulse doesn't travel at the same speed in every type of cable. The size of the wires, type of insulation, and external shielding all affect the speed of the electrical pulse. A factor called the *nominal velocity of propagation* (NVP) is the ratio between the speed of an electrical pulse in a specific type of cable and the speed of light. The scanner must apply the appropriate NVP to the cable to accurately measure the cable length. Scanners should contain a table that has the NVP for a variety of cable types, but you also might want to measure the NVP for a particular spool or lot of cable to get more accurate distance measurements.

The scanner can calculate the cable's NVP if you know the cable length, so it is wise to carefully measure a few hundred feet of cable from the typical 1,000-foot spool and to use what is usually called the scanner's calibration function to measure the NVP of that known length of cable. Modern cable checkers allow you to enter that figure (typically between 0.6 and 0.9) into a memory for future use.

Trust us...there's an easier way

After you know the NVP of a cable or obtain a standard NVP from the cable checker's memory, it is easy to determine how much cable is left on a spool. Put a connector on the cable and use the cable checker to test the cable length; it's a lot easier than unrolling the spool and measuring it foot by foot.

The distance measurement is particularly useful for finding open or shorted coaxial BNC connectors on thin ethernet. When a thin ethernet installation is working properly, you should disconnect every T-connector and take a distance measurement on each cable segment. With all T-connectors disconnected from the cable, you'll see a series of readings on the cable tester such as "Cable open at 30 feet." If you record each of these readings and create a network map, you'll be prepared when a crimped connector shorts out or a T-connector doesn't connect and the network crashes. By retesting the cable and applying a little logic to the changed readings, you'll find the bad connector.

In a UTP installation, taking distance measurements assures you of at least minimal quality on your punch-down blocks or cross-connect panels. When you measure distance on a cable, the cable checker sends a wave that is reflected when it encounters the most distant open connection. If you measure through the punch-down block or cross-connection, you'll know whether the cable check detects a large lump of impedance, like an open circuit. If the cable checker reports the distance to the punch-down block or cross-connect point instead of detecting some more distant point, then you know you have an equipment or connection problem.

Some cable checkers come with a special port for an oscilloscope. If you use a good scope with a 200 MHz bandwidth, you can see the TDR pulse put out by the cable checker, measure its return, and obtain a much finer measurement of cable distance and quality. If you are experienced, the scope trace will show lumped impedances—perhaps marginal connectors—that the cable checker might miss.

Wire Map

Some cable testers offer a wire map function among the distance measurement features, and others make it a standalone function. *Wire map*, a feature unique to twisted-pair installations, shows you which wire pairs connect to what pins on the plugs and sockets. This test quickly detects whether an installer connected the wires to a plug or jack in reverse order—a common problem. It is also valuable for detecting the most common cause of data problems in twisted-pair cabling: split pairs. The split pair condition is shown in Figure 11.3. A similar crossed condition called crossed pairs is also troublesome. You can only spot split pairs through visual inspection or by seeing the effect of a split-pair condition in the crosstalk measurements.

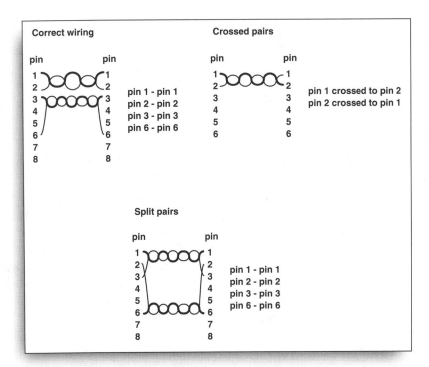

FIGURE 11.3
The conditions called crossed pair and split pair are similar, but slightly different. A crossed pair reverses the tip and ring. A cable checker that does a wire map will detect this condition. However, split pairs will check out OK on a wire map and can only be detected by checking the near-end crosstalk.

The twisting in wire pairs shields the desirable signals from external signals. This shielding only occurs if the wires in the pair are part of the same circuit. Unfortunately, it's common for the wires in a pair to be accidentally split so they are part of different circuits. A current can flow in a circuit and the system appears to work—particularly over short distances and in limited trials—but no self-shielding is protecting the signals, and eventually near-end crosstalk becomes a problem. (Near-end crosstalk is discussed in detail later in this chapter.)

Attenuation

Various electrical factors, primarily resistance, reduce the power of the signals as they pass through the copper wire. Other factors such as capacitive and inductive reactance drag down the signals at different frequencies. Overall, engineers talk about the attenuation of the signal by the cable. Cable testers measure signal attenuation at several frequency bands.

Typically, a tester measures attenuation on a signal received from a signal injector—a small box about the size of a deck of playing cards that attaches to the far end of the cable. Testers often measure attenuation at 64 KHz, 256 KHz, 512 KHz, 772 KHz, 1 MHz, 2 MHz, 4 MHz, 5 MHz, 8 MHz, 10 MHz, 16 MHz, 20 MHz, 32 MHz, 62.5 MHz, and 100 MHz. Measurements are made up to 16 MHz for Category 3 cables, up to 100 MHz for Category 4 and 5 cables, and up to 300 MHz for Category 6 cables.

Attenuation is measured in decibels (dB) and the lower the number, the better. Because the dB scale is logarithmic, even a change of 1 or 2 dB indicates a significant change of power. As an example of the range, the 10Base-T specification allows for a maximum of an 11.5 dB loss in the 5 to 10 MHz band on the 328 feet (100 meters) of wire from the hub to the desktop. The EIA/TIA 568 specification addresses the attenuation problem in more detail. For example, horizontal UTP is measured at ten frequency points, and it allows for a maximum attenuation of 2.8 dB per 1,000 feet at 64 KHz, 7.8 dB per 1,000 feet at 1 MHz, and 40 dB per 1,000 feet at 16 MHz.

Near-End Crosstalk

Near-end crosstalk is the feed-over of electrical energy between wire pairs in the same cable. Cable scanners use a signal injector to properly terminate the far end of the cable, and then sweep through a set of frequencies to measure how much signal leaks between the active wire pair carrying the injector's signal and the inactive pair.

Crossed pairs are the most common cause of high levels of near-end crosstalk. The wire map test performed by a cable scanner can identify those pairs for you, but it cannot identify split pairs. Other causes of near-end crosstalk include twisted pairs that are untwisted when attached to cross-connect devices, untwisted patch cables, and cables that are pulled so tightly around a sharp corner that the pairs change position inside the jacket.

Be sure to test all pairs

When testing twisted-pair cables, be sure the tester switches between all cable pairs in the cable. Sometimes this is a manual task, so it's easy to overlook a pair.

Like attenuation, near-end crosstalk is measured in a series of frequency steps going up to 100 MHz. But unlike attenuation, higher numbers are better. A higher near-end crosstalk number indicates a greater difference between the size of the induced signal and the size of the induced crosstalk.

Network Monitoring and Protocol Decoding

Some cable checkers have the capability to monitor network traffic and, in some cases, to even look inside the network frames to report specific types of messages or activity—a function called *protocol decoding*.

Traffic monitoring is particularly useful for detecting unusually high or low levels of traffic. Many cable checkers can generate an audible alarm if the traffic exceeds programmed limits in either direction. You can also often hear a click when a frame goes through the checker—a handy clue to network operation.

Traffic monitoring is also a useful technique for pinpointing loose cables or other problems (such as an ethernet adapter that malfunctions and broadcasts) without first listening to the cable—a condition called *jabbering*.

You'll need a specific device to monitor an ethernet network and a different one for a token-ring network. Ethernet and token-ring monitors must each act like a node to their respective wiring hubs in order for the hubs to let them access the networks.

Protocol decoding requires a sophisticated program and much more processing power than you'll find in the average cable checker, so these devices cost a lot more. However, if you want to carry all of your troubleshooting devices in one hand, then a cable checker with protocol decoding is a must.

Noise-Level Test

While near-end crosstalk is defined as the signals from adjacent wire pairs, many other signals can impose themselves on wire pairs. These signals from commonly found electrical sources often occupy specific frequency bands, as listed in Table 11.1

Table 11.1	Typical Sources and Frequencies of Near-End Crosstalk	
TYPE	RANGE	SOURCE
Low frequency	10 KHz to 150 KHz	Fluorescent lights, heaters
Medium frequency	150 KHz to 100 MHz	Radio, electronic devices, air cleaners
High frequency	16 MHz to 1,000 MHz	Nearby radio and TV transmitters, computers, electronic devices, motion sensors, radar
Impulse	10 KHz to 100 MHz	Motors, switches, welders, auto ignitions

Electrical noise on a cable is measured in millivolts (one-thousandth of a volt), abbreviated mV. Instead of measuring the peaks of the pulses, the measurement is made on a weighted scale called root mean square (RMS), so typically a cable checker will display a noise reading in mV RMS. The lower the number of millivolts, the less the electrical noise.

When you take a noise reading, you'll have the cables disconnected from the computer equipment. If the cable checker reports high readings, try unplugging electrical devices until you find the source of the noise. Note that simply turning off a device doesn't necessarily work. One of our most frustrating experiences arose from a printer's power supply that generated a large amount of electrical noise and transferred it to a nearby 10Base-T cable when the printer was *off*. When the printer was on, the level of electrical noise was very low. There are always new surprises lurking in every installation.

Programmed Standards

Raw numbers on the attenuation, near-end crosstalk, and noise don't mean much without a reference. If you're buying a cable checker, we strongly suggest getting one that is programmed with reference tables for every standard you will use in your network. This might be IEEE 802.3 10Base-T or IEEE 802.5 token-ring, or it might include high-level tests for EIA/TIA Level 5 cabling. It might even include new evolving standards for 100 megabit and faster signaling over UTP.

Special Features

Cable checkers can come with many special features and management functions. Printing is a feature common in most of them, but look for checkers that print while monitoring; they require more processing power but save time. The ability to print a variety of pre-programmed reports is also a useful option.

Some cable checkers can also serve as cable tracers, sometimes with the addition of a few add-on devices. A cable tracer follows an electrical signal injected into the cable, so you can physically find the cable behind walls. Of course there are less expensive, special-purpose devices that do this, and many people elect to use the special-purpose tracer for this job rather than adding more features to the cable tester.

Remember, standards are constantly evolving, and your cable tester is programmed with information that is likely to change. Some devices offer a method of upgrading the internal software through a modem and a telephone call. This upgradability might cost a little more, but it extends the tester's life and avoids the inconvenience of sending the device back to the factory for an upgrade.

Testing Fiber

Optical cable testers cost more than those designed for copper cables, primarily because the test environment is more complex. Fiber-optic cable testers use optical time-domain reflectometry, which depends on the backscattering of light to find the end of the fiber. This backscattering is weak, and the device must make repeated measurements to ensure accuracy. Fiber-optic cable is discussed in more detail in Chapter 10.

It is also much more difficult to measure attenuation in fiber, but it is also less important than in copper cables. A fiber-optic cable tester often includes a power meter to measure the strength of the light signal at the end of the cable. This factor is more important than attenuation, since the power of the light source can often be adjusted within limits to overcome attenuation. This adjustment is part of the power budget computation for the circuit.

Baseline and Certification

Cable testers are useful tools for any network manager and are absolutely necessary for every cable installer. A network manager should receive a set of baseline measurements for every cable when the cable system is installed and should periodically check it to ensure the continued quality of the system. Certification to specific IEEE or EIA/TIA standards is critically important to an expanding network and whenever new technology is introduced to the system. Test your cables when you install them and on a periodic basis, and you'll have a secure and effective network system.

chapter

12

Wireless Communications

Air Willy ●

Going Wireless ●

Wireless LAN Topology ●

Solving Other Wired Problems ●

Air Willy

"OK 1," the OK Cable dispatcher crackled over the truck's radio, "would you meet the crew at the courthouse? They want to talk to you about a problem."

Willy confirmed the radio call and reviewed what he knew about the courthouse job, which wasn't much. Basically, the county clerk wanted to have a networked PC installed down at the loading dock for checking in packages and getting them distributed without the delay of going through the mail room. OK Cable had installed the original LAN cable system in the clerk's office on the third floor, but the added vertical distance for the new node wouldn't pose a problem.

When Willy pulled up to the courthouse loading dock, he found his crew combing the building plans with the county's network administrator, a retrained deputy sheriff on a disability desk job.

"We got a problem, Willy," his lead installer said. "Between this loading dock and the wiring closet on the new third floor, there's the original first floor built in 1862 with granite walls and marble floors. Of course there are no conduits and practically no space between the walls. I'm glad they don't build buildings like this anymore!"

Willy surveyed the plans, smacked his palm into a granite wall once to confirm that it was really there, shook his head, and then turned to the administrator. "How much data are you going to move over the network? How much network activity will this PC have?"

"Well, they collect all the official mail, packages, and freight for the county here. They probably get three or four shipments in a day, so maybe three to four dozen separate packages or freight shipments. Maybe 50 database entries and about 25 checks against invoices a day, I'd guess." Obviously, the administrator had been doing his homework.

"I'll bet wireless would cost less and do the job," Willy suggested.

The administrator, who was familiar with the pros and cons of police radios, said, "You mean like a cellular telephone or something?"

"Well," Willy replied, "some cellular telephone systems offer one kind of wireless data system, but that's not what I had in mind.

There's a wireless system called 802.11 HR. It's based on an IEEE standard so it has lots of industry backing that lets you network without cables. It should work great in a situation like this."

The network administrator liked the idea of a wireless link, and Willy promised to work up a proposal. When he returned to his truck to leave, he found the two cable installers leaning against it.

"Wireless?" the bigger one asked with his hands folded across his chest. "Something going on here we should know about?"

Willy nodded sagely. "Yup. You should know that wireless is a good alternative when it's too far or too expensive to install cable. We could install ten normal cable runs for what a single wireless node will cost, but in this case it's a good alternative. Wireless networking isn't as fast as networking over cables and it costs a lot more, so copper cables aren't going to disappear any time soon. But in this case, at least you don't have to spend the next week drilling through granite—assuming the folks in the local committee for historic preservation would let you do that in the first place."

The installers nodded as they took in this new information and then packed up to move to the next job.

Going Wireless

Wireless: It's the hottest word in networking. But the term means very different things to different people. There are at least five major types of wireless network connectivity:

- Point-to-point
- Wireless LANs
- City/region
- Nationwide (within the United States)
- Worldwide

Each type of wireless networking is supported by a separate group of companies and, to confuse things even more, the categories of networks often overlap. But before we delve too deeply into this topic, we want to make one point clear: *Wireless networks in every category are always an extension of cabled networks, not a replacement.* Few wireless networks are totally wireless.

The rules of physics apply to wireless connections just as they do to cable, but they impose more restrictions on the wireless environment. Radio waves traveling through space face a much more hostile environment than electrons moving through copper. You can have long distance connections, fast connections, and inexpensive connections over wireless, but not all three at once. Distance and signaling speed always work against each other, and raising either of those parameters while holding the other one steady always raises the cost. This relationship means that it's very difficult to field a wireless system that is less expensive than one based on copper cables, and it's also difficult to create one that is faster than copper. In wireless systems, you can generally have it fast, long distance, or inexpensive; pick any two.

So, to use wireless systems successfully, you should deploy them in niche situations where copper is at some disadvantage. The two most fruitful niches for wireless are in contexts where it is awkward to install copper cables and where people need or are willing to pay for mobility.

Any number of situations can arise that make it difficult to install copper cable. For example, you might want to extend the network out to a lone PC in a warehouse or in some other part of the building where the distance limitations exceed the single span of LAN cable. A repeater would solve the problem, but it would also substantially increase the cost of connecting that single node. In this case, a wireless link could be less expensive and much easier to install.

You might also encounter situations where the type of building construction or the inability to gain a construction right-of-way blocks the cable installation. Or, you might need a temporary network connection for a special project. Wireless connections are useful for these cases, too.

Wireless networking and mobile computing serve quite different needs, but so-called "cordless" networking does bring the two technologically closer. Today, the city/region, nationwide, and worldwide connections systems are aimed solely at mobile users. The need for a mobile installation is driven by a different set of factors than the need for wireless connections; because mobile computing network nodes are on the move, direct connection through a fixed cable isn't even a consideration. People who need these services must tolerate low data rates and/or high costs, so cost and performance comparisons with cable are largely moot. Since mobile systems don't compete directly with cable installations, we don't address them in this book, but we will examine several wireless network solutions that compete with and extend cabled services into a local or campuswide area.

These systems fall into two broad categories: wireless bridges and wireless LANs.

- Wireless Bridges use microwave radio signals to link two or more LANs located in different buildings. The wireless connection acts as a wide area network bridge, connecting LANs in physically separate locations. The wireless bridge is invisible to users on the LAN, since it allows them to connect to remote computers and networks services as if they were directly connected to the local LAN.

- Wireless LAN systems (also called indoor wireless systems) link one or more portable or dislocated computers into a LAN. A wireless LAN usually includes one or more devices, typically called an *access point*, that allow wireless computers to communicate with an existing LAN, providing seamless connectivity between all the wired and wireless computers in a building.

Wireless Bridges

Wireless bridges can connect LANs in two or more buildings into a single LAN, often in place of a dedicated T1 or other high-speed leased data line. These products use microwave radio signals and highly directional rooftop antennas to provide reliable connections between two or more locations at speeds up to 10Mbps while covering distances up to 15 miles.

There are two basic types of wireless bridge systems. Point-to-point links connect two locations, while multipoint systems connect three or more locations. The basic difference between the two is in the way the antennas are deployed. In point-to-point systems, both ends typically use directional antennas aimed at one another. Multipoint systems usually use a combination of directional and nondirectional antennas arranged in a "star" configuration, with the nondirectional antenna in the center of the star.

Figure 12.1 shows a typical wireless bridge.

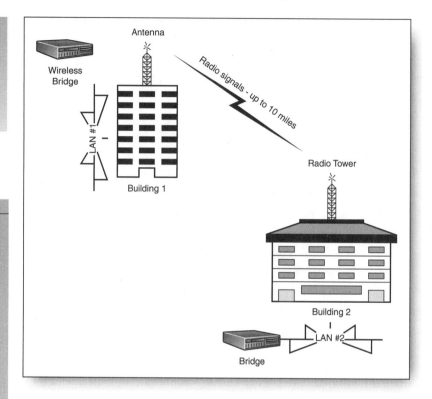

On the plus side of the ledger, wireless bridges can be installed in just a few days, require little or no ongoing maintenance once installed, and are free of monthly usage charges. These three factors make them an attractive alternative to T1 and other high-speed leased lines, especially in areas where leased line circuits are expensive or unavailable.

Although wireless bridges are most often used to cover relatively long distances, they can also be used to solve tricky inter- and intra-building cable problems. The microwave radio signals used by these systems can penetrate brick, concrete, and other wall structures, making them a viable alternative to long vertical cable runs in multi-story buildings, especially where it's difficult or impossible to drill holes and pull cable.

Wireless bridge systems are often used in multi-building campus environments. We strongly recommend using fiber-optic cables to link buildings, because it removes the risks of lightning entering the building and of electrocution due to differences in building ground potentials. However, it is sometimes impossible to get the right-of-way to install any type of cable between buildings, and wireless links can serve to interconnect buildings in another way. It many be cheaper and easier to set up a wireless link than to dig up a parking lot to run cable, but the cable—especially fiber-optic cable—will provide much higher bandwidth and more "headroom" for future expansion.

Physically, wireless bridge systems consist of an equipment cabinet and antenna at each site. The bridge connects to the LAN via an ethernet or token-ring connector. Depending on the distance to be covered, the antenna may be a simple 6-inch "rubber duck" flexible antenna mounted on the back of the wireless unit, or it may be a 2- by 3-foot parabolic dish mounted on the rooftop and connected to the wireless bridge with a thick coaxial cable or waveguide. The small antennas provide a very limited area of coverage, while the larger, external antennas provide increased range and reliability.

Figure 12.2 shows an example of point-to-point bridging used to connect two adjacent buildings.

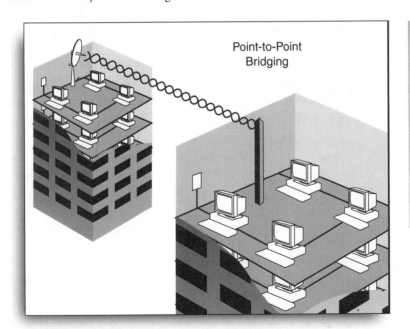

Point-to-Point Bridging

FIGURE 12.2
Virtually all wireless bridges provide protocol-independent, MAC-layer bridging, so they can be used on mixed IP, IPX, and AppleTalk networks. Most bridges provide protocol filtering and routing tools that help maximize throughput on the link by eliminating unnecessary LAN traffic.

233

Wireless LANs

Imagine this: You're setting off on a cross-country business trip. You begin your morning at home, checking your email on your notebook PC while sitting at the breakfast table. On your way out of town, you spend a few minutes in the airport departure lounge, where you turn on your notebook to check the latest news and stock prices. When you arrive at your destination, you check into your hotel, where you once again connect to your corporate email server over the Internet. The next morning, you attend a meeting at your company's west coast offices. During the meeting, you give a presentation on your notebook, using files stored on the LAN back at your home office.

Notice that while we mentioned being connected in all these places, we didn't mention anything about cables. That's because your notebook, home, and offices are on a wireless LAN.

Just a few years ago, wireless LANs were far too expensive for all but the most demanding applications. The few products that were available used proprietary technologies, so products from one vendor couldn't communicate with products from another.

Today, virtually all wireless LAN products are based on one of two IEEE standards. The IEEE 802.11 standard covers wireless communications at 1 and 2Mbps, and the newer 802.11 HR (for High Rate) specification defines an 11Mbps wireless system. All 802.11 HR products can also operate at the slower 802.11 speeds, providing a measure of backward compatibility with existing wireless LANs. Like their wireless bridge cousins, 802.11 wireless LANs don't require an FCC license.

The 802.11 specification defines three classes of wireless technologies, including Direct Sequence Spread Spectrum (DSSS), Frequency Hopping Spread Spectrum (FHSS), and Infrared technology. The vast majority of 802.11 equipment on the market uses DSSS technology because it offers better performance than DSSS. FHSS technology reduces the potential for receiving and creating interference and improves the security of the signals. The spread spectrum technology transmits and receives over a bandwidth of several megahertz. The equipment can ignore the common, narrower pulse signals within the bandwidth, even if they are quite strong.

Do you care if your signal hops or spreads?

Does it really matter to you if you use direct spread spectrum or frequency-hopping? No, probably not. However, we believe that the industry will get behind the DSSS standard and that the "hoppers" are a dead end. Watch for industry alliances that talk about interoperability between equipment from different vendors. Those are the products you want.

Because wireless LAN signals may extend outside of your physical premises, it's possible for an interloper to gain access to your LAN using an 802.11-equipped portable computer outside of your building. An extension to 802.11 called the Wireless Encyption Protocol, or WEP, provides tight security for data transmissions by scrambling the data before it is transmitted over the radio waves.

While initial 802.11 products suffered from inter-vendor compatibility issues, the manufacturers have diligently worked together to smooth out the problems. 802.11 HR is getting off to a smoother start, thanks in large part to the Wireless Ethernet Compatibility Alliance (WECA), a group of six companies that have banded together to promote adoption of 802.11 as a worldwide standard. The six companies—3Com, Aironet, Intersil, Lucent Technologies, Nokia and Symbol Technologies—will ensure true multi-vendor interoperability by creating a certification laboratory to make sure that systems from different manufacturers can be used within the same wireless infrastructure. Thanks to the high degree of compatibility, you can deploy wireless LAN products in your organization without being married to a single-vendor solution.

The rapid emergence of 802.11 HR products has sparked the development of public access wireless Internet access systems. Several companies, including market pioneer MobileStar Communications, are creating publicly accessible 802.11 HR Internet connections in airports and hotels nationwide.

Wireless LAN Topology

While it's possible to create a LAN using only wireless devices, most wireless LANs operate as an adjunct to an existing ethernet or token-ring LAN. The basic building block of a wireless LAN is a device called an Access Point, or AP. The AP units connect to your existing LAN through an ethernet or token-ring connection and provide wireless connectivity for all the wireless PCs within 200 to 500 feet. Depending on the size of the space you wish to cover, you may need one or more APs.

A lesson learned the hard way

While most wireless vendors offer WEP encryption security, it's not always enabled by default. One company we know found this out the hard way. A few weeks after moving into new offices in New York City, an IS director received a call from someone in an apartment building across the street. This person had just turned on a brand-new, wireless-equipped Macintosh notebook and found himself connected to the IS director's in-house LAN.

Fortunately, the caller wasn't a malicious hacker, and he helped the IS people track down the cause of the security leak. One of the access points in a conference room was installed with the default settings, and those default settings set WEP to OFF. If you're concerned about network security (and you should be!), check and then double-check the security settings on every access point in your organization.

For example, you might install an access point in each conference room so that laptop-carrying conferees can plug in to the network from their seats. Two or three access points might cover a warehouse so that people equipped with handheld computers could access the network to check inventory and update the status. One access point could economically provide all the network connectivity required by five to ten people in a temporary office.

Figure 12.3 shows an example of a wireless network.

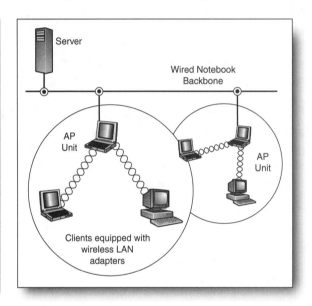

FIGURE 12.3
Each wireless PC will need a network adapter card. Most manufacturers make network adapters for ISA, PCI, and PC Card computers, so you can connect virtually any desktop or notebook PC to a wireless LAN. Some vendors also offer serial and parallel wireless connection units; these allow you to connect printers, scanners, and other peripheral equipment to the wireless LAN.

Solving Other Wired Problems

Wireless networks solve the problem of how to get connections into places where you don't have LAN cables. A slightly different type of wireless system provides practically the ideal solution to the problem of connecting to the last mile of the Internet. These wireless systems also solve the problem of bringing high-speed access into buildings that aren't served by fiber-optic or cable modem connections. Two technologies are available. The Multichannel Multipoint Distribution System (MMDS)—the so-called "wireless cable"—operates in the 2GHz band. The Local Multipoint Distribution Services (LMDS), or "wireless modem" operates in a huge slice of extremely high frequencies between 26GHz and 30GHz. The advantage of LMDS is that it has so much bandwidth that it's easy to provide fast throughput (ideally 500 Kbs, but nominally 300-500 Kbs per end node) without the need for complex engineering of adjacent cells 2–4 miles apart.

We're betting on LMDS as the access technology for 2001 and beyond. A lot of development, horse trading, and legal battling has to be done before LMDS rolls out, but it still promises to provide an excellent way to soar above last mile connection problems. Note that LMDS takes care of the last mile and campus-wide or neighborhood roamers. Other 2001 and beyond solutions will take care of wider roamers.

Right now, several acronym-laden connection technologies compete in the wireless portable digital connection market, but data throughput is about what we got from 14.4 analog modems several years ago. The goal of the third generation cellular systems, fielded in 2001 and beyond, is to connect large numbers of moving customers at 64Kbs.

The higher data rates and innovative services for roaming communicators will come from Low Earth Orbit (LEO) satellite systems. The technology of clusters of small satellites moving across the Earth 800 miles up isn't new. LEO systems have been doing store and forward communications—first for military and intelligence agencies, and recently for container freight shippers—since the 1980s. But real-time relays and large ground gateway services will make the difference in 2001 and beyond.

Motorola's Iridium was the first of the modern LEO systems to get off the ground and as of this writing has 51 satellites in orbit. However, Iridium is aimed at servicing low-speed data needs in unconnected areas. Iridium had some financial problems, but that's basically because cellular systems undermined the market for voice communications that was Iridium's target. Motorola's follow-on system, called Celestri, is a blend of high-orbiting high-capacity satellites and low-orbiting readily available data connections.

Two other big players are Teledesic and Globalstar. Teledesic, backed by Bill Gates and Craig McCaw, is aimed squarely at being the Internet in the Sky. Globalstar, founded by Loral Space & Communications, Ltd. and QUALCOMM Incorporated, has a deep well of digital communications technology to back it up. Any, and likely all of these systems will be bypassing wired connections and

---

Ad-hoc coverage

Connecting PCs without an access point is called *ad-hoc* connectivity. It's possible to connect PCs ad-hoc on an airplane, in a hotel room, and in a conference room. It's a handy feature for moving files. All of the products that conform to the 802.3 standards can create an ad-hoc connection, but often it takes several steps. Before you bury the manual in the bottom of a drawer, check in to how you set up an ad-hoc connection. It could make you a corporate hero at your next meeting.

servicing roaming customers in 2001. It's easy to predict that competition will lead to aggressive pricing with complex menus of satellite services. The sophisticated gateways planned by the satellite companies should make it easy to forge a seamless integration with the terrestrial wireless systems like LMDS. Abundant wireless data connections will drive many commercial and social changes in the next decade.

GLOSSARY

10Base-F IEEE's specification for running CSMA/CD networking (ethernet) over fiber-optic cable. This specification contains several subcategories for low-cost, plastic, interrepeater, and other links.

10Base-T IEEE's specifications for running CSMA/CD networking (ethernet) over unshielded twisted-pair cable. (*See also* IEEE 802.3.)

10Base-2 IEEE's specifications for running CSMA/CD networking (ethernet) over thin coaxial cable.

10Base-5 IEEE's specifications for running CSMA/CD networking (ethernet) over thick coaxial cable.

66 block A punch-down block for the interconnection of cables. The rectangular block, made from plastic or nylon, has connectors in four columns of 50 pins each. Each wire is placed in a pin and then pushed down (punched) into place. The pins pierce the wire's insulation and make an electrical connection. Caution: old 66 blocks do not conform to the Category 5 specifications.

802.3 An IEEE standard describing CSMA/CD networking. The standard contains many subelements, including 10Base-T.

802.5 An IEEE standard for token-ring networks. The standard describes a method of passing a token message between nodes to ensure delivery.

802.11 An IEEE standard for wireless LAN signaling. The basic standard introduced signaling at 1–2Mbps. The 802.11 HR standard introduces signaling at 11Mbps.

100Base-FX The IEEE Fast Ethernet standard for 100Mbps CSMA/CD over single-mode fiber-optic cable.

100Base-T A generic term for the three fast ethernet standards: 100Base-FX, 100Base-T4, and 100Base-TX.

100Base-T4 The IEEE fast ethernet standard for 100Mbps CSMA/CD operation over Category 5 cable (4 pairs of cable). This is not commonly used, but it can provide full-duplex operation for data streaming.

100Base-TX The IEEE Fast Ethernet standard for 100Mbps CSMA/CD over Category 5 cable using 2 pairs of wire within the cable. This is the most common form of fast ethernet.

110 block A punch-down block similar to the 66 block described above, but of more modern design and conforming to more critical technical specifications such as Category 5.

239

Active hub   In ARCnet, a wiring hub used to amplify network transmissions for greater distances. (*See also* passive hub.)

Alternating Current (AC)   An electrical signal or current that reverses direction periodically. AC is the form of electrical power found in residential and commercial buildings.

American National Standards Institute (ANSI)   An organization that develops and publishes standards for codes, data alphabets, and signaling schemes.

Anixter   A worldwide manufacturer of wiring system products. Anixter developed a model for cable classification.

ARCnet   (Attached Resources Computing Networks) A networking architecture (marketed by Datapoint Corporation and other vendors) using a token-passing bus architecture, usually on coaxial cable.

ARCNETPLUS   A 20-megabit signaling scheme version of ARCnet developed and marketed by Datapoint Corporation.

Asynchronous   A method of transmission in which the time intervals between characters are not required to be equal. Start and stop bits may be added to coordinate the transfer of characters.

Asynchronous Transfer Mode (ATM)   A method of network transmission using very small packets. ATM's primary advantage is the ability to carry time-sensitive packets, such as video or voice, without substantial delay. ATM networks will expand smoothly from local to wide area networks.

Attachment Unit Interface (AUI)   A 15-pin D-connector located on the network adapter used to connect cables to fiber-optic, coaxial, or 10Base-T transceivers.

Attenuation   The decrease in power of a signal as it travels along the cable. Attenuation is undesirable because it reduces the changes in voltage that signal a one or a zero in the digital signaling stream.

Attenuation to Crosstalk Ratio (ACR)   In cable testing, an indication of how much larger the received signal on a cable pair is compared to the noise on the same pair.

Attenuator   A device that is used to intentionally decrease, or attenuate, the signal. In fiber optics, a device that dims the light passing through it.

Automatic node discovery   Also called autodiscovery—the process of monitoring the LAN to discover all of the operational nodes.

Backbone   The high-speed link (often over fiber) used to connect separate networks or wiring closets.

Balun (BALanced UNbalanced)   An impedance-matching device that connects a balanced line (such as twisted-pair) and an unbalanced line (such as coaxial cable).

Bandwidth   The range of frequencies a circuit will pass. Analog circuits typically have a bandwidth limited to that of a human voice (about 3KHz). The square waves of digital sound require higher bandwidth. The higher the transmission rate, the greater the bandwidth requirement. Fiber-optic and coaxial cables have excellent bandwidth.

Baseband   A network that transmits signals as a direct-current pulse rather than as variations in a radio frequency signal.

Bell Standard Practices (BSP) A set of procedures designed before the breakup of the Bell Systems. The BSP described in detail how installers should cut, twist, and attach every wire, and how to secure every cable span.

BNC connector A small coaxial connector with a half-twist locking shell. BNC is an acronym for Bayone-Neill-Concelman.

Broadband signaling A network that carries information riding on carrier waves rather than directly as pulses, and provides greater capacity at the cost of higher complexity.

Broadcast To send a message to all stations or an entire class of stations connected to the network.

Carrier-Sense Multiple Access with Collision Detection (CSMA/CD) A media-sharing scheme in which stations listen in to what's happening on the network media; if the cable is not in use, the station is permitted to transmit its message. CSMA is often combined with a means of performing collision detection, hence CSMA/CD.

Category 3 cable (Cat 3) A voice-grade UTP cable used for digital telephone private branch exchanges and for local area networks. Now often used as premise telephone wiring in new homes, but should not be used in new office installations—use Cat 5 instead.

Category 5 cable (Cat 5) Nominally the highest grade of unshielded twisted-pair cable used for LANs. However, various vendors are promoting Cat 5e (enhanced) and even Cat 6 cable—essentially cable that is testing to more stringent standards for frequency response and NEXT.

Chassis hub A wiring hub contained in one self-contained box. The definition has gotten fuzzy at the high end, but at the low end, a chassis hub has become a hand-sized device for quick and economical network connection.

Cladding The material, usually glass, that surrounds the core of the optical fiber. Light bounces off the interface between the cladding and fiber and returns to the fiber.

Coaxial cable A type of network media. Coaxial cable contains a copper inner conductor surrounded by plastic insulation and then a woven copper or foil shield.

Common Management Information Protocol (CMIP) A structure for formatting messages and transmitting information between reporting devices and data collection programs. Developed by the International Standards Organization and designated as ISO 9596.

Conductor Any material that is capable of carrying an electrical current.

Controlled Access Unit (CAU) The IBM name for an intelligent wiring hub used in IBM Token-Ring networks. In common use, pronounced "cow."

Copper Distributed Data Interface (CDDI) A specification developed by Crescendo Communications that uses the FDDI techniques over unshielded twisted-pair.

Cross-connect device A device that terminates a cable or group of cables and makes the termination available for interconnection to other cables.

Crosstalk The spillover of a signal from one channel to another. In data communications it is very disruptive. In cable systems, crosstalk comes from adjacent cable pairs.

Crossover cable   In ethernet, the standard connection cable has the transmit pairs on pins 1 and 2 of the connector and the receive pairs on pins 3 and 6 on both ends of the cable. This is termed a straight-thru connection. However, sometimes you might wish to connect two ethernet units directly (hub-to-hub, for example). This can require a crossover cable that is connected with transmit-to-receive and receive-to-transmit. You should label any crossover cables because they will not work in normal applications.

Data-link layer   The second layer of the OSI model. Protocols functioning in this layer manage the flow of data leaving a network device and work with the receiving station to ensure that the data arrives safely.

DB-15   A standardized 15-pin connector used for ethernet connections.

DB-9   A standardized 9-pin connector used for token-ring connections.

Direct Current (DC)   An electrical current that travels in only one direction. DC is most commonly used in electronic circuits and is the signaling medium for all networks.

Distortion   Any change to the transmitted signal. May be caused by crosstalk, delay, attenuation, or other factors.

Distributed capacitance   The electrical property of capacitance developed within a cable that stores a direct current charge while passing an alternating current charge. This has the effect of diminishing the low frequency portion of transmitted signals.

Distributed inductance   The electrical property of inductance developed within a cable that stores an alternating current charge while passing a direct current charge. This has the effect of diminishing the high frequency portion of transmitted signals.

DIX connector   The connector used on the AUI socket and the transceiver cable.

EIA RS-232   An electrical standard for the interconnection of equipment, established by the Electrical Industries Association. (*See also* serial port.)

EIA/TIA-568   The EIA/TIA's Standard for Commercial Building Telecommunications Wiring. The EIA/TIA-568 standard describes a set of performance classifications and installation parameters for network cable. This standard is scheduled to be replaced with the similar EIA/TIA-568A.

EIA/TIA-569   The Commercial Building Standard for Telecommunication Pathways and Spaces.

EIA/TIA-570   The Residential and Light Commercial Telecommunications Wiring Standard.

EIA/TIA-606   The Administration Standard for the Telecommunications Infrastructure of Commercial Buildings. The EIA/TIA-606 describes the method for numbering and labeling cabling, pathways, and spaces.

Electromagnetic Interference/Radio Frequency Interference (EMI/RFI) Outside sources of potential interference on your network cable. EMI/RFI sources include radio transmitters, electric relays and switches, thermostats, and fluorescent lights.

Electronic Industries Alliance (EIA)
An organization of U.S. manufacturers of electronics parts and equipment. The organization develops industry standards for the interface between data processing and communications equipment.

Ethernet A network cable and access protocol scheme originally developed by Xerox that uses a carrier-sense multiple access (CSMA) media access control scheme. Described and expanded in the IEEE 802.3 standards.

Fault A physical or logical break in a communications link.

Fiber Distributed Data Interface (FDDI) A specification for fiber-optic networks operating at 100 megabits per second. FDDI uses wiring hubs, and the hubs are prime candidates for monitoring and control devices.

Fiber optics A data-transmission method that uses light pulses sent over glass cables.

Fiber-Optic Interrepeater Link (FOIRL) IEEE specification for running ethernet over fiber-optic cable. Typically used between transceivers or between wiring hubs. Easily confused but not interoperable with devices conforming to 10Base-F specifications.

Four-wire circuit A transmission arrangement where two half-duplex circuits (two wires each) are combined to make one full-duplex circuit.

Full-duplex The capability for communications to flow both ways over a communications link at the same time.

Ground An electrically neutral contact point.

Half-duplex Alternating transmissions: Each station can either transmit or receive, but cannot do both simultaneously.

Hertz (Hz) The number of electrical cycles (vibrations) per second. An Hz is equal to one cycle per second. The human voice typically operates between 30 and 3000 Hz. Cables are typically tested at 100 MegaHertz (MHz) or better.

Home Phoneline Networking Association (HPNA) An organization that has developed standards for using existing telephone wiring for home network data transmission. The technique allows a phoneline to simultaneously carry standard voice and fax traffic. Standards exist for 1 and 10Mbps transmission.

Horizontal wiring The cable that runs between each wall jack and its associated wiring closet.

IBM type 1 connector A connector used with shielded twisted-pair cable in a token-ring network.

IEEE 802.3 An IEEE standard describing CSMA/CD networking. The standard contains many subelements, including 10Base-T.

IEEE 802.5 An IEEE specification that describes a LAN using 4 or 16Mbps signaling, token passing media access control, and a physical ring topology. It is used by IBM's Token-Ring systems. (*See also* Token-Ring.)

Impedance A complex opposition to the flow of an alternating current in a circuit. Elements of distributed inductance, distributed capacitance, and resistance combine to create impedance.

Institute of Electrical and Electronics Engineers (IEEE) A standards-making organization responsible for many LAN-based standards and rules.

Integrated Services Digital Network (ISDN) As officially defined by CCITT, "a limited set of standard interfaces to a digital communications network." The result is a network that supplies end users with voice, data, and certain image services on end-to-end digital circuits. The plan is to provide two 64Kbps channels and one 16Kbps channel over digital telephone lines to desktops worldwide.

Interface The interconnection point, usually between equipment.

International Consultive Committee on Telephone and Telegraph (CCITT) An international organization responsible for developing communications standards.

International Standards Organization, Paris (ISO) An organization that developed the seven-layer Open Standards Interconnect model.

Jacket The outside layer of network cabling. The jacket protects the cable, and usually carries markings describing the cable. Various cable jackets are available for interior use, buried use, and use in areas where smoke or flames would create dangerous fumes.

Kevlar An aramid fiber that is used to provide crush resistance and pulling strength in a fiber-optic cable. Kevlar is a trademark of the DuPont Company.

Linear bus topology A topology where the nodes connect to the cable and the cable proceeds in a linear fashion between the nodes.

Local Area Network (LAN) A computer communications system limited to no more than a few miles and using high-speed 2–1000Mbps connections.

Main Distribution Frame (MDF) MDF, also called the cross-connection point, is a wiring point used primarily to distribute circuits coming in from outside a building.

Management Information Base (MIB) A database containing specific elements of information pertaining to the operation and performance of a specific piece of equipment, program, or function. A processor holds data in the format of the MIB until it is polled for the information. An MIB is a key part of the SNMP management system.

Media The cabling or wiring used to carry network signals. Typical examples are coax, fiber-optic, and twisted-pair wire. Plural of medium.

Media Access Control (MAC) The rules that LAN workstations abide by to avoid data collisions when sending signals over shared network media. Often used as "the MAC layer" to mean the access control layer of protocols.

Media Attachment Unit (MAU) A transceiver that attaches to the AUI port on an Ethernet adapter and provides electrical and mechanical attachment to fiber, twisted-pair, or other media.

MIC connector The Medium Interface Connector (MIC) was adopted by ANSI as part of the FDDI architecture. The MIC connector contains two fibers and is keyed to prevent attaching the MIC the wrong way.

Micron One micrometer, or one millionth of a meter.

Multimode fiber A fiber large enough to carry multiple modes of light. The type of fiber most commonly used in local area networks.

National Electrical Code (NEC) A code established by the National Fire Protection Association. The NEC basically describes the classification and installation of electrical power and signal cables.

N-connector The large-diameter connector used with thick ethernet cable.

Near-End Crosstalk (NEXT) Interference measured on a wire that is located adjacent to the wire in which the signal is being sent. NEXT measurements show the amount of signal leaking between pairs when measured close to the signal generation point. If the NEXT is too high, it will overcome signals coming from the far end that are also weakened by attenuation.

NetView A network-management product designed by IBM and 3Com. NetView is a specific network-management and control architecture that relies heavily on mainframe data collection programs, but also incorporates PC-level products running under OS/2.

Network A continuing connection between two or more computers that facilitates the sharing of files and resources.

Network Interface Card (NIC) Also called a LAN adapter. This device links between the relatively high voltage serial data environment on a LAN cable and the low voltage parallel data environment on a PC. You must get a NIC with software appropriate to your operating system, electrical connections appropriate to your computer, and connectors appropriate to the LAN.

Noise Any extraneous noise that invades the transmission of electrical pulses or frequencies along a cable. Noise is measured as impulse or root-mean-square (RMS).

Nominal Velocity of Propagation (NVP) The ratio between the speed of an electrical pulse in a specific type of cable and the speed of light.

Ohm Primarily a unit of resistance, but also can be used to express impedance.

Online Connected to a network or host computer system.

Open Systems Interconnection (OSI) reference model A model for networks, developed by the International Standards Organization, that divides the network functions into seven layers. Each layer builds on the services provided by those under it.

OpenView Hewlett-Packard's suite of network management applications, a server platform, and support services. OpenView is based on HP-UX, which complies with AT&T's UNIX system.

Passive hub A wiring hub that does not amplify network transmissions, but only segments the transmissions between several nodes (*See also* active hub.)

Patch panel A panel built into a cabinet that contains jacks that terminate individual cables. Jumper cables make connections between the individual jacks. A patch panel makes it easy to change network cable connections.

Plenum cable Cable certified to be fire resistant and to produce a minimum of smoke. It can be installed in the space between a false ceiling and the floor or ceiling above, called the plenum.

Polyvinyl Chloride (PVC) Used as an insulating material in coaxial cables between the solid core and the outside braid.

Premise Distribution System (PDS)
A building-wide telecommunications cabling system. AT&T, Northern Telecom, and other vendors have specified PDS architectures.

Private Branch Exchange (PBX) A telephone system serving a specific location. Many PBX systems can carry network data without the use of modems.

Protocol A specification that describes the rules and procedures that products should follow to perform activities on a network, such as transmitting data. Protocols allow products from different vendors to communicate on the same network.

Punch-down block A central termination point for twisted-pair cable. See 66 block and 110 block above.

Repeater In ethernet, a device that amplifies and regenerates signals so they can travel farther on a cable.

RG-58 A coaxial cable connector that has a 50-ohm impedance and is used with thin ethernet.

RG-62 A coaxial cable connector that has a 93-ohm impedance and is used with ARCnet.

RJ-45 An 8-pin connector used for data transmissions over telephone twisted-pair wire.

Remote Network Monitoring (RMON) A specification for an SNMP monitoring system with multiple monitoring devices throughout the LAN.

Sag A decrease of below 80 percent in normal line voltage. Also known as a brownout.

SC connector An acronym for style connector, this connector is often used in fiber-optic cable splices.

Screened Twisted-Pair (SCTP)
Twisted-pair cabling with an outer foil shield to reduce EMI. It has performance and operating characteristics similar to UTP.

Serial port An I/O port that transmits data 1 bit at time, as compared to a parallel port, which transmits multiple (usually 8) bits simultaneously. EIA RS-232 supports serial signaling.

Shielded Distributed Data Interface (SDDI) A specification promoted by IBM and other vendors to run FDDI protocols over shielded twisted-pair cable.

Shielded Twisted-Pair (STP)
Twisted-pair cabling with an overall shield to prevent the entry of outside interference, and individually shielded and twisted pairs to prevent crosstalk.

Simple Network Management Protocol (SNMP) A structure for formatting messages and transmitting information between reporting devices and data-collection programs. Developed jointly by the Department of Defense, industry, and the academic community as part of the TCP/IP protocol suite.

Single-Mode fiber A fiber that has a very small core, allowing only one mode of light to enter and propagate. Single-mode fibers do not suffer modal dispersion and are the best choice for very long runs requiring high data speeds.

SMA connector A type of fiber-optic connector used extensively in telephone installations before the introduction of the ST-type connector. It is still popular. Originally an acronym for Sub-Miniature Assembly.

SNMP (Simple Network Monitoring Protocol) A standard for network management control that includes devices and monitoring or management consoles.

Spike   A power impulse that lasts between 0.5 and 100 microseconds and possesses an amplitude over 100 percent of peak line voltage.

Spread-spectrum   A method of radio transmission that spreads the signal out over a wide bandwidth, typically 1 or more megahertz. Spread-spectrum signals are much less susceptible to interference from pulse noise and from other radio signals. Widely used in short-range wireless LAN systems.

ST connector   A fiber-optic connector developed and trademarked by AT&T; it is the type of connector most commonly used in fiber local area networks. The acronym orginally stood for Straight Tip.

Stackable hub   A special type of hub that can be stacked or combined with other hubs to form a single ethernet repeater. The hubs connect directly through a high-speed interface so they don't suffer the timing delays associated with multiple ethernet repeaters.

Star topology   A network connection method that brings all links to a central node, or wiring hub.

Station cable   The cable that connects the network node to the wall jack.

Surge   A voltage increase above 110 percent of normal power voltage.

Systimax   The Lucent/AT&T specification for installing and planning network cable.

Tap   A connector that couples to a cable without blocking the passage of signals down the cable.

T-connector   A coaxial connector, shaped like a T, that connects two thin Ethernet cables while supplying an additional connector for a network interface card.

Thick ethernet   A cabling system using large-diameter, relatively stiff cable to connect transceivers. The transceivers connect to the nodes through flexible multiwire cable.

Thin ethernet   A cabling system using a thin and flexible coaxial cable to connect each node to the next node in line.

Time-Domain Reflectometry (TDR)   The technique of sending an electric pulse down a cable and then timing its reflection back from the other end. Most cable scanners use TDR to determine the length of the cable.

Token   A message that gives a node permission to transmit.

Token passing   An access protocol in which a special message (token) circulates among the network nodes, giving them permission to transmit.

Token-Ring   Refers to the wire and the access protocol scheme whereby stations relay packets in a logical ring configuration. This architecture, pioneered by IBM, is described in the IEEE 802.5 standards.

Topology   The map of the network. The physical topology describes how the wires or cables are laid out, and the logical or electrical topology describes how the messages flow.

Transceiver   In networks, a device that connects a specific type of cable, such as coax or fiber, to a network adapter card through the AUI connector.

Transmission Control Protocol/Internet Protocol (TCP/IP) Originally developed by the Department of Defense, this set of communications protocols has evolved since the late 1970s. Because network communications programs supporting these protocols are available on so many different computer systems, they have become an excellent way to connect different types of computers over networks.

Trunk segment In ethernet, a piece of cable with a terminator at each end.

Twisted-pair wiring Cable comprised of two wires twisted together to provide increased bandwidth. Some telephone wiring, but by no means all, is twisted-pair.

Underwriters Laboratories (UL) An organization, founded by the National Board of Fire Underwriters, that specifies safety standards.

Uninterruptible Power Supply (UPS) A backup device designed to provide an uninterrupted power source in the event of a power failure. UPSs should be installed on all file servers and wiring hubs.

Unshielded Twisted-Pair (UTP) Twisted-pair cabling that does not have individual or overall shielding.

Vertical wiring The cable that forms the backbone between the wiring closets and the main cross-connection point in the building.

Volt A unit measure of electrical force.

Wide Area Network (WAN) A system for connecting LANs together over a wide area such as a city, region and so on. Devices such as routers or switches have one port on the WAN and one port on a LAN and serve as a gateway between the two. WAN speeds are generally slower than LAN speeds.

Wiring closet An area in a building provided for the punch-down blocks, patch panels, and wiring hubs. It serves as a central point for network or telephone cabling.

Wiring hub A cabinet, usually mounted in a wiring closet, that holds connection modules for various kinds of cabling. The hub contains electronic circuits that retime and repeat the signals on the cable. The hub may also contain a microprocessor that monitors and reports on network activity.

INDEX

Symbols

10Base-FL ethernet, 82

10Base2 (thin) ethernet, 16

10Base5 (thick) ethernet, 16, 83-85

10BaseF ethernet, 16

10BaseT ethernet, 16, 86-87
  802.3i standard, 18-19
  chassis hubs, 88-91
  repeaters, 91-92
  stackable hubs, 88, 91
  wiring hubs, 87-88

50-pin telco connectors (harmonicas), 135-137

100-ohm shielded STP (shielded twisted-pair) cables, 40-42

100BaseT (fast) ethernet, 16

106A Systimax cables, 59

110 Connector System Configurator (software), 135

110 Cross-Connect System (Systimax), 61

110 Jack Panel System, 135

110 Patch Panel System (Lucent), 61-62

150-ohm shielded STP (shielded twisted-pair) cables, 40-42

802.3i 10BaseT standard, 18-19

1090 Systimax cables, 60

2061A Systimax cables, 59

2290 Systimax cables, 60

A

Access Floor Workstation Module (Amp), 66

Access Points (APs), 235

accounting management, 105

Accumax Systimax cables, 60

ad hoc cabling systems, 52, 237

agents, 107-110
  MIB (Management Information Base), 110

American Wire Gauge (AWG) standards, 38

Amp products, 63, 66
  Amp Access Floor Workstation Module, 66
  AMPIX Cross-Connect system, 66-67
  information outlets, 168

Anixter Wire and Cable products, 67-69

Apple Computer (LocalTalk) standards, 74

APs (Access Points), 235

ARCnet, 20-21, 96-97
  size considerations, 22
  topology, 21-22

Asynchronous Transfer Mode (ATM), 73

AT&T 258A UTP (unshielded twisted-pair) wire standards, 174

AT&T/Lucent Systimax cables, 58-59
  Lucent 110 Patch Panel System, 61-62
  plug and jack standards, 62-63
  Systimax 106A and 2061A LAN, 59
  Systimax 1090 and 2290, 60
  Systimax 110 Cross-Connect System, 61

ATM (Asynchronous Transfer Mode), 73

Attached Resource Computing. See ARCnet

attenuation, 13, 221-222

AUI (attachment unit interface) sockets, 83

AWG (American Wire Gauge) standards, 38

B

backbones, 123
  cable types, 131-132
  selecting closet locations, 127, 130

backplanes, 89

baluns, 170

baseband signaling, 12-16

baseline measurements, testing/troubleshooting cable systems, 226

Bell Standard Practices (BSPs), 58

blades, 89-90

249

BNC connectors, 12, 182-184

bridges, 80

broadband signaling, 12-14

broadcast architecture, ethernet, 17

browser front ends, network management, 112

BSPs (Bell Standard Practices), 58

C

cabinets for patch panels and wiring hubs, 137, 140

cables
  baseband and broadband signaling, 12-14
  backbone, 123, 126-127
    cable types, 131-132
    selecting closet locations, 127, 130
  cancellation, 32
  coaxial, 34, 37
  connectors
    BNC, 182-184
    RJ-45, 171-172, 176, 181-182
    token-ring, 183-185
    types, 12
    UTP (unshielded twisted-pair) wires, 171, 175
  costs, 26-27
  defined, 9
  distance limitations, 92
  elements above cabling, 10
  fiber-optic, 42-44, 201-202
    connectors, 204, 207-208
    construction, 202
    FDDI (Fiber Distributed Data Interface) standard, 208-209

FOIRL (fiber-optic interrepeater link) standard, 209-210
installation suggestions, 211
ordering options, 203-204
single-mode and multimode, 203
horizontal, 123
impedance, 34
jackets, 34
LAN adapters, 11-12
MACs (media-access controls), 14
managing/troubleshooting, 102
MTD (maximum total cable distance), 93-95
PDSs (premises distribution systems), 51-54
  Amp, 63, 66-67
  Anixter Wire and Cable, 67-69
  AT&T/Lucent Systimax, 58-63
  IBM Cabling System, 54-58
  Molex Premise Networks, 63, 66-68
power supply problems
  dangers, 148
  grounding, 148, 152-155
  normal or common mode conductor problems, 156
  source of problems, 148
  spikes, surges, and sags, 156-157
  surge suppressors, 157-158
  UPSs (uninterruptible power supplies), 158, 161-162
selection considerations, 44-45
shielding, 32

signals
  degradation, 31-32
  protection techniques, 32-34
standards
  EIA/TIA (Electronic Industries Alliance/ Telecommunications Industry Association), 71-73
  influences, 52-53
  LocalTalk (Apple Computer), 74
  NEC (National Electrical Code), 69-70
  network element interactions, 49-51
  UL (Underwriters Laboratories), 73-75
STP (shielded twisted-pair), 40-42
  guidelines, MTD (maximum total cable distance), 95
systems
  information outlets, 168-169
  station cables, 169-170
  weak links, 167
trays, 123-126
troubleshooting system problems, 215
  attenuation, 221-222
  baseline measurements, 226
  cable distance, 219-220
  certification standards, 226
  fiber-optic cables, 225
  hand-held testers, 216-218
  near-end crosstalk, 222-223
  near-end crosstalk noise levels, 223-224
  network monitoring, 223
  procedures, 216

protocol decoding, 223
testers based on standards, 224
testers with special features, 225
wire maps, 220-221
types, 30-31
UTP (unshielded twisted-pair), 37-38
  advantages/disadvantages, 38
  guidelines, MTD (maximum total cable distance), 95
  shielded, 42
  versus telephone wire, 38-40
value checklist, 9
wire maps, 220-221
wiring closets, 119-121
  backbone wiring, 123, 126-127
  cabinets and racks, 137, 140
  cable trays, 123-126
  cable types, 131-132
  conduits, 123-126
  cross-connect panels, 132-135
  EIA/TIA (Electronic Industries Alliance/ Telecommunications Industry Association) standards, 122
  horizontal wiring, 123
  IDFs (Intermediate Distribution Frames), 120
  importance in networks, 143
  major equipment, 132
  MDFs (Main Distribution Frames), 120
  octopus with harmonica, 135-137
  selecting locations, 127, 130

TIA (Telecommunications Industry Association) standards, 122
ties, 141-142
UPSs (uninterruptible power supplies), 142-143
wall-jack systems, 122
wiring hubs, 87-88, 102

Canadian Standards Association (CSA), UPSs (uninterruptible power supplies), 162

cancellation, 32-34

Carrier-Sense Multiple Access with Collision Detection. *See* CSMA/CD (Carrier-Sense Multiple Access with Collision Detection)

Category 1-5, EIA/TIA (Electronic Industries Alliance/Telecommunications Industry Association)-568 cable-performance specifications, 71-73
  Cat 5E (enhanced) cables, 73

CAUs (controlled access units), 23

CCITT in French (International Consultive Committee on Telephone and Telegraph), 15

certification standards, testing/troubleshooting cable systems, 226

chassis hubs, 88-90
  advantages/disadvantages, 91

Cheapernet. *See* thin ethernet

Cisco Systems, Copper Distributed Data Interface (CDDI), 209

cladding, 44, 202

CMIP (Common Management Information Protocol), 108

CMOT (Common Management Information Protocol over TCP/IP), 108

coaxial cables, 34, 37
  BNC connectors, 12
  connectors
    BNC, 182-184
  selection considerations, 44-45

collisions, 80-81

Common Management Information Protocol over TCP/IP. *See* CMOT (Common Management Information Protocol over TCP/IP), 108

Common Management Information Protocol, *See* CMIP (Common Management Information Protocol)

common mode problems, electrical conductors, 156

conduits, 123-126

configuration management, 105

connectors
  BNC, 12
  fiber-optic cables, 204
    FDDI (Fiber Distributed Data Interface) standard, 208-209
    FOIRL (fiber-optic interrepeater link) standard, 209-210
    low-cost, 207-208
    MIC (Medium Interface Connector), 206-207

connectors

SC (Small Connector),
206-207
SMA, 205-206
ST, 12, 205
IBM Data Connector,
57-58
IBM type 1, 12
RJ-45, 12, 171-172
telco, 135
types, 12
UTP (unshielded twisted-
pair) cable wires, 171, 175

console software, 109-111

controlled access units. See
CAUs (controlled access
units)

Copper Distributed Data
Interface (CDDI), Cisco
Systems, 209

costs of cables, 26-27

cross-connect panels,
126-127, 132-135

Cross-Connect System
(Systimax 110), 61

crosstalk, 13, 32
near-end, 222-223
noise levels, 223-224

CSA (Canadian Standards
Association), UPSs (unin-
terruptible power supplies),
162

CSMA/CD (Carrier-Sense
Multiple Access with
Collision Detection) proto-
col, 16-18

D

Datacom Technologies,
hand-held cable testers,
216, 218

Datapoint Corporation, origin of ARCnet, 20

degradation of signals, 31-32

drop cables, 85-86

duplex ethernet (full), 18

E

ECL (equivalent cable
length), 94

EIA (Electronic Industries
Association), 15
Preferred Commercial
Building Specification
standard for UTP
(unshielded twisted-pair)
wires, 174

EIA/TIA (Electronic
Industries
Alliance/Telecommunications
Industry Association),
52-53, 122
568 standard, 71-73, 122
569 standard, 122

electrical sources. See power
supplies

Electronic Industries
Association (EIA), 15

EMI/RFI noise (electromagnetic interference/radio
frequency interference), 32

equivalent cable length
(ECL), 94
10BaseT, 86-87
chassis hubs, 88, 90-91
repeaters, 91-92
stackable hubs, 88, 91
wiring hubs, 87-88

ethernet, 15, 80, 84
fast, 16
home networks, 190, 192
size considerations, 18, 20
thick, 83-85
thin, 36, 85-86

ethernet-type signaling,
802.3i 10BaseT standard,
18-19

F

fast (100BaseT) ethernet, 16

fault management, 105

FDDI (Fiber Distributed Data
Interface) architecture, 206
standards, fiber-optic cables,
208-209

fiber-optic cables, 42-44,
201-202
backbone wiring, 131-132
connectors, 204
FDDI (Fiber Distributed
Data Interface) standard,
208-209
FOIRL (fiber-optic interrepeater link) standard,
209-210
low-cost, 207-208
MIC (Medium Interface
Connector), 206-207
SC (Small Connector),
206-207
SMA, 205-206
ST, 12, 205
construction, 202
installation suggestions, 211
ordering options, 203-204
selection considerations,
44-45
single-mode and multimode,
203
testing/troubleshooting, 225

fly leads, 133

FOIRL (fiber-optic interrepeater link), 210
standards, fiber-optic cables,
209-210

frames, 22

full duplex ethernet, 18

G

Globalstar LEOs (Low Earth Orbit), 237

ground planes, 153-155

grounding power supplies, 148, 152-155
dangers, 148
source of problems, 148

H

hand-held cable testers, 216-218

harmonicas (50-pin telco connectors), 135-137

Hewlett-Packard's OpenView, 110-111

High Speed Token-Ring (HSTR), 93

High-End Cat 5 cables, 73

home networks, 189-190
Ethernet, 190-192
phone and power lines, 193-198
wireless systems, 193-195

horizontal wiring, 123

HSTR (High Speed Token-Ring), 93

hubs, 87-88, 102
chassis, 88-90
advantages/disadvantages, 90-91
stackable, 88, 91
token-ring protocol, 23-24

I

IBM Cabling System, 53-56
advantages/disadvantages, 57-58
SDDI standard, fiber-optic cables, 209
wire types, 54, 57

IBM Data Connector, 57-58

IBM type 1 connectors, 12

IBM's Token-Ring networking system, 92-93
MTD (maximum total cable distance), 93-95
STP (shielded twisted-pair) cables, 40-41

IDFs (Intermediate Distribution Frames), 120

IEEE (Institute of Electrical and Electronics Engineers), 15, 52-53
10Base-T standards, UTP (unshielded twisted-pair) wires, 175
802.5 token-ring system, 92-93
MTD (maximum total cable distance), 93-95

impedance, 34

in-band signaling, 110

information outlets, cabling systems, 168-169

Institute of Electrical and Electronics Engineers (IEEE), 15, 52-53

Intel's LANDesk Manager, 111

Intermediate Distribution Frames (IDFs), 120

International Consultive Committee on Telephone and Telegraph (CCITT in French), 15

International Electrotechnical Commission (IEC) Joint Technical Committee 1, 75

International Standards Organization (ISO), 15, 75

Iridium (Motorola), 237

ISA expansion cards, compared to PCI, 190

ISO (International Standards Organization), 15, 75

J

jack and plug standards, Lucent, 62-63

jackets (cable), 34

John Fluke Manufacturing, hand-held cable testers, 216-218

K

key telephone system, 39

Krone, Inc., patch panels, 134

L

LAN-Line Thinnet TapAMP, 65

LANDesk Manager (Intel), 111

LANs (local area networks), 7
adapters, 11-12
baseband signaling, 14
homes, 189-190
Ethernet, 190-192
phone and power lines, 193-198
wireless systems, 193-195
wireless, 231, 234-235
topologies, 235-236

latency, 92

LEO (Low Earth Orbit) satellite systems, 237

link lights, 87

LMDS (Local Multipoint Distribution Services), 236

Lobe Attachment Modules, 25

lobes, 25

local area networks. *See* LANs (Local Area Networks)

Local Multipoint Distribution Services (LMDS), 236

LocalTalk (Apple Computer) standards, 74

Low Earth Orbit (LEO) satellite systems, 237

Lucent 110 Patch Panel System, 61-62, 135

Lucent plug and jack standards, 62-63

M

MACs (media-access controls), 14
   CSMA/CD (Carrier-Sense Multiple Access with Collision Detection) protocol, 16-18

Management Information Base (MIB), 110

managing networks, 102-103
   agents, 109-110
   architecture, 106-107
   browser front ends, 112
   cables, 102
   components, 103-105
   console software, 109-111
   device setup, 111-112
   functions, 105-106
   modules, 109
   RMON (Remote Network Monitoring) MIB, 112, 115

standards, 107-108
   CMIP (*Common Management Information Protocol*), *108*
   CMOT (*Common Management Information Protocol over TCP/IP*), *108*
   SNMP (*Simple Network Management Protocol*), *108-109*
troubleshooting problems, 115

Manchester encoded digital baseband signaling, 13, 16

MAUs (multistation access units), 23

maximum total cable distance (MTD), 93-95

media filters, 93

media-access controls. *See* MACs (media-access controls)

Medium Interface Connector (MIC) connectors, 206-207

MIB (Management Information Base), 110

MIC (Medium Interface Connector) connectors, 206-207

microbends, 211

Microsoft Systems Management Server, 111

Microtest Corporation, hand-held cable testers, 216-218

MLT-3 (Multi-Level Transmission-3), 209

Molex Premise Networks, 63, 66
   information outlets, 168-169
   library of publications documenting installation, 137
   Universal System Outlet, 67-68

monitoring networks, troubleshooting cables, 223

Motorola's Iridium, 237

MTD (maximum total cable distance), 93-95

Multi-Level Transmission-3 (MLT-3), 209

multimode fiber-optic cables, 203

multistation access units. *See* MAUs (multistation access units)

N

National Fire Protection Association (NFPA), NEC (National Electrical Code), 69

near-end crosstalk, 222-223
   noise levels, 223-224

NEC (National Electrical Code of the United States), 53, 69-70

NETCONNECT Open Cabling System (Amp), 64

network architectures
   standards, 79-80

network cabling systems. *See* cables

network interface cards (NICs). *See* LAN adapters

network management, 102-103
   agents, 109-110
   architecture, 106-107

browser front ends, 112
components, 103-105
console software, 109-111
device setup, 111-112
functions, 105-106
RMON (Remote Network
Monitoring) MIB, 112,
115
standards, 107-108
*CMIP (Common
Management
Information Protocol),
108*
*CMOT (Common
Management
Information Protocol over
TCP/IP), 108*
*SNMP (Simple Network
Management Protocol),
108-109*
troubleshooting problems,
115

network media. *See* **cables**

**Network Peripherals, SDDI
standard, fiber-optic cables,
209**

networks
homes, 189-190
Ethernet, 190-192
*phone and power lines,
193-198*
wireless systems, 193-195
LANs (Local Area
Networks), 7
monitoring, troubleshoot-
ing cables, 223
size considerations, 8
WANs (Wide Area
Networks), 7
wireless, 229-231
wireless bridges, 231-233
*wireless LANs, 231,
234-236*

**Newton Instrument
Company, retailers of
wiring closet brackets,
racks, and cabinets, 140**

**NFPA (National Fire
Protection Association),
NEC (National Electrical
Code), 69**

**NICs (Network Interface
Cards).** *See* **LAN adapters**

**Nominal Velocity of
Propagation (NVP), 219**

**normal mode problems,
electrical conductors, 156**

Nortel Networks
FDDI (Fiber Distributed
Data Interface) over UTP
standard, fiber-optic
cables, 209
SDDI standard, fiber-optic
cables, 209

**Norton Administrator for
Networks (Symantec), 111**

**Novell's NetWare network
management, 110**

**NVP (Nominal Velocity of
Propagation), 219**

O

octopus, 135, 137
ohms of impedance, 34
**OpenView (Hewlett-
Packard), 110-111**
out-of-band signaling, 110
OVADMIN, 111
OVDRAW, 111

P

**Panduit Electrical Group,
surface raceways, 126**
patch cables, 135
**Patch Panel System (Lucent
110), 61-62**
**PCI expansion cards, com-
pared to ISA, 190**

**PDSs (premises distribution
systems), 51-54**
Amp, 63, 66-67
Anixter Wire and Cable,
67-69
architecture, 51
AT&T/Lucent Systimax,
58-63
IBM Cabling System, 54-58
managing, 103-105
functions, 105-106
Molex Premise Networks,
63, 66-68
opposites, 52

**performance management,
105**

**phone lines, home networks,
193-198**

Photophen, 43

physical topology, 83

**plug and jack standards,
Lucent, 62-63**

**ports, USB (Universal Serial
Bus), 11**

**power lines, home networks,
193, 198**

power supplies
dangers, 148
grounding, 148, 152-155
normal or common mode
conductor problems, 156
source of problems, 148
spikes, surges, and sags,
156-157
surge suppressors, 157-158
UPSs (uninterruptible
power supplies), 158,
161-162

powered wiring hubs, 93

**premises distribution sys-
tems.** *See* **PDSs (premises
distribution systems)**

**protocol decoding, trou-
bleshooting cables, 223**

protocols
ARCnet, 20-21
size considerations, 22
topology, 21-22
ethernet, 15-17
CSMA/CD (Carrier-Sense
Multiple Access with
Collision Detection),
17-18
size considerations, 18-20
network standards, 107-108
CMIP (Common
Management
Information Protocol),
108
CMOT (Common
Management
Information Protocol over
TCP/IP), 108
SNMP (Simple Network
Management Protocol),
108-109
token-ring, 22-24
size considerations, 25
STP (shielded twisted-
pair), 25
UTP (unshielded twisted-
pair), 25
wiring hub, 23-24
punch-down blocks, 133-135
punch-down tools, 133

R

racks for patch panels and
wiring hubs, 137, 140
reactance, 31
Remote Network
Monitoring (RMON) MIB,
112-115
repeaters, 81, 86, 91-92
resistance, 31
rings, 172
RJ-45 connectors, 12,
171-172, 176, 181-182

RMON (Remote Network
Monitoring) MIB, 112, 115
RMON probes, 113-114
RMON2 specification, 114
Rolm and Digital Equipment
Corporation, standards,
UTP (unshielded twisted-
pair) wires, 175

S

sags (power fluctuations),
156-157
SC (Small Connector) con-
nectors, 206-207
SCS (structured cable sys-
tems), 51
SDDI standard, fiber-optic
cables, 209
security management, 105
shielded twisted-pair. *See*
STP (shielded twisted-pair)
shielding, 32-34
signal reference grounds,
153-155
signaling
baseband, 12-14
Manchester encoded digital,
16
broadband, 12-14
degradation, 31-32
fiber-optic cable standards,
FDDI (Fiber Distributed
Data Interface), 208-210
protection techniques,
32-34
Simple Network
Management Protocol. *See*
SNMP (Simple Network
Management Protocol)
single-mode fiber-optic
cables, 203
SMA connectors, 205-206

Small Connector (SC) con-
nectors, 206-207
SNMP (Simple Network
Management Protocol), 108-
109
South Hills Datacomm, retail-
ers of wiring closet brackets,
racks, and
cabinets, 140
SP-2840 (EIA/TIA (Electronic
Industries
Alliance/Telecommunications
Industry Association) 568)
standard, 71-73
spikes (power fluctuations),
156-157
SPSs (standby power systems),
161
ST connectors, 12, 205
stackable hubs, 88, 91
Standard Microsystems
Corporation, origin of
ARCnet, 20
standards
cables
Amp, 63, 66-67
Anixter Wire and Cable,
67-69
AT&T/Lucent Systimax,
58-63
EIA/TIA (Electronic
Industries
Alliance/Telecommunicatio
ns Industry Association),
71-73
IBM Cabling System, 54-58
influences, 52-53
LocalTalk (Apple Computer),
74
Molex Premise Networks,
63, 66, 68
NEC (National Electrical
Code), 69-70
network element interactions,
49-51

PDSs (Premises Distribution Systems), 51-54

SCS (Structured Cable Systems), 51

UL (Underwriters Laboratories), 73-75

network architectures, 79-80, 98

network management, 107-108

CMIP (Common Management Information Protocol), 108

CMOT (Common Management Information Protocol over TCP/IP), 108

SNMP (Simple Network Management Protocol), 108-109

Standards Committee 25, International Standards Organization (ISO), 75

standby power systems (SPSs), 161

station cables, 169-170

connectors

BNC, 182-184

RJ-45, 171-172, 176, 181-182

token-ring, 183-185

STP (shielded twisted-pair) cables, 25, 40-42

guidelines, MTD (maximum total cable distance), 95

IBM type 1 connectors, 12

selection considerations, 44-45

structured cable systems. See SCS (structured cable systems)

surface raceways, 126

surges (power fluctuations), 156-157

suppressors, 157-158

Symantec's Norton Administrator for Networks, 111

Systimax

106A and 2061A LAN cables, 59

110 Cross-Connect System, 61

1090 and 2290 cables, 60

Accumax cables, 60

T

TDR (time-domain reflectometry), 219

telco connectors, 135

telco splice blocks. See punch-down blocks

telecommunications outlets. See well-jack systems

Teledesic LEOs (Low Earth Orbit) satellite systems, 237

telephone wires, versus UTP (unshielded twisted-pair) cables, 38-40

thick ethernet (10Base5), 16, 83-85

thin ethernet (10Base2), 16, 36, 85-86

thresholds, 105

TIA Standards Proposal 4195-B (called SP 4195-B), Additional Transmission Performance Specification for 4-Pair Enhanced Category 5 Cabling, 122

ties for cables, 141-142

time-domain reflectometry (TDR), 219

tips, 172

token-passing, 22

Token-Ring (IBM) networking system, 92-93

cables

MTD (maximum total cable distance), 93-95

STP (shielded twisted-pair) cables, 25, 40-41

UTP (unshielded twisted-pair), 25

connectors, 183-185

protocol, 22-24

size considerations, 25

wiring hub, 23-24

topologies

ARCnet, 21-22

wireless LANs (), 235-236

total internal reflection, fiber-optic cables, 44, 202

transceivers, 83

transfer time, SPSs (standby power systems), 161

transients, 32

transitions, 13

transmission medium. See cables

troubleshooting problems

cable systems, 215

attenuation, 221-222

baseline measurements, 226

cable distance, 219-220

certification standards, 226

fiber-optic cables, 225

hand-held testers, 216-218

near-end crosstalk, 222-223

near-end crosstalk noice levels, 223-224

network monitoring, 223

procedures, 216

protocol decoding, 223

testers based on standards, 224

testers with special features, 225
wire maps, 220-221
network management alerts, 115

trunk cables, 80, 86

trunk segments, 80

Type-66 blocks. *See* **punch-down blocks**

U

UL (Underwriters Laboratories) standards, 52, 73-75
UPSs (uninterruptible power supplies), 162

uninterruptible power supplies. *See* **UPSs (uninterruptible power supplies)**

Universal Serial Bus (USB) ports, 11

Universal Service Order Code (USOC) standards, UTP (unshielded twisted-pair) wires, 173

Universal System Outlet (Molex), 67-68

unpopulated trunks, 82

unshielded twisted-pair. *See* **UTP (unshielded twisted-pair)**

UPSs (uninterruptible power supplies), 142-143, 158, 161-162

USB (Universal Serial Bus) ports, 11

USOC (Universal Service Order Code) standards, UTP (unshielded twisted-pair) wires, 173

UTP (unshielded twisted-pair) cables, 25, 37-38
advantages/disadvantages, 38
backbone wiring, 131-132
connectors, 171, 175
RJ-45, 12
guidelines, MTD (maximum total cable distance), 95
selection considerations, 44-45
shielded, 42
versus telephone wire, 38-40

V

VA (volt amps) ratings, UPSs (uninterruptible power supplies), 142-143

vampire taps, 83

vertical wiring. *See* **backbone wiring**

VF-45 (system of cables and connectors), 44

volt amps (VA) ratings, UPSs (uninterruptible power supplies), 142-143

voltage interruptions
normal or common mode conductor problems, 156
surge suppressors, 157-158
surges, spikes, and sags, 156-157

W

wall-jack systems, 122

WANs (Wide Area Networks), 7
broadband signaling, 14

wireless bridges, 231-233

wireless LANs, 231, 234-235
topologies, 235-236

wireless modems. *See* **LMDS (Local Multipoint Distribution Services)**

wireless networks, 229-231
home networks, 193-195
problems solved, 236-238
wireless bridges, 231-233
wireless LANs, 231, 234-235
topologies, 235-236

wiring. *See* **cables**

wiring closets, 119-121
backbone wiring, 123, 126-127
cabinets and racks, 137, 140
cable ties, 141-142
cable trays, 123-126
cable types, 131-132
conduits, 123-126
cross-connect panels, 132-135
EIA/TIA (Electronic Industries Alliance/Telecommunications Industry Association) standards, 122
horizontal wiring, 123
IDFs (Intermediate Distribution Frames), 120
importance in networks, 143
major equipment, 132
MDFs (Main Distribution Frames), 120
octopus with harmonica, 135-137
selecting locations, 127, 130
TIA standards, 122
UPSs (uninterruptible power supplies), 142-143
wall-jack systems, 122